THE GAIETY SCHOOL OF ACTING
THE NATIONAL THEATRE SCHOOL OF IRELAND

30th
ANNIVERSARY
ANTHOLOGY

1986-2016

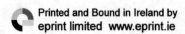
Printed and Bound in Ireland by
eprint limited www.eprint.ie

CONTENTS

Introduction

By

Patrick Sutton, Director

30 years ago, Joe Dowling founded The Gaiety School of Acting - The National Theatre School of Ireland. This important anniversary is being marked on October 23rd 2016. It is a great occasion and one in which we celebrate the actors who have passed through the School and we connect with them as they continue their extraordinarily exciting journey into the theatre, film and television industries and beyond.

We also mark our writers, a small selection of whom are chosen here, to celebrate a vital part of how we pass our actors from the world of training to the world of work. Commissioning new and original work has become a significant part of how we tell our story and I thank all staff and tutors both past and present, our Board of Directors, partners and collaborators for all they have done in working with our actors down all the years. Thanks to Chairman Professor Christopher Murray and Board Member Mary Elizabeth Burke-Kennedy for selecting the chosen plays, and to Maeve Whelan and John Lawless for bringing it all together. Thanks also to those who sponsored the anthology. I also thank you, for your involvement and interest in the School to help it become Ireland's premiere conservatory training ground.

In our 30 years we have commissioned 38 plays. That is a significant record that speaks volumes of our commitment in bringing new writers and new actors together in a creative collision that benefits both.

Enjoy the sample of what we have put together and here's to the next 30 years!

Patrick Sutton
Director
The Gaiety School of Acting - The
National Theatre School of Ireland

October 23rd 2016

The Deer's Surrender

(SELECTED SCENES)

BY

MARINA CARR

The Deer's Surrender: **A Note**

This was Marina Carr's first staged play. With her permission, the editors of this anthology chose seven short scenes as representative of the quality of what was a long script. Had there been world enough and time the author might have revised the play for publication, since in its current state the script is such that it would need authorial editing and rewriting before it could be published in full. Unfortunately, such an option was not available at this time owing to Ms Carr's commitments. She expresses herself happy to allow these scenes to be published here on the understanding that they were written in her early twenties as a specific commission: a graduating play for a group of some sixteen students at the Gaiety School of Acting. In the way of such assignments, she needed to accommodate to the number and gender of these students and yet she was free to give vent to her already appreciable creative talent. It is clear that the play, when staged at Andrew's Lane Theatre, made a big impression. The director on that occasion, Maureen White, writes:

'The set for *The Deer's Surrender*, designed by Liz Cullinane, had a blue floor with white fluffy clouds painted on them, and on the back wall was a framed picture of sky and clouds. A set where heaven and earth are reversed, and no one was ever quite sure where we were was the perfect setting for a play that forces us to see the world differently. The scenes included below give a sense of the wit, energy and irreverence that Marina Carr used in the play to interrogate our notions of men and women, God and religion. Her characters are absurd and recognisable at the same time, and the cast performed with a fierce dedication to the ensemble. What stayed with the audience long after the play was over were not individual performances but rather a storm of energy and ideas and questions – some absurd and some, over twenty-five years later, still challenging us.'

Christopher Murray

The Deer's Surrender

SCENE ONE.

Lights up.
Enter THE CHORUS, *long robes on them of different colours. They disperse themselves at random around the stage.*

1 CHORUS: Once upon a time there was a time.

2 CHORUS: And before that time there was a time before that.

3 CHORUS: Called one time, which was nearly the time we want to talk about.

4 CHORUS: But after that time called one time, there was a time beyond that.

5 CHORUS: Which was before once upon a time and after one time.

6 CHORUS: Now though it was after one time and before once upon a time, don't let that mislead you, we're still not remotely near the time we want to tell you about.

1 CHORUS: Anyway in and around that time, the Earth was wonderful.

2 CHORUS: Everything was in tune with nature.

3 CHORUS: And all that kind of lovely imagery one associates with the best tales.

4 CHORUS: To cut a long story short. There were mothers,

5 CHORUS: And there were daughters.

6 CHORUS: And the mother said to her daughter,

1 CHORUS:	In the beginning there was nothing, then God said,
2 CHORUS:	Grand, let's leave it that way.
3 CHORUS:	But some concoction had arisen out of the slime.
5 CHORUS:	And that specimen said,
6 CHORUS:	I have ribs.
5 CHORUS:	But no one to cook them. What am I going to do?
2 CHORUS:	And out of nothing God created the oven.
4 CHORUS:	And on the seventh day after he had created the snakes and the rats, the skunks and the snails, God said to the specimen, I'm hungry, cook me something to eat.
3 CHORUS:	And the specimen put the rib in the oven and the oven blew up.
1 CHORUS:	And out of the ashes arose the most despicable creature ever seen.
6 CHORUS:	I can't possibly eat that, God said, throw it in the bin!
4 CHORUS:	I'm sorry, the creature replied, but I'm a woman.
5 CHORUS:	You're a what? God said.
3 CHORUS:	I can't help it, the creature wailed.

4 CHORUS: You've ruined everything! the male specimen roared. It was to be me and God and the eternal soul! You weren't in our plans!

5 CHORUS: You certainly were not, God whimpered.

6 CHORUS: Well I'm here now, so what are you going to do about it? the woman asked as she put on her lipstick. But before God or the man could reply she had a baby, a girl baby on top of the oven.

1 CHORUS: God went into shock.

2 CHORUS: So did the man.

3 CHORUS: And so did the woman.

4 CHORUS: How did you learn to do that? God asked.

5 CHORUS: He was jealous.

6 CHORUS: I don't know, the woman replied and had twins.

3 CHORUS: You're out of control! God yelled. I won't stand for this. I'm the one who creates around here.

2 CHORUS: And after God, I'm the next creator, the man skulked. You've no business doing this in front of our very eyes!

1 CHORUS: Don't be annoying me, the woman said. I've post-natal depression, and she went for a nap on the door of the oven and had triplets while she slept.

4 CHORUS: God was in an awful state. Suddenly the world had gone mad. He couldn't fit the woman into his logical, rational principles. He couldn't

	classify her as an animal, but he was loath to classify her as human.
5 CHORUS:	The man agreed with him. What in the name of God are we going to do, God? the man asked.
6 CHORUS:	It's certainly a problem, God replied, and needs careful thinking out. In the meantime, let's just keep her down.

SCENE TWO.

BLESSED VIRGIN:	Once upon a time there was a girl in the East who fell in love with a young man. He was her first and only love. After a while she realised she was with child. Some say there is no greater happiness for a woman to carry the child of the man she loves. At night they would meet in secret at the grove. They made plans to run away, where they would go, what they would name the child, how much money they would need. She said they should run now, forget the money, they would manage somehow. He asked her to wait just a little longer, that soon they would be on their way. One night she went to the grove to wait for him as they had planned. She waited four hours and then went home. She went the next night and the next and every night for a month, because she could not believe he would ever do this to her. The swelling increased, the mother cried, the father threw a tantrum, the aunts and uncles raved. The girl didn't care any more. The family decided to marry her off before they would all be disgraced.

Enter JESUS.

JESUS: Mammy, will you hurry up or we'll be late!

SCENE THREE.

Lights up to reveal ALPHA, OMEGA *and* GAMMA *on their crosses.* GAMMA *upside down on hers,* OMEGA *in the centre and* ALPHA *at an angle. Crosses are bright pink.*

OMEGA: What'll we do today?

ALPHA: What do you mean, what'll we do today?

GAMMA: Such a thing to ask!

OMEGA: I had a dreadful night's sleep.

GAMMA: That's a pity.

ALPHA: I had a wonderful sleep. I dreamt about Beta. A wonderful dream.

GAMMA: It was a boring dream. I listened in on it.

OMEGA: Yeah, so did I. Nothing of interest ever happens in your dreams, Alpha. It's a very bad reflection on your person.

ALPHA: At least my dreams are clean. Not like some!

OMEGA: My dreams are spick and span. It's Gama who has the filthy dreams.

GAMMA: You're just jealous because you've nothing to look forward to when you go to sleep. When I go to sleep, now that's a different story.

OMEGA: We know all about it.

GAMMA:	You don't know all about it.
APLHA:	Sure don't we tune in on you?
GAMMA:	You're only spying on the peripheral of my subconscious. You haven't the remotest idea what goes on in the deepest recesses of my soul.
OMEGA:	I suspect not much.
GAMMA:	Laugh away, but let me tell you there are many dimensions to me. I exist on many levels, all of them above the likes of you.
ALPHA:	You've changed since you met that MC fella.
OMEGA:	Yeah, you're full of western intellectual jargon!
ALPHA:	You're too caught up in patriarchy for our liking.
GAMMA:	Well if you must know the truth, I can't stand women's company. If for some reason men became extinct and there were only women left in the world, I'd shoot myself.
ALPHA:	That's an awful thing to say with Omega and myself prostrate on the perpendicular here beside you.
GAMMA:	I was theorising, okay!
OMEGA:	You were not! It was directed at Alpha and myself. You need a good clout, only I couldn't be bothered giving you one.
ALPHA:	(*who has been rooting in her handbag, produces lipstick*) Or I. How do I look, girls?

OMEGA:	Show? (ALPHA *shows*) A bit too much around the edges.

ALPHA *passes the lipstick on.*

GAMMA:	(*putting on lipstick*) I met a man once who didn't understand lipstick.
OMEGA:	(*putting on lipstick*) Very few of them do.
GAMMA:	In all other respects he was an intelligent man, but if he saw a bit of lipstick he lost the run of himself. He wrote a thesis on it.
ALPHA:	No thesis can describe the mysteries of the lipstick.
OMEGA:	Alpha is right. The lipstick has baffled scholars and theologians for centuries.
ALPHA:	Did not your man above (*they all look up*) ravage the blessed virgin and her sixteen, in bed with her lipstick on.
GAMMA:	Did not Christ himself swoon when he first saw Magdalene's painted lips, wouldn't let them stone her!
ALPHA:	Without lipstick there would be no God, no Jesus, no life everlasting.
OMEGA:	Without lipstick we'd all be atheists. Pi loves lipstick on me.
ALPHA:	So does Beta.
GAMMA:	MC never notices, but I wear it anyway. I don't think he likes it. He doesn't like my cross either.

OMEGA:	Don't mind him. That cross is really lovely on you.
GAMMA:	(*delighted*) Do you think?
ALPHA:	Oh yes, the colour is very becoming.
GAMMA:	Thank you. I prefer your crosses any day. They make you look so slim, very elegant.
OMEGA:	(*pleased*) Really?
ALPHA:	I don't think mine suits me. I feel I look a bit dumpy on it.
GAMMA:	You look lovely, doesn't she Omega?
OMEGA:	Very snazzy.
ALPHA:	I want to polish it before Beta calls.
GAMMA:	I could do with a shine, too. Has anyone got any polish?
ALPHA:	We're all out of it. C'mon, we'll go and buy some.

And exit the three, over to BLESSED VIRGIN *and* JESUS.

SCENE FOUR.

Enter the BLESSED VIRGIN *carried on by some of the* CHORUS.

4 CHORUS:	(*who has remained on stage*) You know the thing I could never come to terms with in the Tristan Isolde story is why did they ever leave the cave. I mean if they were that

13

happy, if they were really lovers, why did they have to go back, and if they went back why did they ever run away in the first place. And the other thing that's really annoying me today is the story they're telling. I had a beautiful story prepared and was all set to tell it and they started on this one. I hate the six of us together all the time. I'm an individual with an individual tale to tell and I'll tell it to you even if it kills you. It goes something like this. Once upon a time there was a man who was in love with two women. One was on a life support machine and the other was dead. One day he woke up and said to himself, This can't go on. I have to finish with one of them.

6 CHORUS: Are you telling another story?

4 CHORUS: No, I'm just repeating the main points of the story we're telling.

5 CHORUS: You're not! You're telling that story again about the man and the two women.

6 CHORUS: You know that story is banned.

4 CHORUS: Honestly I was just describing the oven.

6 CHORUS: Carry on!

4 CHORUS: So the man put on his suit and runners and put all his belongings into a paper bag and headed off for the intensive care unit of the graveyard to finish with one of them. On the way he met a woman with a fish in a plastic bag. The woman looked at him and said that maybe he'd like to do the love lie down. I've never yet refused a woman with a fish, the man thought to himself.

Certainly I feel like a lie down with you, the man said as he polished his runners...

2 CHORUS: (*cutting in on her*) Mary Brigid Bernadette Rose was a typist and the company sent her to Cyprus. And the Boss was consumed with a passion for her and Mary Brigid Bernadette Rose fluttered her Catholic eyelashes and said, You won't use me, me Cypriot Boyo, for I come from a land where love has been beaten out of us, where passion is a myth we've forgotten about, where sex is something you bargain with. You want to get into my brown nylons, it'll cost you!

JESUS *has been carried on at this stage, wakes up.*

JESUS: You shouldn't smoke!

BLESSED VIRGIN: Stop telling me what to do!

JESUS: It doesn't look good! It puts me in a very bad light, if anyone saw you!

BLESSED VIRGIN: Let them see me! I'm fed up of this Holy Mary lark! Lies, all of it!

JESUS: Mammy, how dare you? Look at me your darling son, dying on the cross for you.

BLESSED VIRGIN: The cheek of you and all I did for you. I didn't break my back rearing you for you to go off and nail yourself to a cross.

JESUS: I didn't nail myself. I was nailed.

BLESSED VIRGIN: Well you didn't stop them! You're an ungrateful pup, that's what you are!

15

JESUS:	You'd want to watch your language, you forget who you're talking to.
BLESSED VIRGIN:	Don't pull that one on me. You might have fooled the western world for the last few thousand years. But you can't fool me because I'm your mother and I know the stuff you're made of! Sure didn't I make you myself!
JESUS:	I'm telling Daddy on you!
BLESSED VIRGIN:	Tell him!
JESUS:	He'll put you in your place!
BLESSED VIRGIN:	Oh will he now?

Enter PRIEST *in wedding gown, goes straight for* JESUS.

PRIEST:	I've prepared a wonderful sermon!
JESUS:	For the women.
PRIEST:	They're really getting out of hand.
JESUS:	And it's all Mammy's fault. She's sending out bad vibes to them, vibes against you and me and Daddy.
PRIEST:	Don't worry, I'll put a stop to their gallivanting.
BLESSED VIRGIN:	You won't! You're on the way out the pair of you! I'm only surprised you lasted this long.
JESUS:	We're here to stay.
BLESSED VIRGIN:	We'll see about that!
PRIEST:	We are indeed. Do you like my new frock?

JESUS:	White is lovely on you.
PRIEST:	I love white. If I had my way I'd dress the Blessed Virgin in white.
BLESSED VIRGIN:	What is it about virgins that drives men crazy?
PRIEST:	(*prancing around*) The congregation will love it. They like me to dress nice for them, shows I care.
JESUS:	And you do.
PRIEST:	Of course I do.
BLESSED VIRGIN:	You look like a woman!

JESUS *throws a look to* BLESSED VIRGIN*, she looks back smugly at him.*

JESUS:	What's on the agenda for today, father?
PRIEST:	The usual. A few baptisms, a few marriages, a few confessions, a few burials.
JESUS:	A hard day ahead of you.
PRIEST:	I do it willingly for you.
JESUS:	Just as I hang here willingly for you.
PRIEST:	I don't know what I'd do without you.
JESUS:	Or I you.
BLESSED VIRGIN:	What is this? The mutual admiration society?

PRIEST:	(*going over, patting* BLESSED VIRGIN) Of course we couldn't manage without the Blessed Virgin, either!
BLESSED VIRGIN:	Damn right you couldn't!
JESUS:	Mammy, your language!
BLESSED VIRGIN:	Tell him to stop calling me the Blessed Virgin! I'm the Great Mother! I'm the one you should be down on your knees worshipping. Only for me you'd never have been born!
JESUS:	I would so! Daddy would have found someone else to carry me, no problem. I wish he had!
PRIEST:	Is she giving you a hard time again?
JESUS:	The menopause you know!
BLESSED VIRGIN:	The Great Mother doesn't have a menopause. I was fertile before the world began and I'll be dropping eggs long after it's ended.
PRIEST:	Wasn't she lucky to be chosen by our heavenly father? And the painless childbirth she had, few women are that lucky.
BLESSED VIRGIN:	I was in labour three days and three nights with that fella in a stinking cow shed! "Away In A Manger" my eye!
PRIEST:	She didn't suffer a thing.
BLESSED VIRGIN:	You'd swear you had him the way you're going on.

PRIEST:	If only every woman was like the Blessed Virgin. Think of what a paradise this place would be.
BLESSED VIRGIN:	Nanny goat!
PRIEST:	I dream of a world full of virgins all wafting around in blue, and not a word out of them except the odd saintly smile. Instead I'm hounded by miniskirts and low-cut tops, boots, no.7 lipstick, obsession perfume and high heels all colours of the rainbow. I won't stand for it much longer.

Enter the THREE MOTHERS, *crosses on them.*

SCENE FIVE.

Enter the CHORUS.

1 CHORUS:	When the woman woke up from her nap, she discovered that she was tied to the oven by her ponytail.
2 CHORUS:	Needless to say she got a bit of a fright.
5 CHORUS:	Hey, what's going on here? she shouted to the male.
6 CHORUS:	You're not allowed to raise your voice to me, the man said gently.
4 CHORUS:	He could afford to be gentle.
3 CHORUS:	Why am I tied to the oven by my hair?
2 CHORUS:	It's a punishment from me, God replied.

5 CHORUS:	I didn't do anything, the woman said.
6 CHORUS:	You did so! God thundered. You gave life in front of my very nose.
1 CHORUS:	I'll never do it again, the woman pleaded.
2 CHORUS:	Don't lie to me, God said. I hate a liar!
3 CHORUS:	Yeah, God hates a liar, the man echoed.
4 CHORUS:	I have always thought liars quite interesting, the woman ventured.
6 CHORUS:	We're not concerned with what you think, the man replied from a safe distance.
5 CHORUS:	We want our dinner, God said.
3 CHORUS:	So the woman went off hunting with the oven tied to her head.
1 CHORUS:	Meanwhile, your man and God discussed the ontological proofs for their existence.
5 CHORUS:	The woman managed to mow down five buffalo and six deer.
6 CHORUS:	Coming home from the hunt, she met another woman who had two ovens tied to her neck.
4 CHORUS:	I thought I was the only oven in the world, one oven said.
3 CHORUS:	So did I, replied two ovens.
2 CHORUS:	Is there a man and a god in your life as well, one oven asked.

1 CHORUS: There certainly is, two ovens replied. It's on account of the old womb I have. If there was any way I could get rid of it maybe they'd leave me alone. They take turns to watch me every night.

3 CHORUS: Ah sure it's the same with me, one oven said. When God sleeps your man watches and when your man sleeps God watches.

4 CHORUS: Well it was lovely talking to you, two ovens said, but I'd better go now.

6 CHORUS: Yeah, me too, one oven agreed. No doubt I'll meet you on the hunting grounds again.

5 CHORUS: You certainly will, said two ovens. And the pair of them headed home.

2 CHORUS: Walking softly in the dusk each delighted to have met one of their kind.

3 CHORUS: One oven arrived home to find God and the man asleep, exhausted from their intellectual discussion.

4 CHORUS: I could kill them now, she thought to herself, and run away and never come back.

6 CHORUS: Instead she covered them with a buffalo skin in case they got a chill.

1 CHORUS: When dinner was ready the pair woke up and ate their fill and gave thanks to God.

3 CHORUS: Music, let's have some music, God said.

4 CHORUS: And the woman played a song she had heard on the hunting grounds that day, the song of the

wild beast brought low, the song of the buffalo
going down, the song of the deer's surrender.

6 CHORUS: And the man and God looked at the woman as
she made music for them and they grew soft and
almost loved her and crept into her oven and
slept and the woman was happy.

And exit the six.

SCENE SIX.

Jubilant procession on stage of all women. Enter the GREAT MOTHER
and ALPHA *from side. All bow as they enter and get up on the centre
rostrum or altar.*

ALPHA: May the Great Mother be with you.

ALL: And also with you.

BLESSED VIRGIN: My sermon today will be on men and their
desire for a womb of their own.

M1:   Your sermon yesterday was on men!

M2:   And the day before!

ALPHA: SHH!

BLESSED VIRGIN: Now when you're dealing with men, you're
dealing with a dangerous species. They are a
species possessed with one insane desire and
they will stop at nothing to fulfil it. Each and
every one of them would give their right eye for
a womb of their own!

ALPHA:	Now maybe one could forgive their jealousy over the lack of a womb, but it doesn't stop there! No! They won't be happy until they have the eggs and the fallopians as well. Oh, they really want jam on it!
BLESSED VIRGIN:	Now because men couldn't have a womb, in their desperation to have something that resembled a womb, they invented the bomb! Now if you examine this theory closely you'll see the endings of both words are identical! (ALPHA *produces two flashcards with bomb and womb written on them.*) The omb from womb was put into the bomb!
ALPHA:	So you can see clearly that the bomb is the male version of the womb! (*putting aside cards*) Let us approach the argument from another angle. Why do men wear trousers? (*A meaningful pause.*) I'll tell you why. Because they want a womb. They'll stop at nothing to get one! You see their vanity will not permit them to wear a skirt! A skirt isn't good enough for them! No, they have to wear these licentious creations!
BLESSED VIRGIN:	The trouser is designed to show off every curve in the male body. It is designed for the sole purpose of attracting women to them!
ALPHA:	It works like a magnet! You see a pair of trousers and irresistibly you are drawn. And when they sit down, note how the slyness of the design allows the trouser to slide up the leg and reveal one or two hairy calves depending on your luck and the position in which his legs are in! And hence women are plagued!

BLESSED VIRGIN: Their tricks don't stop there! Oh no! Far from it, they've only just begun. What about the perfume they wear? Chanel, Paco Rabane, Brute! And their ties!

ALPHA: Yes, their ties! They're obscene! You see a tie dangling from a man's neck and what do you think of?

Moan from the women.

BLESSED VIRGIN: Yes! Man is a snare to be avoided at all costs!

ALPHA: His sole purpose on this earth is to send the female out of her senses, while all the time at the back of his mind is the insane desire to snatch her womb off her and put it on himself!

BLESSED VIRGIN: But that won't happen! Because there are going to be some changes around here! From now on the trousers is banned as an instrument of pornography!

ALPHA: From now on men will only be found in kitchens and in bedrooms!

BLESSED VIRGIN: From now on all men will be nailed frontways to the cross!

ALPHA: From now on men will rear everyone's children!

BLESSED VIRGIN: And they will never...

ALPHA: I say never...

BLESSED VIRGIN: Never have a womb of their own!

Both out of breath with fanaticism. And into

BLESSED VIRGIN:	Great mother open our eyes! In the name of the mother and the mother and the mother!
ALPHA:	(*delighted with herself*) That went off very well.
BLESSED VIRGIN:	Do you think am I too soft on the men?
ALPHA:	A little bit maybe.
BLESSED VIRGIN:	What else could we do to them?
ALPHA:	I wonder...Ah no, forget it.
BLESSED VIRGIN:	No, go on.
ALPHA:	Well I was just kinda wondering, is there any way we could wipe them off the face of the earth?
BLESSED VIRGIN:	God, that's a brainwave! How did you think of that?
ALPHA:	It just came to me in a flash, a kind of vision.
BLESSED VIRGIN:	A world with just women in it. Wouldn't that be something?
ALPHA:	It certainly would.
BLESSED VIRGIN:	How would we go about it?
ALPHA:	Well we have to find a reason first.
BLESSED VIRGIN:	I have the very reason!
ALPHA:	They're too tall!
BLESSED VIRGIN:	Exactly!

ALPHA:	The cheek of them! How dare they grow so high and leave us looking up at them!
BLESSED VIRGIN:	Did you know that the reason men are so high is because their voices are so low?
ALPHA:	I never knew that.
BLESSED VIRGIN:	Well take it from me!
ALPHA:	Is that why women have long hair?
BLESSED VIRGIN:	Don't be ridiculous! Women have long hair because they use a hair dryer.
ALPHA:	Well Beta uses a hair dryer and he doesn't have long hair.
BLESSED VIRGIN:	But you're forgetting that he's tall.
ALPHA:	He's not! He's small!
BLESSED VIRGIN:	Well according to my theory he's tall.
ALPHA:	Oh I follow you now. The reason his hair is not tall even though he uses a hair dryer is because he gets it cut, and therefore his neck is short and you consider him long. It fits perfectly. It's a wonderful theory.
ALPHA:	Yeah. (*Pause*) I hate men being taller than us, I hate that their feet and hands are bigger, I hate that they have a hairy chest and we don't, I hate that they can have a beard if they want. It's just not fair! All we have is long hair and a womb!
BLESSED VIRGIN:	We used to have beards but they stole them from us.

ALPHA:	Is there any way we could steal them back?
BLESSED VIRGIN:	Of course there is. With the Great Mother everything is possible.
ALPHA:	Really? And is there any way you could make them smaller?
BLESSED VIRGIN:	How small would you like them?
ALPHA:	I'd like them quarter the size they are now and maybe you could fix it so that all babies are born girls.
BLESSED VIRGIN:	No problem. Have you any other ideas for the sermon tomorrow?
ALPHA:	No, just the height and the beard would be fine for the moment. Will we go and write it now? I think the first line should go, 'Women we are gathered here today to recover our height and our beards.'
BLESSED VIRGIN:	(*both going off*) That sounds like a beautiful opening.
ALPHA:	We'll have them in tears with our eloquence.

And off.

SCENE SEVEN.

Last chorus scene.

BLOND:	So one oven reared her children according to the laws. Then one morning she woke up and said to herself, It's years since I've seen two ovens, and

	so she set off for the hunting grounds to look for her.
DYMER:	Mary Brigid Bernadette Rose lay back on the beach and laughed. She laughed so hard she strangled herself on her ball and chain. To this day the Cypriot can be seen on the beach mourning an Irish skeleton in a dark overcoat and elbow-length gloves.
DOLCE:	She reached the hunting grounds to find two ovens waiting for her. I knew you would come in the end, two ovens said when she saw her.
DILL:	Where are your ovens, one oven asked her.
DABID:	Oh those, I haven't worn them in years. Listen, there's a new god in the garden of men that everyone's following, will you come away with me there?
DOOBY:	Ah I'm too old now to change, one oven said. I'm so used to God and your man, I couldn't survive without them.
DOLCE:	But I'll tell me children what you've told me here today.
DYMER:	And so they parted, one oven heading back to God and your man and two ovens heading off to the garden of men and the next god.

And enter ALL.
CHORUS *move aside. First* PRIEST *followed by* THREE MOTHERS. *He takes up position behind* JESUS. BLESSED VIRGIN *takes her stand.* ALPHA *takes middle stand, in her beard. Congregation are around.*

FATHER:	My sermon today will be on the direct relation between the reduction of female souls entering heaven and the increase of the sales of the pill! Now I have thoroughly researched this argument and let me give you the facts! (*Mimes the rest of the sermon, works himself into a frenzy.*)
BLESSED VIRGIN:	The title of my sermon today is 'Is There Anything Men Haven't Stolen From Us Women?' The answer is no! You look around and see that they have stolen everything! (*Mimes the rest, mimes herself into a fury, synchronise* PRIEST *and* BLESSED VIRGIN'S *fury.*)
ALPHA:	The god Shehe asked me to speak to you. Shehe asked me to give you this message, and I quote: 'I cannot promise you life everlasting, who knows what happens when we leave this earth? In fact I can promise you very little but this I will promise you. If you come with me I will lead you beyond the Impasse we have dwelt in for so long. I will show you how the Earth could be heaven, how the heavens dwell in the Earth if we would only allow them. And this I swear to you. I swear I will never discriminate against you on any account, least of all because you are men or because you are women. How can I, when I am both?'

And lights.

Fox And Crow

BY

GAVIN KOSTICK

A play for 18 performers, in 5 Acts. Each actor is supplied with a broomstick, large white cloth which contains such props as candle, matches, knife, bottle, mask, harmonica, hammer and piece of metal. By and large the props for each scene are made out of these.

ACT ONE.

SET.

The main area of the set is a flat, highly stylised chess-board. This is the stage-within-a-stage where the action of the play is performed. The board is surrounded by the kind of junk that might be found in a forest tip. Oil drums, ladders, rope, old tool kits etc. This outer stage is the source for all set and props that are used in the play. In the outer stage there is a table, on which is a chess board, arid chess set, the chess pieces are strewn about as if a game has just ended.

On either side of the table sit a FOX and a CROW.

16 actors are placed about the stage as if they were the pieces from the game.

CROW: You're wrong, Sister Fox. Wrong. The human animal is selfish to the core.

FOX: I am not wrong Brother Crow. Humans in their heart of hearts, are generous.

CROW: Selfish.

FOX: Generous.

CROW: Well then, as we play, I shall tell you a story.

As they speak they set up the pieces. The actors move to their positions exactly as if they are being set up by the FOX.

CROW: (*continuing*) And the events of this story will force you to admit that greedy self-interest is embedded in the human, like a stone in a cherry.

FOX: Clack all you like. I won't admit it.

CROW: You will, sister. I bet you will.

FOX:	You bet?
CROW:	Whatever you like.
FOX:	Supper?
CROW:	Supper it is.
FOX:	Brother.
CROW:	Yes?
FOX:	To make things even, why don't I tell you a little story that I have in mind. It's nothing much, a trifle, but I'm willing to bet that by the end of it, you will confess to me that generosity blossoms in the breast of the human, like a rose in the wilderness.
CROW:	Agreed. So. The rules are, each of us tells a story. If you are forced to agree with me, you provide supper.
FOX:	And visa-versa.
CROW:	Who goes first?
FOX:	White begins?

They select pieces. FOX *gets white.*

From here on throughout the entire play the FOX and CROW are playing chess. What we see in this scene are the white (i.e. the FOX'S) pieces only. They move exactly as the FOX moves them, and if they are taken in the game, the actor is killed on the spot on the stage.

FOX:	Dawn rose on an army that was disposing itself for battle. Camp fires were extinguished. (*all the candles are blown out*) And the forces allayed.

As the opening moves are played out the following dialogue takes place. The central pawns should include DARRAGH.

FOX: Why, when or where the battle took place does not really matter. What matters is that although at first the two armies were as near equal as can be imagined, one side at first gained a tactical advantage, then a material advantage. Attacks were pressed home, defence became a retreat, a retreat became a rout and the rout became a bloody slaughter. By the time the sun had set, one of the two armies had been destroyed to a man.

FOX clicks fingers, all the pieces fall down. Sounds of dying.

FOX: Death walked out. Taking the souls from the dead, and plucking the breath from the living.

CROW: Did she? Did she?

FOX: She did.

Enter MEDBH.

FOX: As did a distressed young maid, by the name of...

CROW: Medbh. Medbh. I'm right, I'm right aren't I?

FOX: You are.

CROW: And Medbh's looking for her sweetheart, Darragh, who's been stabbed.

FOX: She has. You've heard this before.

34

CROW:	Not only that, it is the *very* same beginning as the *story* I have for you. You're a fool sister. If you carry on this way I will be victorious.
FOX:	This *story* proves generosity.
CROW:	Fiddle.
FOX:	Perhaps our narratives will diverge shortly.
CROW:	True. Tell me. Does your story have a dragon in it, near the end?
FOX:	It does.
CROW:	So does mine.
MEDBH:	Oh Darragh! Oh my sweetheart!
FOX:	A chill was on Darragh's forehead.
MEDBH:	You're cold, so cold.
FOX:	The old crone, Death had reached his side.
DEATH:	He's mine, child.
MEDBH:	We are to be married.
DEATH:	The world is full of tragedies.
MEDBH:	It should be my sweet lips that kiss him, not yours, so old and dry and bitter.
DEATH:	My kiss may be bitter to the taste, but at the end of it lies sleep.
MEDBH:	It should be my clean arms that hold him, not yours so fierce and tight.

DEATH:	My grip is fierce, but those I hold find peace.
MEDBH:	Bring him sleep when he is grey headed and nodding by the fire. Bring him peace when our grandchildren play about our knees. Take him then old Mother and I'll thank you as is right and proper. But pass by him today.
DEATH:	Shall I spare this boy alone, and so many others must go down in the clay?
MEDBH:	Yes, gentle Mother, for none else is loved here, as I love him. Our love is sure that if he must die, I shall surely stretch myself out by his side and never stir again.
DEATH:	Go home, to your village where there are those that will love you and comfort you and in time...
MEDBH:	Never, never, never, never.
DEATH:	And what would you promise me in return for the gift of his life?
MEDBH:	Anything. Everything.
DEATH:	Very well. In a short time you shall have a daughter. On the day you are to give her her name, you must place her in the arms of every man and woman and child in the village. Should any single person choose to kiss your baby before she is named, you must give your daughter away to that person at once and without question or complaint.
MEDBH:	Is that all?
DEATH:	It is.

MEDBH:	Then you have my word. With all my heart. With all my thanks.
DEATH:	Take him home.
MEDBH:	Oh love. Wake up. Wake up, Darragh.
DARRAGH:	Medbh. I've had such a bad dream.
MEDBH:	Shh. We're going home, love.

FOX and CROW continue playing. The battlefield becomes a bustling village, complete with a variety of occupations, couples, families etc. DEATH settles down at the back to watch. Perhaps when a character is thoroughly identified with a chess piece then the way it is taken on and off the board can be integrated with the actor going on and off the playing area of the stage.

CROW:	You've stolen chickens from this village, haven't you?
FOX:	Many times. And rabbits from an ancient warren nearby. The fields are flat and open, but the ditches and hedgerows are good for cover. The village was neither big nor small, and all of its citizens were delighted with Medbh's return, and the return of their young hero.

The village celebrates. DARRAGH and MEDBH are at the centre of attention. More congratulations, the village prepares the festivities. Everyone is delighted to see him home safe, except the SMITH. He bustles around the crowd, trying to get to MEDBH on his own. He is a dark, brooding character.

MICHEAL:	They're back. They're back.
SHIELA:	Where?
MICHEAL:	There. Look. Was it a glorious victory Darragh?

DARRAGH:	It was not Michael Óg. It was a sad disaster. But for Medbh, I should have died on the field.
SHIELA:	Are you wounded, so?
DARRAGH:	Not a piece of me Shiela.
SHIELA:	And when will you be married?
MEDBH:	As soon as ever we can.
MICHEAL:	Tell us about war Darragh. Did you kill many?
DARRAGH:	I did not. I won't claim to have played the hero, so I won't live to be named a liar.
MICHEAL:	It must have been an adventure all the same. Settle down and tell us the while.
VILLAGERS:	Go on Darragh.
DARRAGH:	If you will have it. Here it is...

DARRAGH *talks to the villagers.*

CROW:	You said all the citizens were delighted sister.
FOX:	So they were brother, all save one alone. (*Places* SMITH *on the board. A black castle perhaps*)
CROW:	And who was this one alone?

The SMITH *takes the chance to talk to* MEDBH *on his own.*

SMITH:	Medbh. Medbh.
MEDBH:	(*still delighted*) Smith. My dear Smith. Are you happy for us?

SMITH:	I'm happy to see you back safe. You should not have run off so without warning.
MEDBH:	It was Darragh who went to war. I only went to find him.
SMITH:	Medbh.
MEDBH:	What?
SMITH:	I made something for you. I've had it a time, and now I'd like to give it you.

He passes her a ring.

MEDBH:	It's beautiful.
SMITH:	I made it for you.
MEDBH:	It's too much. I have a ring already, but I'll set this on a necklace.
SMITH:	Medbh. It's from me to you. It means I love you and I want to marry you. I want to be your husband.

SHIELA *overhears this. She eavesdrops the rest of the conversation.*

MEDBH:	I can't accept this.
SMITH:	I love you, and I always have.
MEDBH:	Stop.
SMITH:	I'm no hero, no dancer or story-teller. But I would do anything for you Medbh.
MEDBH:	Anything?

SMITH:	Yes.
MEDBH:	Then be my friend.
SMITH:	When Darragh went away I got down on my knees and prayed that he would never come back.
MEDBH:	Stop.
SMITH:	I prayed that you would fly to me and I would comfort you like a little chick, and you would understand that I have loved you more than he ever could.
MEDBH:	Smith.
SMITH:	I prayed for this so much I believed it was true.
MEDBH:	Silence.
SMITH:	Look at him Medbh. Look at me. Which of us loves you more?
MEDBH:	Have I ever led you on?
SMITH:	Marry me.
MEDBH:	I don't love you. I love Darragh.
SMITH:	You sat on the ledge of my forge. Swinging your ankles the light of the sun...
MEDBH:	I'm sorry ever did.
SMITH:	Don't say that.
MEDBH:	Friends Smith. That's what we are.

SMITH:	Lovers.
MEDBH:	No. Never.
SMITH:	You must have known.
MEDBH:	I didn't. I swear. Let us be friends.
SMITH:	Friends.
MEDBH:	Yes.
SMITH:	If I can't have you.
MEDBH:	You! Have me!
SMITH:	If we can't be together...
MEDBH:	Enough now. I am going to marry the man I love. And that man is Darragh. And I'm sorry for what you've said, because it means I've lost the bestest friend of my childhood, which was you and now can be no more. Here.

MEDBH returns the ring and goes to DARRAGH. The SMITH calls after her.

| SMITH: | What have I done? I've lost her. |

The SMITH exits. Three or four VILLAGERS who have overheard, are talking. They are getting on with preparations for the wedding as they chat.

MICHEAL:	It's a disgrace. An insult to a war hero.
SHIELA:	A man can propose to whomever he likes.
MICHEAL:	Breaking up a couple.

SHIELA:	He was better to say it out than wait for her to be wedded and gone.
MICHEAL:	He was always slipping her little gifts and trinkets.
VILLAGER 1:	Then it's Medbh' s fault for encouraging him.
SHIELA:	She did not.
VILLAGER 1:	She's turned poor Smithie's head and that's a fact. She should never have seen so much of him.
MICHEAL:	Darragh should be told.
SHIELA:	You will not tell him. Medbh has spurned the Smith, and that's enough.
MICHEAL:	And why does Medbh not tell Darragh herself. She's wants them both...
SHIELA:	Speak no ill of Medbh, Micheal Óg, not on her wedding day.

The preparations have finished and **MEDBH** *and* **DARRAGH** *are married.*

SHIELA:	The bride and groom.

The SMITH is going to leave, but he takes one last look at MEDBH. Wedding ceremony.

VILLAGERS:	Speech! Speech!
MEDBH:	I have the strangest kind of speech for you all. It's a kind of request. Darragh and I thank you for sharing so deeply in our happiness.

SHIELA & OTHERS: Hooray.

MEDBH: And should we have the joy, one day of a little baby. On the child's naming day we shall put that baby into the arms of each and every one of you. All that we ask is that you do not kiss that baby on its face nor any part of it at all.

VILLAGERS: Why Medbh?

Ad lib curiosity.

MEDBH: Swear to this first. Then we shall tell you.

VILLAGERS, one after another and then in a throng, "I swear". Not the SMITH.

SHIELA: There. That's all of us.

MEDBH: Everyone?

VILLAGERS: Everyone.

MEDBH *starts to tell the story.*

MEDBH: Well, I'll tell you so.

FOX: And in the sweet joy of her marriage day, Medbh told them all exactly what had passed.

CROW: Good, agreed. Three seasons pass.

FOX: Summer, autumn and winter themselves. The gentle and much beloved Medbh began to swell. The villagers looked on and were pleased

CROW: But the soul of the Smith was tainted.

FOX: Exactly.

CROW:	A knot had tied itself inside him. He might have loosened it, if he had tried. For he was not so ugly, nor so clumsy as he supposed. But bitter fruits have a pale skin, and he bit deeply.

SMITH *is at anvil.*

SMITH:	Oaf. Fool. Unlovable rogue. Never be loved. Never be loved. She laughed at me. Laughed at me. Laughed at me.
CROW:	The Smith, like all Smiths at that time had a magic in his forge.
FOX:	Of which he himself had only been faintly aware.
CROW:	But now the clanging of his anguish began to sour the milk...
FOX:	...wilt the crops...
CROW:	...lame the horses.
FOX:	And the hurt coiled inside him and tightened and tightened, until, in his desolation he beat his heart right out of himself.
CROW:	Then he hid it.

A child is born.

DARRAGH:	It's a girl! We have a daughter.
ALL:	A girl. A girl. Let us see.
MEDBH:	Pass her around. Pass her around. Bless her, pet her, but please, do not kiss her. Remember your oaths.

SHIELA: Me first! Me first!

She takes the baby. Beams at her and passes it on. The VILLAGERS sing a collective lullaby, begun by SHIELA, which ends as the baby is returned to the mother. The VILLAGERS pass her around. Perhaps one pretends to kiss then refrains. At some point, DEATH re-enters, she is not recognised by the VILLAGERS. At last the child is returned to her mother.

MEDBH: That's everyone.

SHIELA & OTHERS: Everyone.

MEDBH: Then I name this child...

Enter the SMITH.

SMITH: You have forgotten me.

MICHEAL: We have not. You are no longer part of the village Smith.

SMITH: I am.

MICHEAL: You have not come down to the market this past year.

SMITH: I have been working and thinking. I have wronged you Darragh, and so I have made you this torque.

DARRAGH: How have you wronged me?

SMITH: I have loved Medbh, and tried to steal her away from you.

DARRAGH: When was this?

MEDBH:	Before we were married. And I have not seen him since.
SMITH:	Will you accept my apology?
DARRAGH:	I will of course. It's no crime to have loved Medbh. How could I of all here say that?
SMITH:	Will you try it on?
DARRAGH:	I will. Of course.
SMITH:	May I hold the child? My understanding is that she must be passed to each and every one of us.
MEDBH:	Smith. Here is my child. Hold her. I'm glad the unhappiness has gone from your mind.

The SMITH *takes the child.*

SMITH:	Medbh. Was there ever a time when you might have loved me?
MEDBH:	What?
SMITH:	Could you ever have loved me?
MEDBH:	I don't believe so.
SMITH:	Never at all?
MICHEAL:	Take off the torque Darragh.
DARRAGH:	Smith. Give back my daughter now.
MICHEAL:	Darragh.
DARRAGH:	Give her back.

The SMITH stares at DARRAGH, and he recoils. The SMITH kisses the baby, and at the moment he does so the torque begins to strangle DARRAGH.

SMITH: The baby is mine. Her name is Aurora and I shall cover her in gold.

MICHEAL: Villain.

MICHEAL goes for the SMITH. Other villagers help DARRAGH or go to MEDBH. MEDBH rushes at the SMITH and wrests the baby from him. General confusion.

MEDBH: No! You can't have her. Even if you kiss her you can't have her.

At that exact moment DEATH enters and there is total silence and stillness.

DEATH: You cannot break your oath Medbh.

MEDBH: A bitter oath. My child gone and my husband too.

DEATH: You cannot break it. The Smith must take the child.

MICHEAL: Never.

MEDBH: I take it back. I deny it.

VILLAGERS: Never! Never!

MEDBH: Please gentle Death. My husband to die and my child taken from me. It's too much.

SHIELA: Release her. We beg you.

VILLAGERS:	Release her!

The VILLAGERS *kneel to* DEATH. *Only the* SMITH *is left standing.*

MICHEAL:	If the child must be taken it must. But do not let Darragh be murdered.
DEATH:	Do you all wish this?
VILLAGERS:	We do.
SMITH:	I do not.
DEATH:	He is a much loved man. He won't die. None of you shall die today, but all will sleep. Put down roots. Push up shoots. Heavy headed, flower-bedded, poppies one and all.

DEATH transforms the VILLAGERS into poppies. DEATH is left regarding the SMITH and the baby.

DEATH:	And here you will stay. Until time ends. No more alive than dancing flowers. Unless a mortal shall come who, of their own free will, pours out their life blood, and waters your roots from their very heart.
SMITH:	And what of me and the child?
DEATH:	You have made no oath.
SMITH:	Good. Little Aurora. Sweet child. Then you and I shall live together. And I shall bring you up, just as I wish, and you shall never know any man but me.

The Poppies shudder.

SMITH: Quiet. Or I'll take my sickle to a whetstone and that'll be the end of you. Aurora. Aurora.

Exit SMITH, *singing lullaby to child.*

CROW: The Smith set off to raise the girl, and the poppies were left to sway and sag in the breeze. Death left...

DEATH is still in the field of poppies. Enter three travelling entertainer /rogues. HELTER, SKELTER and LITTLE SAM...

HELTER: Hold old woman!

SKELTER: She is weak, she is tired, I pity her frail joints.

HELTER: Little Sam. A chair for the crone.

LITTLE SAM becomes a chair for DEATH. HELTER pushes her so that she sits down sharply.

HELTER: Are you comfortable?

SKELTER: She can never be comfortable, her bones are so old.

SKELTER: Little Sam. Adjust yourself. There madam.

LITTLE SAM: She's comfortable.

SKELTER: She looks unwell. Are you sure Little Sam?

LITTLE SAM: I'm sure.

Each of them sings their names, trying to harmonise with the other. This takes some doing.

HELTER: Helter.

SKELTER: Skelter.

LITTLE SAM: And Little Sam.

The three of them begin a song/do a routine to entertain DEATH. This involves card tricks, eggs out of ears, find the lady etc. DEATH (disconcertingly for the three), is never fooled, e.g. is always picking the right card. As they do their routines they sing something like the following in three part harmony. See separate song sheet. HELTER, SKELTER and LITTLE SAM's song.

They end the routine by all holding out their caps for a coin. DEATH gives them nothing.

SKELTER: She's old and poor and she hasn't a farthing.

HELTER: Well if she has nothing, she can at least tell us of
                       a village hereabouts.

SKELTER: She's a kind one, she'll tell us.

HELTER: Well old mother. We've heard of a christening,
                       and we mean to make some money there. So
                       which way to the village, and we'll drink to you
                       later?

DEATH: You're here.

HELTER, SKELTER and LITTLE SAM, *look around elaborately.*

HELTER: Have we offended you, madam, that you mock
                       us this way?

DEATH: You have reached the village.

SKELTER: Her wits are astray.

HELTER: The sun has got to her.

50

LITTLE SAM:	I'll box her ears.
HELTER:	Little Sam. Her brain will only be rattled more. Where is the village old woman?
DEATH:	All around you, in the form of poppies. Listen, they're singing.
LITTLE SAM :	She's right.
SKELTER:	The poor dears. How terrible. *(They're off key)*
HELTER:	Who has done this to them?
DEATH:	Why, Death.
ALL THREE:	And who is Death?
DEATH:	Have you never met Death?

HELTER, SKELTER *and* LITTLE SAM *go into a huddle and consult.*

ALL THREE:	No. We never have. Tell us about Death.
DEATH:	Well, Death is she that puts an end to life. She puts her hand on the baby's face as she sleeps. She breaks the branches on which the children swing. She blocks up the heart of a man in his prime. She wets the stone steps so the old women will fall. Death plays all these tricks and countless others besides.
HELTER:	Monstrous!
SKELTER:	Contemptible!
LITTLE SAM:	*(too angry to speak)* Ooo!

HELTER:	And tell us, crone, where this scoundrel Death may be found. For I think I speak for us all...
SKELTER & LS:	...You do! You do!
HELTER:	When I say, we three swear that we shall track down this murderous Death wherever he...
DEATH:	She.
HELTER:	She you say. Worse and worse. Where-ever she may be found.
SKELTER:	Where can we find Death?
DEATH:	You can find Death not far from here. She rests in a wood, under a tree which has five roots, like the fingers of a man's hand.
HELTER:	(*shaking* DEATH's *hand and exiting*) Shouldn't be too hard to find. Thank you.
SKELTER:	(*shaking* DEATH's *hand and exiting*) Thank you.

LITTLE SAM also shakes DEATH'S hand almost leaves, then in a moment of emotion goes back and kisses her on the cheek, and then exits. The FOX and CROW set up the battlefield again, so the poppy field vanishes. Enter a few SOLDIERS.

Battlefield setup.

CROW:	Meanwhile, in the aftermath of the same battle in which Darragh had so nearly died, the small band of brothers who had won the field exulted in their good fortune.
SOLDIERS:	Hurray! Hurray! Hurray!

CROW: These were men, tied by nothing but their conquest. It is no surprise that once they had divided their spoil, they went their separate ways. One warrior, (*picking out a piece – the* WARRIOR, *who has a sackful of gold as spoil, other soldiers shake his hand and leave*) a fierce and tested knight who was far from his homeland, set out into the evening, only to find himself lost in a dismal wood.

A dark wood is created. The WARRIOR makes his way cautiously along. The bag of gold he has is very heavy. The wood is malignant and causes him to trip and fall. Perhaps he has a horse which is spooked. And flees.

CROW: Even for a bird, it is not an easy place to tread. And the crooked ways are dogged by wicked creatures.

CROW adds another piece. It is a SIDHE (pronounced Shee), who holds up a candle.

WARRIOR: Who's there?

SIDHE: He's lithe!

WARRIOR: Shelter!

The SIDHE shields the light, hiding it from him. She moves elsewhere and reveals it again.

WARRIOR: Halt. Who are you?

SIDHE: He's quick!

The light is hidden and revealed a third time.

WARRIOR: Sanctuary!

SIDHE: He's a handsome man.

53

WARRIOR: I can pay. I have gold.

SIDHE *hides light.*

SIDHE: He's a fool.

The WARRIOR *stumbles in the darkness and drops his bag of gold. He looks for it but cannot find it.*

WARRIOR: To the devil with you.

The SIDHE *teases and tricks him. He begins to chase them, then to run away from them. Then at last she is by him. She has led him to her house.*

SIDHE: To the devil is it? And me lonely and looking for company, and you out in the darkness. Put up your sword.

WARRIOR: Who are you?

SIDHE: Step into my house.

The house appears. It has a cauldron. It rains.

SIDHE: It's not a night to be spent outdoors. Will you eat?

WARRIOR: I will, old hag.

SIDHE: Here.

WARRIOR: What is it?

SIDHE: Game stew.

WARRIOR: It's good.

The WARRIOR *eats. The* SIDHE *stares at him unnervingly. She is very ugly.*

54

WARRIOR:	What are you thinking?
SIDHE:	How will you pay me now?
WARRIOR:	What a warrior can do for you mother, shall be done.
SIDHE:	Then lie with me.
WARRIOR:	You being an old hag mother, and me being young and sweet, I shall not.
SIDHE:	You promised payment.
WARRIOR:	I did. And as I have no gold or silver, it may be I shall pay you out with iron.
SIDHE:	That would be unkind.
WARRIOR:	To suggest I might take to your bed is worse.
SIDHE:	What is it that you find so repugnant about me?
WARRIOR:	There is not one part of you that is not vile.
SIDHE:	Each and every part of me?
WARRIOR:	Each and every part. A glance shows your teeth to be green and rotted, with evil points.
SIDHE:	And what should they be, if you were to like to look upon them.
WARRIOR:	White, and even and rounded.
SIDHE:	Like this?

As he speaks, the SIDHE *transforms herself.*

WARRIOR:	And if you should have no bristles upon your chin, but your skin were to be smooth and soft.
SIDHE:	Feel here. Soft skin I have.
WARRIOR:	And if your dugs were not flat and fallen, but ample and high.
SIDHE:	Here. The candle smoke must have smothered your gaze. Let the white moon shine out. See, are my breasts not both ample and high?
WARRIOR:	They are.
SIDHE:	Speak on. What would you call beauty?
WARRIOR:	A back to put an arm around. A slender ankle to stroke the leg. A broad back-side to clutch. A delicate waist to grasp at. A soft hand to caress me. And a single dimple to make it complete. Now I would lie with you, if it were not for my beloved who waits at home for me.
SIDHE:	Lie with me, and the boy I'll bear you will be straight as a reed and strong as a bull, and a mightier warrior than his father.
WARRIOR:	My own true love can promise me that.
SIDHE:	Lie with me, and the boy we'll have will be straight and strong, a warrior and wise. I'll teach him the paths of the wild, to track and to kill.
WARRIOR:	I'll teach my own child those skills.
SIDHE:	Lie with me and he shall be straight and strong, a warrior and wise, and if he will be governed by me, he shall become one of the Sidhe and never grow old, nor know any pain.

WARRIOR: Well, I'm glad for what you say pretty lady, for
                  my true love cannot promise me that, and so I
                  will lie with you.

The WARRIOR *and the* SIDHE *kiss, and are covered by a sheet.*

CROW: Lust. Lust, lust, lust, lust. Lust, lust. Shameful.

FOX: Is it? I have always regarded lust as benign.
                  After all, where would we be without it?

CROW: Well I can't say I approve.

*When the bodies under the sheet are still, the SIDHE take the
WARRIOR'S sword. She feels all over the WARRIOR'S body until she
locates his heart exactly. She plunges the sword through him and he
cries out.*

SIDHE: I shall call our child Luhan. Son of the moon.
                  And farewell to you.

Exit SIDHE *and* WARRIOR.

*Enter HELTER, SKELTER and LITTLE SAM. They are counting tree
roots. They cross from one side of the stage to the other. Ad lib scene
around them using only the words 1,2,3,4,5. At one point they find a tree
with five roots, but by the way they shape their hands, it's nothing like
the right shape.*

*Exit all, save FOX and CROW as usual. Enter a DOVE. As she
speaks/sings, she is tracked by the HUNTER.*

DOVE: The man who stripped me, covered me in
                  feathers, He cast me down, and I flew up with
                  wings. A mouth once soft, is a beak, unyielding,
                  My hands once white now yellow claws. My
                  voice is all that lives unchanging, To sing and
                  sigh my sorrowful fall.

HUNTER:	Hold still little dove, you must die today.
DOVE:	Mercy!
HUNTER:	I will not show mercy.
DOVE:	I'm poor eating.
HUNTER:	Eat you is it? I don't care to eat you, all I intend is to kill you.
DOVE:	I have a husband who will weep and sigh.
HUNTER:	What's that to me?
DOVE:	Don't you care for the sorrow he will feel?
HUNTER:	Milk and dribble, I do not. I'm only sorry I can't kill him also.
DOVE:	What has made you so cruel and unhappy? (HUNTER *draws bow*) Tell me, I know many secrets. Perhaps I can help you.
HUNTER:	You, help me?
DOVE:	It's a strange and topsy-turvy world.
HUNTER:	You have the truth of it there. Well then. Once I had a wife, and when I had a wife, I was not so cruel.
DOVE:	And did you love her?
HUNTER:	I did, and she me. Indeed, our love was so great that as we slept we sang duets in our slumber.
DOVE:	Was there no discord between you?

58

HUNTER:	There was not. Save only that she was sorry for the creatures that I slew for our survival. But I told her, wife, I am a hunter, and we must have meat.
DOVE:	What did she say to that?
HUNTER:	She said nothing. But one night I awoke to silence and the bed cold, her gone and her nightdress thrown down on the floor.
DOVE:	Where was she gone?
HUNTER:	Out. To release the animals from my traps.
DOVE:	Are you sure?
HUNTER:	I am. How else to explain how I had caught nothing in the weeks gone by?
DOVE:	Did you chase her so?
HUNTER:	I did not. I thought it better to wait, and confront her – and she slinking in naked from the darkness. So I took her gown and I hid it. And I closed my eyes and gloated. And when she did come in I pretended to sleep.
DOVE:	Why?
HUNTER:	To make her suffer of course. So she must wake me, to have her gown. You see.
DOVE:	And did she wake you?
HUNTER:	She did not. In she walked, and she wailed and she sighed, and she said, 'if my husband loved me without flaw he would lay out my gown for me,' but I was in a rage and I kept my eyes tight

59

shut, and I waited for her touch. And then. And then. She was gone. And never a track left by the door. And so, little dove, that is why I am so cruel and unhappy and that is why you must die.

DOVE: Wait. If you spare me, I shall tell you how you can learn of your wife's whereabouts.

HUNTER: How?

DOVE: Spare me.

HUNTER: Tell me first.

DOVE: Not far from here is a pool. Not broad, but so deep its bottom is salt and reaches to the ocean. Over the pool grows a crooked hazel.

HUNTER: I know it.

DOVE: Throw down hazel-nuts into the well and a salmon will rise. Ask it any question and it will tell you true. But be warned, once the question is made and answered the salmon will slip away and you will never catch him again.

HUNTER: It's good advice you've given me. It's sorry I am that you must die.

The HUNTER shoots the DOVE. He goes to the pool, and summons up the SALMON as instructed.

HUNTER: Tell me, where is my wife?

SALMON: Where you have shot her of course, wounded and bleeding.

Exit SALMON, HUNTER *and* DOVE.

CROW: The Sidhe and Luhan.

FOX: Aurora and the Smith.

The four characters enter, but remain on separate parts of the stage.

FOX: The years begin to pass.

The SMITH and the SIDHE sing a lullaby. It has the same tune, but opposed lyrics, so an unconscious duet takes place.

FOX: Slow at first, then quicker. Then year on year, falling thick, like a snow flurry.

CROW: Aurora's companion. The silent mannequin.

FOX: When Aurora was eleven or twelve years old.

AURORA: (*as child*) Smith! Smith! I'm bored. I want a friend.

SMITH: I am your friend.

AURORA: One of my own.

SMITH: But there are only the two of us in the whole wide world.

AURORA: Then I shall pine away and die.

SMITH: Wait. I'll make you a friend.

FOX: And so he did.

The SMITH sets about making a female friend (the MANNEQUIN).

SMITH: Now, a heart. A heart? I do very well without one. But how can it be in a toy? I shall make her

a mechanical heart, and set it to love for Aurora.
There. Child! Child!

The MANNEQUIN *comes to life.*

AURORA: She's lovely. How do you do?

The MANNEQUIN *curtsies.*

AURORA: What's your name?

Silence.

SMITH: I gave her a tongue.

AURORA: If she doesn't want to speak yet she doesn't. She
                       might be shy. She'll speak when you want to,
                       won't you dear?

Silence.

ACT TWO.

SCENE ONE.

Onstage; FOX AND CROW; LUHAN and SIDHE; AURORA, MANNEQUIN and SMITH.

CROW:	Sister?
FOX:	Yes?
CROW:	You were lost in thought.
FOX:	Was I?
CROW:	You were
FOX:	There's such a lot of pain in the world brother.
CROW:	What's that to scavengers like us?
FOX:	Nothing, I suppose. Nothing.

Focus of scene shifts to LUHAN and SIDHE. They are in the cottage with the cauldron.

SIDHE:	Son of mine. I must be away now to fetch my two sisters. While I am out, you must obey my one command.
LUHAN:	(*insolently*) Don't look in the pot.

Suddenly twisting his ear.

SIDHE:	Don't cross me Luhan. Don't look into the pot, or it'll be the worse for you.
LUHAN:	Yes mother.

SIDHE: Mother knows best.

LUHAN: Mother knows best.

The SIDHE *exits.*

LUHAN: Don't look in the pot. Don't look in the pot.

He kicks the pot. It gives a kick back.

LUHAN: Well that's news.

He knocks it. It knocks back.

LUHAN: One would swear there was something strange
                        here.

He plays with knocking the pot. It knocks back.

LUHAN: Hush now. There's thinking to be done. There's
                        something in the pot that mother doesn't want
                        me to see. That's plain enough. And if mother
                        doesn't want it seen, it must be bad for me. (*pot
                        bangs*) Hush. But why have it at all in the house
                        so? If it's so very bad, she'd have it thrown out.
                        It might be that what is in the pot is not a bad
                        thing, but a good thing. A good thing that
                        mother wants to keep all for herself, and not
                        share with me at all. That makes sense. Perhaps
                        she keeps her magic in the pot. I'll look in so. I
                        will not. For it might be dangerous. But if it's
                        dangerous, why, that's my own risk, and I've an
                        urge to test myself against danger. So, that's me
                        done with thinking, and that's a relief.

*He lifts the lid of the pot. A pair of human feet run out. He slams the lid
down. He runs to prevent the feet from running out of the door. He shuts
windows etc. The feet (which have been boiled) stand nervously in the
corner.*

64

LUHAN: A fine pair of feet you are. Just as broad and strong as my own. But I've nothing to be gained from letting you out, so it's back you must go.

The feet run and cower, and LUHAN has a hard job tracing them down. At last he lifts the lid to put them back, but instead a pair of legs jump out and land on top of the feet.

LUHAN: A fine pair of legs you might be – just as powerful as my own – but back you must go.

LUHAN goes to get the legs back in they resist. Some ad libbing might go on as he tries to wrestle them in. Each time he opens the lid of the pot another body part comes out (hips, torso, arms).

LUHAN: This is a disgrace. It's as big and strong as myself you might be, but in the end I'll wrestle you back.

The nearly complete body seems to nod.

LUHAN: I've gone this far. I'll be hung for a sheep as a lamb.

He opens the pot. A head comes out. It is the WARRIOR.

LUHAN: And who might you be? To be found in bits and pieces in my mother's pot.

WARRIOR: Your father.

LUHAN: That's hardly likely.

WARRIOR: It's true all the same.

LUHAN: Say your piece.

WARRIOR: I will and quickly. Son, though your mother is a Sidhe, I, your poor father was a mortal man, tricked and killed long ago, and left to stew in that pot for all the years of your childhood. You yourself have one foot planted in the faery world and the other planted in the human. Tonight you mother will offer you to eat from my skin and bones. And if you do that, son, you shall become a Sidhe itself, just like her, and the human part will be burned away.

LUHAN: Mother has promised me joy and youth and strength. Why should I not be a Sidhe?

WARRIOR: It's true that Sidhe are forever young, and it's true they have a wild joy, but a Sidhe can't know love or hate or pain or the true taste of life at all. Your mother makes the life of a faery sound a delightful thing, but it is not, it is twisted and cold, and they see only in strange ways and though you are not dead, still you will never savour the world as a human can. Do not eat tonight, no matter how much they beg, Luhan.

LUHAN: Everlasting youth is a hard thing to lose, father.

WARRIOR: True love is a hard thing to lose.

LUHAN: And might it be that you're lying to me, creature from the pot.

WARRIOR: Make up your own mind, son of mine. Question the sisters closely, Luhan. And if you want to be sure, hold cold iron to their necks. Witches hate that more than anything.

LUHAN: I have no iron.

WARRIOR: My sword is buried under the bed.

LUHAN *goes to look and finds it.*

LUHAN:	It is. It is poor father mine.

The WARRIOR hears the witches coming and jumps back into the pot. LUHAN hides the sword just in time (possibly in the pot). The three sisters enter. They are all Sidhe. The second sister is a WaterSidhe and the third is a BanSidhe.

SIDHE:	Kiss your aunts Luhan.
LUHAN:	Yes mother.
WATERSIDHE:	What red lips he has.
BANSIDHE:	What soft cheeks he has.

The BANSIDHE begins to cry.

SIDHE:	Don't cry sister, I couldn't bear it.
BANSIDHE:	We were once so young, and now we never see each other at all.
WATERSIDHE:	We're here now.

The SIDHE is handing out bowls.

LUHAN:	How is it that you live apart?
WATERSIDHE:	Well dumpling. Once we three were inseparable, but time went by, and, just like you, we had to choose to take our places in the wilderness. Your mother here took up her lantern and laid strange trails through the woods. Your aunt, commenced to wash and became a Ban Sidhe of ill omen, and I, I dived down into streams and ponds to snatch at the ankles of children as they swim by.
LUHAN:	Do you drown them?

WATERSIDHE:	I do if I catch them.
LUHAN:	And do they feel pain?
BANSIDHE:	That's the human part talking, bless him.
WATERSIDHE:	I expect they do.
LUHAN:	And your wailing, aunt, is it only for those who deserve it?
BANSIDHE:	Oh no. I bring a curse on the evil and the innocent alike.
LUHAN:	Is that fair?
WATERSIDHE:	Where did he get such ideas?
SIDHE:	Not from me.

SIDHE *puts meat in each bowl.*

LUHAN:	What's this, mother?
SIDHE:	Tonight you eat meat for the first time.
WATERSIDHE:	And when that is done child, you will be a fit member of the Midnight Court.

All have bowls now.

SIDHE:	Eat Luhan.

Pause.

LUHAN:	Without saying grace?
All SIDHE:	Thankful truly us make Beelzebub the may receive to about are we what for.

SIDHE:	So. Eat son of mine, and join the Sidhe. Be happy.
LUHAN:	Am I not a Sidhe already, mother?
WATERSIDHE:	You are at the threshold, one mouthful and you may choose your place in the revels.
LUHAN:	What can I choose?
WATERSIDHE:	If I'd been a boy, I'd have been a Redcap.
SIDHE:	Sister. Let him alone.
WATERSIDHE:	A Redcap, Luhan, is a sprite that lives on cliffs and castle battlements. You throw boulders down on unwary travellers, and smash their skulls to pieces. Then you hippety hop your way down, and dip your cap into their blood. And so you will live forever, just so long as your hood is even the slightest bit damp.
BANSIDHE:	If that doesn't appeal, you might be a House-Brownie.
WATERSIDHE:	Oh please.
BANSIDHE:	It's a very comfortable profession. We have an uncle who is a House-Brownie but, but (*nearly cries*)
WATERSIDHE:	He had to leave.
BANSIDHE:	The humans where he stayed gave him a dish of milk and a suit of clothes, and at the merest hint of gratitude he had to flee far away, we never...
LUHAN:	Perhaps I might want to be a warrior.

BANSIDHE:	Then you must travel to the faery court across the water, but then... (*she begins to cry*) we should never see you at all.
LUHAN:	Suppose I want to be a human warrior.
WATERSIDHE:	Is he often like this?
SIDHE:	Eat your food. You shall be a Pooka, Luhan and race under the night skies. I have set my heart that you should be a Pooka.
LUHAN:	Your heart mother.
WATERSIDHE:	It's a figure of speech.
LUHAN:	Do you have a heart mother?
SIDHE:	Who have you been talking to?
LUHAN:	You don't do you?
SIDHE:	Hearts! Eat, and you will be one of us. And that is so much the better.
LUHAN:	I will not.
BANSIDHE:	You should really dear.
LUHAN:	Never!
SIDHE:	Eat now. I command it.
LUHAN:	You don't command me.

He grabs the sword and holds it across all three throats at once.

ALL SIDHE:	It burns! It freezes!

70

LUHAN:	Tell me the truth. Did you murder my father?
SIDHE:	Ungrateful!
WATERSIDHE:	He's mad.
SIDHE:	So. Luhan. The Sidhe are never old, never sick, never tired.
LUHAN:	But will I ever be able to love or hate mother? Tell me that?
WATERSIDHE:	He's a disgrace.
BANSIDHE:	He's hurting us.
LUHAN:	Will I mother? Will I?
BANSIDHE:	I'm going to scream.
LUHAN:	Tell me the truth.
SIDHE:	Luhan. Up on the beam of the house there's a jug.
LUHAN:	What?
SIDHE:	I took the truth years ago and put it in a jug.
LUHAN:	Where?
SIDHE:	Up above you. Look higher.
LUHAN:	The truth's in a jug...?

But as he looks up, the Sidhe escape. SIDHE kicks over the pot. The body comes out in pieces.

SIDHE:	That's for you.

They smash up WARRIOR. LUHAN *flies into a rage.*

LUHAN: Mother! Then this is for you, and you.

In rage and disgust, he attacks them, but only kills the WATERSIDHE and the BANSIDHE.

SIDHE: You've cursed yourself Luhan. Not human, not Sidhe. It's the worst of both worlds you'll have. You're cursed.

SIDHE *exits.*

WARRIOR: (*dying*) Luhan. Find out the Salmon of Knowledge Luhan. The Salmon can guide you.

LUHAN: I will father.

He exits. A breathing then a gasping. Then the BANSIDHE *wails.*

BANSIDHE: Vengeance! Vengeance! Vengeance!

SCENE TWO.

The wail of the BANSIDHE merges into the clanging of the SMITH at his anvil. AURORA is covered with the gifts she has received over the years. Also in the room is the female MANNEQUIN that she has as a companion/guard. The MANNEQUIN still doesn't speak, but moves during the scene. She performs menial junctions, and is secretly in love with the SMITH.

FOX: Brother?

CROW: Yes?

FOX: You see the way I am about to checkmate you?

72

CROW:	No.
FOX:	Well, suppose just suppose, I am.
CROW:	For the sake of argument.
FOX:	I might use any of a number of pieces to make the final move.
CROW:	True.
FOX:	Well, I wonder if in the same way, although we are telling only the one story, perhaps we are each looking at a different character as the centre of our tale.
CROW:	Oh. In that case I make no bones about saying that humans are selfish, and it is the Smith who is the most selfish of all.
FOX:	Oh dear, oh dear. Humans are generous and it is the Smith who is the most generous at that.

Focus of scene shifts.

SMITH:	Are you happy Aurora?
AURORA:	Happy?
SMITH:	Yes.
AURORA:	Should I be?
SMITH:	On the evening before your wedding, you should be happy.
AURORA:	Are you happy then?
SMITH:	I am. Very.

AURORA:	Tell me what you feel like.
SMITH:	I'm trembling inside.
AURORA:	Yes.
SMITH:	My breath is tight.
AURORA:	Yes.
SMITH:	I'm dizzy with expectation.
AURORA:	Is happiness like anxiety then?
SMITH:	No. Perhaps a little.
AURORA:	And who will marry us?
SMITH:	The mannequin if you like.
AURORA:	But she won't speak.
SMITH:	We shall say the words, and she shall put our hands together, and that will be enough.
AURORA:	And you love me?
SMITH:	I do.
AURORA:	And I am very beautiful?
SMITH:	You are.
AURORA:	Smith. How do you know I am beautiful?
SMITH:	The way you can see that I am handsome. By looking.

AURORA:	Then look at my hand. And look at your hand. Red. White. Calluses. Smooth. Thick, broken nails...
SMITH:	From making you presents. Look. Today I have made this for you.
AURORA:	Thank you.
SMITH:	Haven't I given you everything you've ever wanted.
AURORA:	You have. I think.
SMITH:	I have. And I will go on giving you everything until the day we die.
AURORA:	Tell me about the other humans.
SMITH:	They've all gone. There are no humans.
AURORA:	But you remember them.
SMITH:	They were wicked. And the devil punished them. But because I was good, and because you were innocent, we were saved. An angel put love in my heart for you, and an angel put love in your heart for me, so that we could start our race all over again. And so that we should be happy together...
AURORA:	...(*who has heard this story*) the angel made you young and handsome and strong, so that we would be well matched. So you tell me. Will you describe my mother?
SMITH:	She was as beautiful as you. But she fell into the hands of a bad man who corrupted her. It was a

sad thing. It was him who brought evil to the village.

AURORA: And what was his name?

SMITH: It doesn't matter. They're all gone.

AURORA: All dead.

SMITH: Yes. All dead.

AURORA: And what shall I wear for my wedding?

SMITH: Why. The dress I have for you.

AURORA: Let me see.

The SMITH snaps his fingers and the MANNEQUIN gets the dress. The MANNEQUIN may do other tasks, such as combing AURORA'S hair, or fetching drinks.

SMITH: There.

AURORA: That is not good enough.

SMITH: Aurora!

AURORA: I am beautiful.

SMITH: Yes.

AURORA: The most beautiful of all women that have ever been.

SMITH: I think so.

AURORA: Then my dress must be made out of sunbeams, and studded with stars that are so fresh from the sky that they twinkle.

| SMITH: | Sunbeams and stars that twinkle. |

He taps his anvil thoughtfully.

| SMITH: | I should have to go a long way for that. |

| AURORA: | You refuse me on my wedding day? |

| SMITH: | No, Aurora. Child of the sun. You shall have sunbeams and stars. You deserve such a wedding dress. Sun and stars, and if I pass the moon on my way I shall net it, and place it on your breast here. And then we shall be married. |

| AURORA: | Yes. You will really make me such a dress. |

| SMITH: | Of course. You've asked me. |

| AURORA: | Thank you. |

She kisses him on the cheek. He is elated for a moment, then exits. During the following speech the MANNEQUIN is thoroughly involved.

| AURORA: | Gone. Now you, if you sneak to him I shall de-spring your metal heart. Understand me? (*takes down a book*) S. T. Traps. Triggers. Truth. See Compass. Compass. Magnetic compass for the Cardinal points. What do you suppose the Cardinal points are? Like a priest. For finding priests. What good is that? Compass for finding lost objects. Compass for finding the truth. Here goes. |

AURORA uses the anvil. She is scared at first that the SMITH might hear and return, and she is initially clumsy.

| AURORA: | (*to MANNEQUIN*) More heat. A little brass. A human hair. A golden needle. The letter T. for Truth. An L. for lies. Careful now. Stand at one |

end, any lie at all. 'I have two left feet'. And a
truth at the other. Any truth. 'I...' What? Oh, the
truth. 'I want to know more about my mother
and father.' Look. Look. I made it work. Now
you stay here.

*AURORA sits the MANNEQUIN down where she (AURORA) began the
scene, and begins to load her with her jewellery – the gifts of the SMITH
over the years.*

AURORA: Now for your face.

She makes up the MANNEQUIN'S face.

AURORA: Don't worry. Sit still. I'm only going for a little
walk. So what if my parents were wicked? I
should like to see where they are buried at least.
What can be the harm in that? Now, hold this
note. If I'm not back in time, hold it out to him.
There. You look just like me. Why don't I wait
for him? Oh. Don't you see. I want to do
something on my own. At least once. I'll be back
for the wedding. Goodbye now.

AURORA *exits, leaving the worried* MANNEQUIN.

*After AURORA has left the MANNEQUIN looks around. She starts to
sing. Her song tells of how she loves the SMITH and how she wishes she
were truly his bride, and not just a shadow.*

SCENE THREE.

*Enter HELTER, SKELTER and LITTLE SAM. They are in the forest,
near where the WARRIOR lost his bag of gold. LITTLE SAM still carries
all the provisions.*

FOX: Helter, Skelter and Little Sam had searched the wood for twenty one years.

Focus shifts to HELTER, SKELTER *and* LITTLE SAM.

HELTER: I'm shattered. Halt.

LITTLE SAM: We must go on until we find Death.

SKELTER: My feet hurt.

HELTER: We need a rest. Troops. Halt.

They throw themselves down.

HELTER: Little Sam. Pillow duty.

HELTER *and* SKELTER *use* LITTLE SAM *as a pillow.*

LITTLE SAM: Ow! Ow! Ow! Ow! Ow! Aahh! That's better.

HELTER: What's better?

LITTLE SAM: Well this root was digging into me.

HELTER: Was it?

LITTLE SAM: So I moved. But then this root dug into me as well.

SKELTER: That's two roots.

LITTLE SAM: Then there was this one and this one.

HELTER: Four roots.

LITTLE SAM: Four uncomfortable roots.

SKELTER: That's it. Four.

LITTLE SAM:	Except there is one more little root, about half the size of the others.
HELTER:	Half the size.
LITTLE SAM:	Yes. And that little root isn't comfortable either. So I padded myself with this old bag.
HELTER:	What old bag?
SKELTER & H:	(*Leaping up*) Death! We've found you!

Looking at bag.

SKELTER:	Death's very small.
HELTER:	But dangerous, remember.
SKELTER:	True. Little Sam. Now is your moment of greatness. I give to you the honour of unmasking Death.
LITTLE SAM:	Really?
SKELTER & H:	Really.
LITTLE SAM:	I could cry.
HELTER:	Get on with it.

LITTLE SAM *looks in the bag.*

LITTLE SAM:	Death's not here. It's only a bag of gold.
SKELTER:	Little Sam's right. It's an old bag, full of gold.
ALL:	Gold! (*They cheer wildly*)

HELTER:	That crone was sadly mistaken. To confuse a bag of gold and Death.
SKELTER:	Her mind is quite gone.
LITTLE SAM:	How much is there?
HELTER:	Enough for all of us, Little Sam, Enough for all of us. Except it's too heavy to lift.
LITTLE SAM:	Let me try.
HELTER:	You know I'm stronger than you, Little Sam.
LITTLE SAM:	But I pushed it just now.
HELTER:	Pushing's not the same as lifting. The bag's too heavy, isn't it Skelter? (*meaningfully*) Isn't it?
SKELTER:	Yes. Far too heavy Helter.
HELTER:	I have an idea. Little Sam. You run to the village and find us some spades. Then we'll take as much as we can carry, and bury the rest so we can come back for it later. Hurry Little Sam. Hurry, as fast as your little legs will go.
LITTLE SAM:	I'll be as fast as ever I can Helter.

LITTLE SAM *exits.* HELTER *and* SKELTER *wave.*

SKELTER:	Brilliant, Helter. And now we two simply make off.
HELTER:	We do not. We wait here.
SKELTER:	Why Helter. Why split the gold three ways when two is better?

HELTER:	We will split it two ways Skelter. Listen. If Little Sam comes back and finds us gone he will hunt us to the ends of the earth. We must make an end of him here. We will bury something Skelter, (*pulling out knife*) but it won't be gold.
SKELTER:	(*pulling out knife*) Poor Little Sam. He was my best friend. Apart from you.

ACT THREE.

Scene changes. Exit all except FOX and CROW. Enter the HUNTER placing traps. After he has passed, the FOX and the CROW put themselves into the traps. The FOX a metal 'man-trap' type arrangement, and the CROW a noose which has him hanging by the leg. If the FOX is stage right, and the CROW stage centre, then stage left is the SALMON's pool. The HUNTER places a cloth over it, so the hazel nuts cannot fall in, then conceals himself.

HUNTER:	If you won't answer me, it's starve down there you will, starve surely.

AURORA *enters.*

FOX:	Help! Help! Kind lady, if you do not free me a hunter will surely cut my poor throat.
AURORA:	You probably deserve it.
FOX:	I do not. Please help me.
AURORA:	No time. No time at all.

She passes to where the CROW *is hung.*

CROW:	Help! Help! Kind lady, if you do not free me a hunter will surely cut my poor throat.
AURORA:	You probably deserve it.
CROW:	I do not deserve it. Please help me.
AURORA:	No time. No time at all!

She passes on to the well. But as she goes to touch it the HUNTER appears. He has a sword.

AURORA:	What are you?
HUNTER:	A hunter.
AURORA:	What are you doing?
HUNTER:	I'm guarding this well.
AURORA:	Why?
HUNTER:	If you throw hazelnuts on the surface of this well a salmon will appear. Grasp the salmon by the gills and you may ask it any single question you like and it will answer truthfully.
AURORA:	(*to compass*) It worked. Well then.
HUNTER:	But you must ask it the question I tell you to.
AURORA:	Why?
HUNTER:	This is my forest, you will do as I say.
AURORA:	Out of my way.
HUNTER:	I will not.

AURORA:	I shall ask what I want, and piffle to you.
HUNTER:	Then I shall bind you up until you change your mind.
AURORA:	Impertinent! Help! Smith! Help! Anyone!
CROW:	Ha! So there!
FOX:	That'll teach you!

The HUNTER *binds her up and hides her. Enter* LUHAN.

FOX:	Help! Help!
LUHAN:	Helping you, won't harm me.

He frees her.

FOX:	If you need me. Whistle.

FOX gives example whistle and goes to regular story telling place. LUHAN passes on.

CROW:	Help! Help!
LUHAN:	Helping you, won't harm me.

He frees the CROW.

CROW:	If you need me. Whistle.

CROW *does as* FOX. LUHAN *passes on. He arrives at pool. Enter* HUNTER.

LUHAN:	What are you?
HUNTER:	A hunter.

84

LUHAN:	What are you doing?
HUNTER:	I'm guarding this well.
LUHAN:	Why?
HUNTER:	If you throw hazelnuts on the surface of this well a salmon will appear. Grasp the salmon by the gills and you may ask it any single question you like and it will answer truthfully.
LUHAN:	Good. Then I'm here.
HUNTER:	But you must ask it the question I tell you to.
LUHAN:	Why?
HUNTER:	This is my forest, you will do as I say.
LUHAN:	I will not.
HUNTER:	Then you'll be bound up until you change your mind.

They fight. LUHAN *defeats the* HUNTER *and captures him.*

HUNTER:	Who are you that has beaten me so?
LUHAN:	Luhan.
HUNTER:	Put an end to me, Luhan. My miserable life is done.
LUHAN:	I will not. Until I'm satisfied as to your strange behaviour.
AURORA:	Help, you there! He tied me up.

LUHAN:	Well. I'll have to think again and that's a fact. You (the Hunter) are waiting by this well. The well which has the Salmon in it.

He uncovers the well. SALMON *rises.*

SALMON:	Feed me. Feed me.

LUHAN *does so.*

LUHAN:	And now I've the right to ask you a question, brother?

SALMON:	One and one only.

LUHAN:	I should go ahead so. Why not, I've earned it. I want to know...(*looks at* HUNTER *who is looking at him beseechingly*) A moment. What would your question be?

HUNTER:	I want to know how I may cure my poor wife, whom I have injured with my own hand.

Enter LITTLE SAM. *Unseen. He still has the three loads of him and his friends. Plus spades.*

LITTLE SAM:	What's this?

LUHAN:	Is she greatly hurt?

HUNTER:	She has lain twixt life and death these many years, and each breath is a mortal agony.

LUHAN:	Mortal agony. What are these?

HUNTER:	Tears.

LUHAN:	Why?

HUNTER:	I have failed her, and now she will not be cured.
LUHAN:	I can't have tears. Salmon. How may this man cure his wife?
AURORA:	What a waste.
SALMON:	Easy enough.
LITTLE SAM:	A talking fish.
SALMON:	He must take a bottle of water from this well and go home to his wife. Then he must take the night-gown he stole from her, and has hidden by his heart, and lay it over her. Then he must sprinkle the water upon her, and put a little to her lips and she will be cured.

The astonished HUNTER takes out the shift, from where he has it tucked away next to his heart. He takes a bottle of water very carefully. He runs away.

LITTLE SAM:	That's wisdom. Perhaps there's something in this for Little Sam.
AURORA:	There. He didn't even thank you.
LUHAN:	Neither have you yet.
AURORA:	Oh. Thank you.

AURORA feeds the SALMON.

AURORA:	Here little fish. I have a question. Where is my mother?
SALMON:	In a poppy field, Aurora, not far from this well. Follow the scent.

LUHAN:	Friend Salmon...
SALMON:	I'm sorry Luhan, I've answered your question. And one is all. If there's any other way I can help you. Whistle. (*Pops down. Pops back up*) But about your problem. I'm not saying anything, I'm just thinking out loud. If eating from your mortal father would make you a Sidhe. Then I wonder what you could do to make you a man?

AURORA *is sniffing the air.*

LUHAN:	What are you doing?
AURORA:	Can you make out the scent of Poppies? I don't know one flower from another.
LUHAN:	Don't know one flower from another? They're this way. Come on.

They exit together. LITTLE SAM *approaches the well.*

LITTLE SAM:	'Little Sam -pillow.' 'Little Sam -chair.' 'Little Sam -chest of drawers'. Well perhaps Little Sam has had enough of playing furniture.

LITTLE SAM *feeds the* SALMON *and grabs him.*

SALMON:	Ow!
LITTLE SAM:	Don't wriggle so and tell me. How may I get all the gold for myself?
SALMON:	Nothing simpler. Dip all three of your wine bottles into the well. The two for your friends will come out poison. Yours will be wine, pure and true. Then go back and offer them a toast to your success.

LITTLE SAM: Excellent.

LITTLE SAM *fills up the bottles. He sings a refrain from the song as he does so, 'Helter, Skelter and Little Sam'.*

LITTLE SAM: Helter and Skelter were waiting by a tree. Helter and Skelter took a drink from me.

Exit LITTLE SAM. New Scene between SIDHE and DEATH, at poppy field.

DEATH: You are far from home.

SIDHE: I can go where I please.

DEATH: You're agitated. Why don't you sit down and rest.

SIDHE: I never rest.

DEATH: I do all the time. I often find that sitting and waiting is more productive than hunting.

SIDHE: And what are you waiting for?

DEATH: Not 'what', but 'who'.

SIDHE: Who then?

DEATH: A young man. Here he comes.

SIDHE: He's not in young domain Death.

DEATH: Not yet.

SIDHE: You can't command him.

DEATH: Dear me no. I'm going to let him choose for himself. I suggest you do the same.

AURORA and LUHAN arrive in the poppy field. The poppies are gently humming AURORA'S lullaby. DEATH and the SIDHE listen to the scene.

AURORA: My mother must be buried here. It's almost familiar. It's beautiful.

LUHAN: It is.

AURORA: It's a shame. She was wicked.

LUHAN: Who?

AURORA: My mother, my father. All of them.

LUHAN: What did they do?

AURORA: What? I don't know exactly. Something very bad.

LUHAN: And who told you this?

AURORA: My husband to be of course. I'm going to be married tomorrow.

LUHAN: Are you?

AURORA: Yes.

As the conversation goes on the Poppies react to what is being said. The couple are getting around to kissing but not quite.

LUHAN: Many blessings.

AURORA: My husband to be is very handsome.

LUHAN: I see.

AURORA: And young and strong. And I am very happy.

LUHAN:	I'm glad for you.
AURORA:	Are you old?
LUHAN:	I don't think so.
AURORA:	And are you ugly?
LUHAN:	I might be that. I've never seen my reflection.
AURORA:	I apparently, am very beautiful.
LUHAN:	You may well be.
AURORA:	But would you say so?
LUHAN:	Well. All I ever knew was my mother and she looked whatever way she liked. But if I knew what beauty was, I'd say it looked like you.
AURORA:	I've been selfish.
LUHAN:	When?
AURORA:	I should have asked your question for you at the well. You did free me. I should have, shouldn't I?
LUHAN:	Yes. But it's done now, so not to worry.
AURORA:	What did you want to know?
LUHAN:	How I can be cured. I'm under a curse.
AURORA:	Perhaps we can find a cure for you.
LUHAN:	Well the Salmon seemed to hint that...what kind of cure do you have in mind?

AURORA: I've heard in faery tales that if a good man is under a curse, and is given a single, pure...

LUHAN: Single, pure...?

AURORA: You are a good man?

LUHAN: Yes. Undoubtedly.

AURORA: Under a curse.

LUHAN: Wicked, wicked curse.

AURORA: Well single, pure kiss.

LUHAN: Right so.

They close their eyes to kiss. A sound of clanging in the distance. AURORA can hear this, but LUHAN cannot. She pulls away. He leans farther and farther inward. And eventually falls on his nose.

LUHAN: Aurora.

AURORA: It's my husband. The Smith. He's the one who tells me I am beautiful.

LUHAN: Where?

AURORA: He's missing me.

LUHAN: Where? Who?

AURORA: He's generous and kind and good and he's never refused me anything. And he's so upset.

LUHAN: Aurora!

AURORA: Oh goodbye Luhan. I'm sorry.

LUHAN:	My cure.
AURORA:	Let me go.
LUHAN:	What have I done?
AURORA:	Let me go!
LUHAN:	Aurora!
AURORA:	My poor Smith.
LUHAN:	Who? Where? Show me?
AURORA:	Get your hands off me.

She exits, leaving LUHAN *in the poppy field.*

LUHAN: 'A single, pure kiss' she says. 'Get your hands off me' she says. Well enough. If that's what she wants. I've forgotten her already. What was her name? Dawn or something. She is vain and selfish with a mind that swings like a weather vane. Poppies. Nod now if you think I should have been a Pooka, and never troubled myself with love. Or should I be a man, and suffer this stupid pain?

LUHAN starts to sing. The song is chorused by the Poppies. It is to the effect that LUHAN desires to be either fully SIDHE, so he can't feel the pain of love, or fully human, so he can die and forget. Halfway through DEATH enters and harmonises with him. At the very end of the song the SIDHE (LUHAN'S mother), joins in. DEATH enters the scene.

LUHAN: Good evening old mother.

DEATH: That's a sad song you were singing.

LUHAN:	It's a sad way I'm in. I almost have it in me to wish I could join these wicked flowers here and worry about nothing but sunshine and showers.
DEATH:	What wicked flowers?
LUHAN:	These ones.
DEATH:	Wicked are they?
LUHAN:	So Aurora says.
DEATH:	Does she?
LUHAN:	So her husband says.
DEATH:	Married is she?
LUHAN:	Not yet.
DEATH:	Not yet.
LUHAN:	But she loves him.
DEATH:	Oh, well. She loves him. She told you that, did she?
LUHAN:	Well, she...
DEATH:	Yes?
LUHAN:	I'm trying to remember. No. She never said that. But how can I go to her, when I'm all disjointed and turned-about. If I was a man, I'd storm hell's gates themselves to get Aurora. And so we'd be happy.
DEATH:	Until you died.

LUHAN: Old mother, I'd rather die with love, than live
                       forever, and that's final. But how...

Enter SIDHE *to scene, who has heard enough.*

SIDHE: Son.

LUHAN: Mother.

SIDHE: You don't know what you're asking for.

LUHAN: I do mother. I'm asking you to release me. I'm
                       asking you for the tiniest drop of your blood.
                       Mother, I've been turning a riddle over in my
                       mind and it seems to me that even a drop of
                       your blood will change me forever.

SIDHE: It will. Here.

*She cuts herself and he takes a drop. He twists and turns as the Sidhe is
burnt out of him. As the SIDHE looks over him as he squirms, she sings
her old lullaby. Then she and DEATH bow to each other and exit.*

SIDHE: (*to* DEATH) Don't hurry him Death. Give him
                       time.

She exits.

LUHAN: Old woman. Oh I know you now. What's this...

DEATH: It's fear. It comes with mortality. But you
                       needn't worry just yet. As we go, let me tell you
                       about these wicked poppies.

Exit all save FOX *and* CROW.

ACT FOUR.

FOX *and* CROW. *The stage is otherwise bare.*

CROW: Now. At the forge...wait.

Two Sidhe warriors enter. These are rather frightening, alien powerful beings. One is HOTSIDHE, the other COLDSIDHE.

FOX: Brother.

CROW: Wait. Wait. At last. At last we have it.

FOX: Brother.

The FOX looks worried.

CROW: What is this nonsense. I'm disappointed in you, sister. These two don't belong...

He is broken off with a squawk as the HOTSIDHE grabs him by the throat. Note they are the only characters who can break the convention of the play, by addressing FOX and CROW.

COLDSIDHE: Don't belong?

CROW: Urgh!

COLDSIDHE: Don't belong, sister Fox?

FOX: In such humble...

COLDSIDHE: Are you playing chess?

FOX: We are, lady.

HOTSIDHE: Good. I'll pluck him alive until he tells us.

FOX:	Tell you what?
COLDSIDHE:	Who is white?
FOX:	Me, lady.
COLDSIDHE:	(*Looking at pieces*) Very cunning. Yes. Traps all over. Just like a fox. Tell me, little sister. Do you know us?
FOX:	You are knights of the Hy-Brasil. The island over the water. You are deadly.
COLDSIDHE:	Killers, that's right. Have you heard of Om Palace?
FOX:	It is legend.
COLDSIDHE:	Describe the throne room.
HOTSIDHE:	Sister!
COLDSIDHE:	Go on.
FOX:	The throne room is lined with shells, all pink and pearl, and the sounds of the earth are gathered within it.
COLDSIDHE:	And what should we hear, but...
HOTSIDHE:	Vengeance! Vengeance! Vengeance!
COLDSIDHE:	Two unimportant cousins of ours, calling for vengeance. They have been slain by a young warrior called Luhan.
HOTSIDHE:	The Crow won't look at me.

COLDSIDHE:	A fox and a crow are playing chess in a clearing, and as they play, they align. And, far away, in our palace of shells we heard the name.
HOTSIDHE:	Luhan, Luhan, Luhan.
COLDSIDHE:	So where is he sister?
FOX:	Oh that's not us sir. No, there are any amount of foxes and crows that play chess around here. The county's riddled with us. In fact we're thinking of forming a league. No, your Luhan, must be part of some other tale.

Enter the SMITH *beating at his anvil. Enter* MANNEQUIN.

HOTSIDHE:	Is that him?
CROW:	That's a Smith.
FOX:	We were gossiping about a Smith and his bride. They are to be married.
COLDSIDHE:	My animal friends. We have come a long way quickly. And we desire to return again even faster than that. We will find and kill this Luhan, make no doubt of it. And those who have helped us will be rewarded, and those who have hindered us, will be punished. Am I clear?
FOX:	Yes lady.
CROW:	Yes sir.

Exit the SIDHE. The SMITH is finishing the wedding dress. The SMITH is speaking to the MANNEQUIN who naturally doesn't answer. Perhaps she's doing something simple like sewing. The MANNEQUIN has her back to him.

SMITH: I got the sunbeams first. I captured them in a
                          glass jar which I lowered deep into a crystal
                          lake. You know how light shines best as it cuts
                          through deep water. Then I had to climb a steep
                          mountain ridge and knock out stars one by one
                          with a catapult. What are you sewing dear? A
                          surprise. A veil perhaps? I packed them in
                          mountain snow to keep them fresh and
                          sparkling. And then I set to thinking what cloth
                          could they be set in? And do you know what I
                          did, I fished down a strand of the milky way for
                          you. It's like cobwebs. But much finer and
                          stronger. So. Do you remember how I used to
                          tell you stories as you fell asleep. Well. I made
                          all of them up myself. And. I'm very proud of
                          that because once upon a time I was very bad
                          with words. I thought I was the most thick-
                          tongued idiot in the world. I mean. I think I can
                          tell you now we are to be married. I once loved
                          your mother very much. Before she was wicked
                          and corrupted. And, it seems to me, that if I had
                          been better with words, I should never have lost
                          her. Because I would have been able to persuade
                          her away from evil. Finished now. What do you
                          think? (*Shows* MANNEQUIN *dress*) Well?
                          Please, say something. (MANNEQUIN *holds
                          out note*) 'I have vowed that I will only speak
                          again once we are wed. A kiss will seal our
                          marriage'. Very well. Once you've put on the
                          dress. Quickly now. I shall look away. We will
                          have our mannequin help. (*Claps for*
                          MANNEQUIN) Odd. Odder and odder. (*Looks
                          around again suspiciously*). Don't cower away
                          from me Aurora. (*He smears the*
                          MANNEQUIN*'s make-up. He realises the
                          deception, the* MANNEQUIN*'s mouth is
                          working faster and faster; finally she breaks
                          through*)

MANNEQUIN:	I love you! I love you! I love you! I love you!
SMITH:	What!
MANNEQUIN:	Marry me! Marry me! Marry me!
SMITH:	You're a toy. I made you.
MANNEQUIN:	She's a toy. You made her!
SMITH:	She's a human!
MANNEQUIN:	I love you! I love you! I love you!
SMITH:	You're not human. You cannot love.
MANNEQUIN:	You gave me a heart and so I can.
SMITH:	I gave you a heart to love Aurora.
MANNEQUIN:	A heart can't be controlled. I tried, I did.
SMITH:	You're metal. I can't love my own creation.
MANNEQUIN:	You created her.
SMITH:	She loves me. Her feelings are real.
MANNEQUIN:	You've created her as much as you created me.
SMITH:	No! I love her.
MANNEQUIN:	You love no one. You want her for revenge.
SMITH:	That's enough.
MANNEQUIN:	All you'll ever do is possess her, but you could love me.

SMITH:	I'll destroy you first.
MANNEQUIN:	I love you and she does not.
SMITH:	Silence!
MANNEQUIN:	You don't have to be bitter.
SMITH:	I'm not, I love Aurora.
MANNEQUIN:	That's a lie.
SMITH:	If you must talk, tell me where she is!
MANNEQUIN:	I love you and she does not. I love you and she does not.

The SMITH, *in a rage, takes his hammer and smashes the* MANNEQUIN *to pieces.*

SMITH:	Where is she? Where is she?
MANNEQUIN:	She never will! She never will! She never will!

After the MANNEQUIN is destroyed, the SMITH turns to his anvil and starts to beat on it. It is a song of anguish, near despair and longing.

SMITH:	Aurora! Aurora!
CROW:	And that was the clanging that Aurora heard as she stood with Luhan in the poppy field. And so she came chasing home.

AURORA *enters.*

SMITH:	Aurora I went and made you a dress, just as you asked me and you tricked me and ran away.
AURORA:	I came back when you called.

SMITH:	You hurt me.
AURORA:	I wanted to know the truth about my parents.
SMITH:	I told you the truth.
AURORA:	I met someone.
SMITH:	Who?
AURORA:	A man. And he was young and handsome.
SMITH:	No!
AURORA:	Why did you tell me you were young and handsome? You're not.
SMITH:	I was vain and silly. But that's the only lie I've told.
AURORA:	He was gentle too.
SMITH:	You know so little. If he was gentle it was to impress you.
AURORA:	He freed animals.
SMITH:	An easy trick.
AURORA:	He helped me find my mother's grave.
SMITH:	The poppy field.
AURORA:	Yes.
SMITH:	What was this devil's name?
AURORA:	Luhan.

SMITH:	Luhan! Oh my Aurora. He is no human. He is a heartless Sidhe, and a murderer too. Yes. You've had a lucky escape. While you were gone, two Sidhe Knights came by to look for him for punishment, because, he has killed his family and been cursed by his own mother.
AURORA:	His own mother. He didn't say that.
SMITH:	A fair outside Aurora, can hide the blackest of hearts.
AURORA:	You swear.
SMITH:	I do. I do Aurora.
AURORA:	I do know so little.
SMITH:	Here, take your dress now.
AURORA:	Where is my friend?
SMITH:	I sent her away.
AURORA:	That was unkind.
SMITH:	When we are married, we will walk hand in hand down to the poppy field and I will tell the story just as it happened…

End of scene. Exit SMITH *and* AURORA.

FOX:	And you maintain brother, that it is the Smith and the Smith alone who will embody the selfishness of mankind.
CROW:	I do.

FOX:	Well, I am flummoxed if I can see how that will come about.
CROW:	I remain confident.
FOX:	Then let us tie up a loose end or two, so we may approach the final cataclysm with all the pieces set in their final places.
CROW:	In the forest, the hunter had returned to his wife.

Enter wounded WIFE and HUNTER. He places the shift over her, sprinkles the water then gives her some to drink. She wakes.

HUNTER:	My dear. My darling. Wake up.
HUNTER'S WIFE:	Husband. Why have you cured me?
HUNTER:	Why. To see you well.
HUNTER'S WIFE:	Why have you given me back my human form?
HUNTER:	So you may walk where you please.
HUNTER'S WIFE:	Wouldn't you rather I was a dove. So you can come sneaking through the forest after me. So you can lay traps for me, and cold snares, and put poisons on the leaves. That is the life you love. Tell me, isn't that why you have cured me, my husband, so you can enjoy the chase once more.
HUNTER:	It is not.
HUNTER'S WIFE:	And if not me, is it so you can hunt the badger, the dear, the timid rabbit.
HUNTER:	It is not. No more. I have done with that.

HUNTER'S WIFE:	Look me in the eye.
HUNTER:	I have done with that. Even if you leave me, as I think you must, still I will not return to my old ways. I have done hunting, and I will kill no more.
HUNTER'S WIFE:	Who has softened your heart so?

Enter the two Sidhe.

COLDSIDHE:	You. We're looking for a warrior.
HUNTER:	And what's that to me?
COLDSIDHE:	We can reward you.
HUNTER:	What's the warrior's name?
HOTSIDHE:	Luhan.
HUNTER:	I don't know him.
COLDSIDHE:	Will you track him for us?
HUNTER:	I am no longer a hunter.
HOTSIDHE:	Since when?
HUNTER:	Since my wife was healed.
COLDSIDHE:	And how exactly did that come to pass?
HUNTER:	I learnt the secret from the Salmon of Wisdom.
HOTSIDHE:	He's lying.
COLDSIDHE:	Not exactly he's hiding something.

HUNTER:	Begone now, I've answered enough.
HOTSIDHE:	Where is Luhan?
HUNTER'S WIFE:	Leave him.

The Sidhe are circling menacingly.

COLDSIDHE:	He knows.
HUNTER:	Find him love. It was he who softened my heart.
COLDSIDHE:	Well, well.
HUNTER:	Warn him. Warn...(*he is killed*)

The HUNTER's wife runs, with the HUNTER trying to hold off the two Sidhe. With almost contemptuous ease they disarm him and kill him.

COLDSIDHE:	Strange. No footprints.
HOTSIDHE:	Look. Where that dove flutters
COLDSIDHE:	A changeling. Easy enough to follow. Come.

They exit. End of scene. Enter HELTER and SKELTER, waiting by the bag of gold. They whistle uneasily and unpleasantly, this goes on for some time.

LITTLE SAM:	Here's Little Sam, and I've brought...
HELTER & S:	Good!

They leap on him kill him immediately, stabbing him many times.

HELTER:	That's for you.
SKELTER:	Thirsty work.

106

HELTER: Let's see what he's got.

They take out a bottle each.

HELTER: To wealth.

SKELTER: To wealth.

BOTH: Cheers!

HELTER drinks, but at that moment LITTLE SAM groans, and SKELTER puts back the bottle.

SKELTER: Little Sam's alive! The traitor!

HELTER: Well stab him again.

SKELTER: Here, and here.

LITTLE SAM *is finally killed.*

HELTER: I don't feel well Skelter.

SKELTER: That's not like you. Perhaps it's murdering Little Sam has upset your stomach.

HELTER: Perhaps. No. I think it's worse than that, I think. Skelter, will you chink a toast to me...I'm dying. My last request is, drink to me. Go on.

HELTER *dies.*

SKELTER: Now that's a strange request. If I were a suspicious man, I'd say. (*smells bottles*) Why, Little Sam. But you know, it's not your fault. In fact, now that I think about it. That old crone has a lot to answer for.

SKELTER *exits. End of scene.*

FOX:	I love the endgame. Simple. Spare. Decisive.
CROW:	One wrong move and victory becomes defeat. Defeat, victory. And when the game is over. Supper.

SMITH *is at his forge. Enter* LUHAN, *he has his sword.*

SMITH:	And who might you be?
LUHAN:	Luhan.
SMITH:	And what brings you here?
LUHAN:	I've come for Aurora.
SMITH:	Have you now?
LUHAN:	And you won't stop me either.
SMITH:	And if you do take her, I will be destroyed.
LUHAN:	Well I'm sorry for that.
SMITH:	Sorry.
LUHAN:	Well, one of us must be hurt, and that's a shame.
SMITH:	But you'd rather it was me than you.
LUHAN:	I hadn't thought of it like that.
SMITH:	Aren't you scared of me?
LUHAN:	I am not.
SMITH:	I'm a powerful man.
LUHAN:	Love will give me strength.

108

SMITH:	Not strength enough, I think. And perhaps, Luhan. Aurora does not wish to be taken. Aurora! Aurora!

AURORA *enters in wedding dress. The three of them look from one to the other with a mixture of emotions.*

SMITH:	Here is Luhan. Luhan who I say is a black Sidhe. Whom I say, has cut his family down with the sword he holds out now. Who was cursed by his own mother. Who ate from the meat and bones of his own father.
LUHAN:	That's a lie.
SMITH:	A cannibal. A graveyard robber. A black fury in a human form. Sweet of tongue, bitter in deed. A soulless, gutless, horror, wreaking of torment and cruelty.
LUHAN:	Silence!

LUHAN *advances to the SMITH with his sword. The SMITH contrives to be run through to make it seem to AURORA that LUHAN has stabbed him.*

AURORA:	Smith!
SMITH:	You see.
LUHAN:	I didn't mean.

LUHAN *stands agape.*

AURORA:	Murderer!
LUHAN:	No, Aurora.
AURORA:	You're evil.

LUHAN:	It's not so.
AURORA:	Are you hurt?
SMITH:	It's not mortal, child.

He draws the sword back out.

SMITH:	Indeed. He's barely harmed me at all.
LUHAN:	How?

The SMITH *begins to tie* LUHAN *to the forge.*

AURORA:	Smith? It went through your heart, I saw.
SMITH:	Some little magic. Evil can do us no harm in this forge.

The SMITH ties LUHAN to his anvil and gags him.

AURORA:	What will you do with him?
SMITH:	Leave him bound, and when the Sidhe knights pass this way, we shall give him over to be perished by his own kind. That's what he deserves.
AURORA:	Why did he come here?
SMITH:	To steal you away. He didn't know that we had pledged our marriage oaths this morning. Or that tonight is our wedding night.

They kiss, and go to bed. LUHAN *is still bound to the anvil.*

ACT FIVE.

CROW: Would you say that Aurora ever truly loved the Smith?

FOX: It's hard to believe. All I can say is she went to the bridal bed with him. How does any woman choose her first man? I have known it be done a sacrament as revered as first communion, and I have known a convent child take a stranger with foul breath.

CROW: Perhaps it was her way of saying goodbye.

FOX: Perhaps she didn't know why she did it, more than you or I do.

CROW: And the Smith. Should you say he was happy?

FOX: Oh yes. I'm certain that for one night he had perfect happiness.

CROW: Please remember that remark, when we finish our story.

FOX: Aurora burned with all she had seen, all she had heard, with what she had done, and sleep was far from her.

Enter MEDBH *and* DARRAGH. *Ghosts.*

DARRAGH: Why tears child?

AURORA: Who are you?

MEDBH: Your mother.

DARRAGH: Your father.

AURORA:	I went looking for you.
MEDBH:	We know.
AURORA:	Why have you come to me now?
DARRAGH:	Your tears called us. We felt them like spring rain falling on the soil.
AURORA:	I'm so unhappy. Mother. Were you unhappy on your wedding night?
MEDBH:	I cried. But I was not unhappy.
AURORA:	For a moment. When I saw my husband pierced upon a sword. I felt a thrill, like a door flung wide. Father. I think I've become a vain, silly foolish girl.
DARRAGH:	Daughter. It's been hard for you, with none but him to teach you right from wrong.
AURORA:	I tried to believe that once we had lain together, the floodgates in my heart would open and a river of passion would stream through me. Will I ever love him?
MEDBH:	We can't tell you.
AURORA:	I've thrown my life away.
MEDBH:	Your life isn't over. Only if you give up will it end. Do you want to give up?
AURORA:	No.
DARRAGH:	Ask the Smith the truth of why Luhan's blow didn't kill him.

112

MEDBH:	Ask him the truth of that.
AURORA:	Mother. Father. I'll bring flowers for your graves.
MEDBH:	We're not dead child.
DARRAGH:	Just transformed.
MEDBH:	Waiting.

MEDBH *and* DARRAGH *exit.*

AURORA:	Why couldn't Luhan kill you?
SMITH:	It's a secret.
AURORA:	From me?
SMITH:	It's best kept that way.
AURORA:	Then I'm not your wife.
SMITH:	Shh! Shouldn't you be sleeping?
AURORA:	If we are man and wife then there can't be any secrets. You must trust me.
SMITH:	I'll tell you in the morning.
AURORA:	Tell me now. Please.
SMITH:	Years ago I beat my heart from out of my chest.
AURORA:	You have no heart?
SMITH:	Not inside me.
AURORA:	Than how can you love?

SMITH:	I had to hammer it out of me to be safe.
AURORA:	Where is it?
SMITH:	Well, I had no great magic at first, so I squeezed it into an egg.
AURORA:	An egg. That's not very safe.
SMITH:	I thought the same. So when I had more power I put the egg in a hare.
AURORA:	A hare can be hunted.
SMITH:	I thought the same. So I put the hare in a swallow.
AURORA:	A swallow can be preyed upon.
SMITH:	I thought the same. So I put the swallow in a trout.
AURORA:	A trout can be fished up.
SMITH:	I thought the same. So I put the trout in a dragon.
AURORA:	Ah!
SMITH:	And I put the dragon under the earth. And if you should ever wish to meet this dragon, just tap on my anvil with the little silver hammer, which I have hung around my neck. Once, twice and a third time. Once. Twice and a third time. See how I trust you Aurora.

They settle down as if to sleep. AURORA tries to extricate herself, very slowly. She steals the hammer. She is doing her best not to wake the SMITH. She gets to the door.

AURORA goes to LUHAN. The SMITH listens in to the scene.

AURORA:	I'm going to release you. When I do, don't say 'I love you.' Because if you do, I'll have to say, 'I love you too'. And if that happens, I think we'll both have to run away together. But we won't be able to do that because my husband will come for us, and he is so powerful that he will kill you. So we can't run away. Which means, that if you say 'I love you', I shall have to tell you how you can fight him. And the way to do that is to tap this silver hammer on the anvil, once, twice and a third time. It's not that I hate him. He meant everything to me, or nearly. When he stood here, making with his broad hands. I loved him, nearly. But the things he made were always presents for me. And he always had to tell me he loved me and ask me to tell him that I loved him too, and the words destroyed the feeling. So, evil Sidhe, whatever you are, it's very strange, if he had said nothing I might have loved him, but if you...if you...

She ungags him.

LUHAN:	I love you.

AURORA:	I love you too.

LUHAN *takes the hammer and taps the anvil. There is a long pause.*

AURORA:	He lied to me.

Then the SMITH *roars in his sleep.*

SMITH:	Aurora!

From the roar a Dragon raise itself up from the earth. LUHAN fights the dragon and splits it in two. A Trout plops out into a pool. LUHAN whistles.

LUHAN: Brother Salmon! Brother Salmon! Remember Luhan who fed you.

The SALMON chases it and breaks its spine. A Swallow flies out and LUHAN whistles again.

LUHAN: Brother Crow! Brother Crow! Remember Luhan who freed you.

The *CROW* flies after it and tears it apart. A hare falls out – right into the poppy field. Luhan whistles.

LUHAN: Sister Fox! Sister Fox! Remember Luhan who freed you.

The FOX chases the Hare through the field and finally kills it. LUHAN and the SMITH dive for the egg, Luhan has it.

SMITH: Mercy.

A pause. Enter DEATH, enter SKELTER, with gold.

SKELTER: Old woman. Old woman. Old woman.

DEATH: Yes Skelter?

SKELTER: You lied to me. I don't mind about the others, but you lied to me. Death wasn't under that tree. This bag of gold was. By the way, whose is it?

DEATH: By right of inheritance it belongs to Luhan.

SKELTER: Inheritance, schminheritance. If anyone asks...

Enter HUNTER's Wife.

116

HUNTER'S WIFE: Luhan! Is Luhan here? Quickly.

Enter two Sidhe, tracking.

SKELTER: I'm Luhan, and this is my gold.

HUNTER'S WIFE: Run.

HOTSIDHE: You?

SKELTER: That's me. Luhan. No question.

HOTSIDHE: Vengeance.

HOTSIDHE *stabs* SKELTER. LUHAN *runs to* SKELTER.

SKELTER: =Oh villainy. Helter, Little Sam. We didn't find Death. Death found us.

SKELTER *dies. The Sidhe go to exit.*

CROW: What a mix up.

FOX: Brother!

HOTSIDHE: A mix-up?

CROW: Nothing.

LUHAN: Who are you?

COLDSIDHE: Ah. This is our murderer.

The COLDSIDHE *and* HOTSIDHE *go quickly to* LUHAN *and stab him.*

AURORA: Luhan!

DEATH: It's only for a little time. I shall return for you one day. I always do.

The FOX and the CROW go back to their set. The action carries on during their final dialogue.

FOX: And there you have it. The Smith, in his final generosity of heart gave himself up so that Luhan and Aurora might be together. The end. You owe me supper.

CROW: Not at all. The Smith knew his moment of happiness was over forever. Aurora had left him. He'd lost. So he simply contrived a noble death. Selfish to the last. After all, he knew that from his single wedded night a child would be born who...

FOX: He did not know that!

CROW: Supper! Supper! Supper! I insist.

FOX: Do you?

CROW: I do. What do you have prepared? A tasty treat I hope.

FOX: Tasty enough in my opinion.

CROW: What is it?

FOX: The supper I have prepared, is you.

And the FOX *eats the* CROW.

END.

Whose House?

BY

MARY ELIZABETH BURKE KENNEDY

CHARACTERS.

THE RAT QUEEN	SUSIE
THE RAT KING	TOMMY
COMMANDANT JIM	DAVID
LENA, HIS SECOND WIFE	CHARLENE
BECKY	REBECCA
LARRY	STEPHEN
LULU	LOUISE
NIKKI	NICOLE
CLARE	SARAH
CHRISTIE, HER HUSBAND	GORDON
GIRLEEN	SUSIE
BOYO, HER BROTHER	TOMMY
DANIEL O'CONNELL'S AGENT	NICOLE

THE CAST AS A CHORUS PLAY.

THE RATS

THE PARTY GUESTS IN FANCY DRESS

REBECCA'S AND LARRY'S MOTHER

THE COMMUNE

THE PAPARAZZI

THE STORY OF DANIEL O'CONNELL'S VISIT

MIGRANT WORKERS

SETTING.

THE PLAY IS SET TO-DAY IN A LARGE, RESTORED GEORGIAN
HOUSE, ON THE OUTSKIRTS OF A COUNTRY TOWN IN THE
MIDDLE OF IRELAND.

PROLOGUE.

The ruin of a big house. Rats scurry among the fallen masonry. There is a tent/shelter, consisting of pieces of canvas thrown over bent branches. It is night. Windy. The entire chorus sings.

> *Under the stars by the light of the moon we huddle together. By day we scavenge for something to eat in all kinds Of weather. Some people laugh when they see us go by, Some people fear us and our evil eye. Some people just shake their heads and say why Do they live on the road?*
>
> *We've got no answer, that's just who we are, The road is our home. Though it's not easy, it's our kind of comfort, We just have to roam. We'll work if you let us, we'll sharpen your knives. We'll sell pictures of saints to your holy wives. Out, under the sky We'll survive where you'd die, On the road.*
>
> *Hark! Hark! The dogs do bark, The tinkers are coming to town. Some in rags and some in tags, And one in a velvet gown*

RAT QUEEN: The children in the town call me the Rat Queen. They run when they see me coming. "She's got rats in her bag! She's got rats in her hair!" They take dares to come at night, to the ruin where we have our camp. But I don't have to worry. My rat friends protect me. You should see those kids run when they see my friends. You should hear them swear. Such profanity.

She laughs and the rats join in until there is a great chorus of laughter.

122

RAT QUEEN:	*(suddenly serious)* Where would they learn such language?
RAT KING:	They hear their parents talking about us. Blaming us for everything that goes wrong in the town. If there is a break-in, we did it. If there is an outbreak of sickness we caused it with our "dirty ways". We brought the rats, they say.
RAT QUEEN:	The rats were here in this ruin before we ever pitched our shelters. If anything, I contain them. I keep them from plaguing the town. They stay here, around our camp, because I talk to them and feed them.
RAT KING:	That's not what the townspeople think. They want rid of us. A man came out last night and warned me. They're moving us on.
RAT QUEEN:	What will happen to my rats?
RAT KING:	They'll poison them.
RAT QUEEN:	They have no right. We belong here. My Grandmother always used to say we were on this land, long before the English came and built the big house.
RAT KING:	That doesn't matter any more. It's 1955. The English are gone and the Army owns the land and they are going to fix up the house, so the man from the council said.
RAT QUEEN:	That's impossible. All it is, is a few stumps of walls, held together by ivy. It shelters us. That's all it's good for. It's our home.

RAT KING:	The Council man says we have to go. It's a national monument, he says. Daniel O'Connell stayed in this house, he says, and it will put the town on the map if it's fixed up.
RAT QUEEN:	I'm not moving.
RAT KING:	We have no choice.
RAT QUEEN:	It's my house.
RAT KING:	It was never your house.

The chorus create the re-built house.

GORDON:	Built by the Warwickshire regiment when this was a garrison town in 1815 for the Colonel and his family, who couldn't be expected to live in the barracks.
SARAH:	Warwick House was the envy of every householder far and near. Fashion had come to country living.
STEPHEN:	A double-fronted house. With a leaded fanlight over the front door.
CHARLENE:	And glass panels beside the door, that you could peep through into the hall. Or peep out of, to see who was coming up the steps.
TOMMY:	Granite steps sweeping up to the door and wrought iron railings on either side. Elegance never before seen outside of Dublin.
NICOLE:	And yes, the house was elegant-to a degree. The Irish have a way of exaggerating everything.

This house was not English Georgian, it was Irish Georgian, and within that category it wasn't even Dublin Georgian it was Country Georgian, which meant that the builders cut corners wherever they could and it was built of sandstone rather than red brick and the precise mathematical proportions were not observed. A bit hit and miss. You can tell I'm the outsider here.

LOUISE: Not that the details of the architecture mattered to the Colonel and his family. They had plenty of living rooms and bed rooms and dressing rooms, and stables for their fine horses and their carriage, and a basement for their native servants to cook and do the washing, out of sight.

RAT QUEEN: And deeper even than the basements were the cool wine cellars. Where sometimes, there were rats.

RAT KING: But nobody above stairs saw them either.

CHARLENE: The army families came and went until the last colonel was murdered by some crowd of rebels...

DAVID: Peep o' Day Boys.

LOUISE: The very ones. And shortly after that the regiment withdrew and the house was taken over by some big businessman from the town and it was some time after that, that Daniel O'Connell came to stay.

NICOLE: He held a big rally in Ballybother.

SARAH:	(*Correcting her*) Bothar. Ballybothar.
DAVID:	And he stayed in Warwick House.
GORDON:	And that was all that happened to the house until it got burned down during the War of Independence because somebody thought the owner was English.
STEPHEN:	And he was only from Tullamore, but he had gone to school in England so he sounded English and he was in the big house, so they burned it.
GORDON:	The ruin sat there as an eyesore until 1955 by which the barracks was occupied by a regiment of the Irish army.
STEPHEN:	A quick-witted commandant reclaimed the site as Army property and set about persuading the Major General of the time to let him restore it.
DAVID:	It would be an asset to the army. An asset to the town. It would integrate the army and the town in a positive new way. And there would be a blue plaque to Daniel O'Connell, assuring his approval of the project.
SARAH:	The Major-General congratulated the commandant on his vision and the army paid up.
DAVID:	The commandant would oversee the interior decorating and the selection of furnishings, and would himself live there, as a caretaker, you might say.

GORDON:	The town council was delighted with the plan. But it anticipated trouble getting rid of the tinkers that camped there every winter.
STEPHEN:	So the commandant sent out a lorry-load of young privates.
DAVID:	They jumped out of the back waving rifles.
GORDON:	You've no right here.
STEPHEN:	Gather up your stinkin' belongings and go.
DAVID:	Get on out o that with ye.
RAT KING:	There was no arguing with them. So we packed up our bits and pieces and left.
RAT QUEEN:	And when we were down the road a bit we heard them shouting and squealing and shooting. Shooting.
RAT KING:	They were shooting her rats.

SCENE ONE.

CHARLENE *collects a cape a walking stick and a big hat.*

LENA:	The story of the Commandant and the Commandant's Beautiful Wife.

She dresses JIM *as she speaks and she kisses his body as she dresses him.*

	So here he is, the greatest orator in Europe, in his cape and his cane and his hat, and his finely curled hair and his full red lips.

JIM: (Disengaging himself.) That's all right. I'm dressed now. I have to say this fancy dress carry on gives me a pain. Why could we not have had an ordinary party?

LENA: Oh, come on! Have you no fun in you? The whole town is coming here in full regalia to see us and to see our house.

JIM: I don't see the sense of it. Me going as Daniel O'Connell and you going as Scarlett O'Hara

LENA: The point is that we are living in his house…

JIM: It was never his house…

LENA: We are living in his house and you have an imposing figure just like him. And I have a figure like Scarlett O'Hara, or I will have when you lace me into this corset.

She hands him the corset to lace her in.

LENA: Put your arms around me from behind and fit it around my waist. That's right.   Over my hips and under my breasts. Then pull the laces as tight as you can.

JIM: You won't be able to breathe.

LENA:	Wait till you see my costume. The little dressmaker in High Street made it for me. She copied it from the film. The red dress that Scarlett wears when Rhett makes her go to Melanie's birthday after she has been caught making up to Ashley by Miss Mead and India Wilkes. And Rhett leaves her when they get to the door of the house and tells her that she's own her own and she has to face all the gossips by herself and the door opens and she just stands there. Magnificent. In the red dress. With a red satin stole around her shoulders, trimmed with red ostrich feathers. And everybody just gasps.
JIM:	You'll be the one that will be gasping.
LENA:	She had an 18-inch waist. Can you believe that?
JIM:	She didn't exist.
LENA:	Actually no. It was 20 inches and her Mammy said she would never get her figure back to 18 after she had the baby.
JIM:	Scarlett O'Hara is a work of fiction.
LENA:	No it's true. Women at that time did have 18-inch waists.
JIM:	Only because they were trussed up in these contraptions.
LENA:	I think my corset is fabulous. My little woman made this for me too. I'm going to wear it all the time.
JIM:	Nonsense.
LENA:	What's nonsense about it?

JIM:	You can't go round in that thing.
LENA:	I'd have my clothes on over it. No one would know I was wearing it. Only you. You'd have to put me into it. And let me out of it. Wouldn't you like that? You could be commanding, like Rhett Butler when he sweeps Scarlett into his arms and carries her up the stairs to the bedroom….He was really in command that night.
DAVID:	You've got to stop this, Lena. Stop it right now.
LENA:	Stop what? What's the matter with you?
DAVID:	These fantasies. This is not Daniel O'Connell's house. He only spent a night in a house that used to be on this site. And you are not a character out of Gone With the Wind. And neither am I.
LENA:	Oh! For heaven's sake you have to spoil everything. We're dressing up. Everybody in the town is coming here tonight in order to let themselves go and...just pretend.
DAVID:	They won't all have specially made underwear.
LENA:	That's because they haven't got the imagination I have.

The Chorus are the party guests.

LOUISE:	That's the truest word she ever spoke.
REBECCA:	Always known for her imagination, the same Lena.

130

GORDON:	Couldn't ever distinguish between imagining and lying.
SARAH:	Got it from her father.
GORDON:	Used to say he was," In the film business."
REBECCA.	All he did was run the local cinema.
NICOLE:	Admittedly he owned it. And he went to Cannes, once.
TOMMY:	Lena went off to Dublin when she left school. Said she was studying to be a secretary in Sherrie's college. But she was seen working as an usherette in a cinema on Camden Street.
SUSIE:	Had a boyfriend in the Guards. She said he was a detective.
REBECCA:	Then she disappeared for a long time. Her mother said she had gone to her cousins in Yorkshire.
STEPHEN:	When she came back she was subdued. Said she didn't like England. Living in an industrial town.
NICOLE:	Said her nerves were bad.
LOUISE:	No big stories about England. So people made up their own version of events.
SARAH:	And this version involved an amorous Garda Síochána and a nine-month stay in an English convent.
REBECCA:	The people of Ballybothar had imaginations too.

GORDON:	And then a new infantry division arrived at the barracks, with a new Commandant.
TOMMY:	Young to have got so far in rank. Going further everyone said.
SUSIE:	A widower. Marianne, his tragic young wife, had died in a riding accident.
NICOLE:	How romantic could you get? And he looked terrific in his uniform.
STEPHEN:	Lena's imagination kicked back into life. She set off in hot pursuit.
GORDON:	Stormed the barracks and the Commandant fell.
LOUISE:	They took over the big house. It was Lena's palace. She launched her reign in it with a grand fancy dress party.
LENA:	You always said that's what you loved about me. That I was different to the rest of the people in this town. That I had vision. That I was the only one who understood your ambition.
JIM:	Vision for the future is one thing. Living in fantasy-land is another.
LENA:	That's what tonight is all about. And we'll do it better than anyone else. The men will all come as cowboys and the women will all be Marilyn Monroe in peroxide wigs. We will bring a touch of class.
JIM:	Apart from anything else, we can't afford your fantasies any longer. How much does your "little woman in High Street" cost?

LENA:	She's very cheap. God, you should see the house where she lives. Smells of gas. The whole neighbourhood does. And it's so pokey. Can't imagine how she brings up a family. She's glad of whatever I give her.
JIM:	You give her nothing. She doesn't exist anymore than Scarlett O' Hara. You ordered these costumes from London. From a place called Angels'.
LENA:	Have you been spying on me?
JIM:	I see the money going out of our account. I've checked up on it.
LENA:	So I ordered costumes from Angels'. Is that a crime?
JIM:	It's telling lies when you don't have to.
LENA:	It's not as though I'm stealing from you. The money's mine to spend, isn't it Or am I going to have to ask you for an allowance every week?
JIM:	That mightn't be a bad idea. We have to stop throwing money around.
LENA:	I'm not as extravagant as some people.
JIM:	Whatever that means.
LENA:	I don't keep a horse.
JIM:	Leave Marianne out of this argument.
LENA:	I would gladly leave her out, but she's always there, in your head isn't she? The perfect wife. Your soul mate. Like Ashley and Miss Melly.

"Miss Marianne" wore modest frocks too, I suppose, and cameo brooches.

DAVID: How dare you drag Marianne into your stupid games. She's dead. This is going too far.

LENA: All right. I'm sorry. I won't mention her again. I am really sorry. Honestly I am.

DAVID: Why do you say things like that? Do you want to hurt me?

LENA *collapses in floods of tears.*

LENA: I say stupid things only because I can't say what's really on my mind. There's something I have to tell you but I'm afraid to.

JIM: Come on. Out with it.

LENA: I can't now. The people are arriving.

JIM: You should have thought of that before you started this row. I'm not going anywhere until you tell what this is all about.

LENA: First promise that you won't turn against me. Promise that you'll still love me.

LOUISE: Downstairs, the guests had got rid of their coats and the Ballybothar fancy dress ball was getting into full swing, in the new big house.

STEPHEN: All the cowboys were dancing with the Marilyn Monroes.

NICOLE: Everyone had an eye out for the Commandant and Lena.

SUSIE:	Everyone was sure that Lena would make a late entrance down the staircase, to be sure of creating the maximum effect.
GORDON: **SARAH:**	So they danced away and decided to ignore her. Time wore on and it was getting late, even for a late entrance.
REBECCA:	The caterers wanted to set out the running buffet dinner.
TOMMY:	This was the first running buffet ever in Ballybothar.
STEPHEN:	A young captain decided to pop upstairs to see what was keeping the hosts.
STEPHEN:	He knocked and knocked. And then The Commandant answered. In a fury.
DAVID:	We'll be down in a minute.
STEPHEN:	And he banged he door.
SUSIE:	The word got out. Something had happened upstairs.
LOUISE:	Maybe he had found out at last, the kind of her.
NICOLE:	Maybe he had found out about the baby.
REBECCA:	Maybe the Garda Síochána had turned up.
TOMMY:	The detective.
GORDON:	Maybe a nun from the convent in England had shown up.

SUSIE:	What would the Commandant think of his little Lena in that case?
GORDON:	A showdown must have taken place.
TOMMY:	Violence might have broken out. There had been violence...
SARAH:	That's what everybody feared.
REBECCA:	Violence.
LOUISE:	Definitely. That was it.
SUSIE:	They waited for the blood.
JIM:	Oh, for Heaven's sake, stop this tantrum. They'll hear you out on the street.
LENA:	Is that all you care about? Privacy? Well forget it. They probably know all about it already.
JIM:	All about what?
LENA:	Why I ran away to London.
JIM:	I thought you were in Sheffield.
LENA:	A smokescreen. I went to London.
JIM:	Go on.
LENA:	Come and let me kiss you first.

DAVID kneels beside her and kisses her.

LENA:	You do know that I love you more than anything in the world.

JIM:	I do. But you confuse me.
LENA:	I'm jealous of Marianne. She was so good and I'm not.
JIM:	You're just extravagant. It's only a little fault.
LENA:	You don't know what I've done. It's terrible. I can't tell you.
JIM:	I'm a man of the world. You can tell me anything.
LENA:	There was...someone else, another man. Before you.
JIM:	I understand. That's all right.
LENA:	He was in the Guards. I met him at a dance in the Garda club in Dublin. I fell in love with him. He was married.
JIM:	I see. But you weren't to know that.
LENA:	It was the first thing he told me on the night we met. "I'm a married man", he aid. And I told him I didn't care.
JIM:	That was rash of you.
CHARLENE:	When I became pregnant he arranged for me to go to London.
JIM:	Pregnant! I see. That's pretty terrible all right. Terrible for you, I mean. Did you have the baby there? You had it adopted?
LENA:	His sister was a nurse in London. She knew people. She arranged for me to have an abortion.

	He thought that would be a better thing. We both did.
JIM:	Oh my God! What a dreadful story.
LENA:	That's not the end of it. Something went wrong with the...the procedure. I ended up in hospital. I had to have my womb removed. Now you see. *(silence)*. Aren't you going to say anything? *(silence)*. For God's sake speak to me.

JIM *moves to exit.*

LENA:	Where are you going?
JIM:	I'm getting out of here.
LENA:	You said I could tell you anything.
JIM:	This is too much to take in. I need to think.
LENA:	You can't walk out on me now. What will I say to the guests?
JIM:	You'll think of something.

JIM *leaves.*

LENA:	You're running back to Marianne, aren't you Jim? You could only take so much. You've failed me.
GORDON:	The guests were tucking into their sherry trifles by the time their hostess appeared at the top of the grand staircase.
LOUISE:	Alone.
GORDON:	And, it has to be said, magnificent.

REBECCA:	But she was pale and her eyes were cast down. There was something tense about her that made people stop eating.
TOMMY:	She came half way down the stairs to where there was a little landing before the next flight of steps. She stopped and raised her head to speak.
SARAH:	She said she hoped everyone was having a good time.
STEPHEN:	She said her husband had been called away, suddenly, on a family matter. An illness. In his family.
NICOLE:	She urged them all to continue eating and to drink up.
SUSIE:	She moved to continue her descent of the staircase. And then she fell.
LOUISE:	A long, slow, silent fall.
SARAH:	Over and over she tumbled, hitting every step, landing face down, arms stretched out on the floor of the hall.
TOMMY:	Everyone rushed to her aid. The doctor sent for an ambulance, for he was too drunk to be of any use himself.
SARAH:	She was taken away.
LOUISE:	People tried to reconstruct how it had happened.
NICOLE:	Someone swore she had seen her foot catch in the hem of her dress.

SUSIE:	Someone swore she saw a mouse run out in front of her. Or maybe even a rat. There were still rats about that place.
GORDON:	And then someone swore he had seen her deliberately fling herself down the steps.
SARAH:	Whatever was the case, the poor woman suffered for it.
LOUISE:	It transpired that she was pregnant and she lost the baby through the fall.
LOUISE:	Just the same as Scarlett O'Hara.
STEPHEN:	When the Commandant turned up the next day at the barrack and was told what had happened to Lena, he laughed. Just laughed.
REBECCA:	He never went to see her.
STEPHEN:	He asked for a transfer overseas and was refused. He left the army and went to Africa on his own. Became a mercenary it was said.
GORDON:	He never set foot in Ballybothar again.
LOUISE:	The army respectfully requested Lena to leave the big house. She was, after all not their responsibility.
TOMMY:	They could get no tenants among the other officers.
SUSIE:	Their wives all thought the house was jinxed.
BECKY:	After a time they sold it to the doctor, who moved in with his beautiful wife and his daughter.

140

LARRY: And his son was born there. In the house. He delivered him himself.

TOMMY: Sober, that night.

LENA: Lena took over the cinema from her father and re-named it the De Luxe. She worked in the box-office, cleaned it herself. Spent the rest of her life in there. Sometimes, just sitting in the dark.

SCENE TWO.

LARRY: The story of the doctor's house and the doctor's children. 1968.

BECKY. (Whispering) This house is a prison. I wish I was in a real prison. At least I wouldn't have to think. Just do what I was told to do, at the same time everyday. I would be given my food. There would be people to talk to. I could listen but I wouldn't have to talk if I didn't want to. People like good listeners. Prisoners are people with interesting stories. People who have done interesting things. Bad things. People who have stolen things. Taken lives. Committed crimes of their own free will. I've never done anything of my own free will, good or bad. But I am serving my sentence here.

Each member of the chorus is The Mother. Each with a cane to beat the floor before he or she speaks.

SARAH: That's a fine way to talk about living with your mother.

141

NICOLE:	She thinks she can't be heard down there, whingeing and crying.
SUSIE:	Complaining about the one who brought her into the world and who has paid for every bite of food that has passed her lips ever since.
GORDON:	The mother who earned the respect of the town for her business sense and her hard bargaining.
DAVID:	For standing by a degenerate of a husband, paying his debts and seeing him through scandals.
TOMMY:	The mother who never showed preference between her daughter and her son, even though the son was a brilliant artist and her daughter couldn't draw water. They both lived at home, in the finest house in Ballybothar and she supported them.
CHARLENE:	The mother who was a better-looking woman in her day than her daughter ever would be. The epitome of style. The only woman in Ballybothar with a mink coat. A film star.
LOUISE:	The mother who was now cruelly bed-ridden by a stroke. Who could not move but who still had the heart and the mind and the will of a lion.
SARAH:	The mother who knew every thought that passed through her daughter's mind even when she wasn't talking to herself out loud like she was now.
BECKY:	Thump, thump, thump all you like with that cane of yours. I'm not running up the stairs again. (Imitating her mother)"I want a glass of water. Just wet my lips, don't drown me. There's

142

a taste off that water. You didn't wash the glass properly. What was in it? Alcohol. I knew it. You're like your father before you. A lush. He taught you well. He taught you some nice things. Now you've spilt it on my nightdress. You'll have to change me. Be careful of my arm. My arm has a bruise from the last time you changed me. You are so rough. Why can't you learn to do it like the nurses? The nurses are skilful. You could never be a nurse. You could never be anything. Always in a rush to get away by yourself. To talk to yourself. To have sex with yourself. You do that don't you? I've heard you moaning in the night. I suppose you have to resort to that. What man would have you, with your horse face? Now when I was your age I can remember arriving in this town for the first time to take up my teaching job and the schoolmaster saying that I was the most beautiful girl that had ever set foot in Ballybothar." (shouting at the ceiling) Why didn't you marry the schoolteacher, then, instead of the lush. If you could have had your pick, why did you pick my father? (she breaks down) Why did you pick my father? Why didn't you stop him.

LARRY *enters. He has been painting in his studio and drinking.*

LARRY:	What in God's name is going on? I can't hear myself think. Between her banging and you howling at the moon. Would you not just answer her when she calls you?
BECKY:	You do it. You change her nightdress if she's wet. You change the soiled bedding.
LARRY:	Do you think that's what she wants?
BECKY:	More than likely. Can't you smell it?

LARRY:	You're paranoid.
BECKY:	I can smell you too. You're drunk.
LARRY:	It's the turpentine. I was cleaning brushes.
BECKY:	In your mouth?
LARRY:	For fuck's sake, Rebecca.
BECKY:	Don't use that kind of language to me. I'm not one of your art college beatniks.
LARRY:	You should get out, Rebecca. You should broaden your mind.
BECKY:	And when am I supposed to do that? The nurse comes three times a week to bath her and treat the bedsores and while she's here, I sleep. It's the only chance I get when the cane isn't banging on the ceiling.
LARRY:	We need to talk about that. About the nurse I mean. We'll have to look at having her less often.
BECKY:	What are you saying?
LARRY:	Money. She's damned expensive, that nurse. And we simply haven't got the cash. Could you not learn to do what she does?
BECKY:	I don't want to learn to do what she does. I don't want to be a nurse. I don't want to nurse mother. I want to get out of here and it's not just to broaden my mind. It's to keep my mind.
LARRY:	I'm afraid that's a lost cause, my lovely.

144

BECKY:	(whispering) Don't call me that! Don't call me that!
LARRY:	I mean here you sit, talking to yourself and you haven't a clue where the next penny is coming from.

The chorus, as Mother, start to bang on the floor.

SARAH:	Come up to me, my boy. My wonderful, talented boy.
NICOLE:	My boy who has drawn portraits of me, which hang all over the house.
CHARLENE:	Portraits copied from photographs taken in my youth, when I was the most beautiful woman in this town.
GORDON:	Of course when he asks me to let him handle the finances of the family, I let him. I give him power of attorney. He signs the cheques to pay the bills. I can't any longer.
LOUISE:	As for my daughter! She would spend the money on drink. He has a head for figures, inherited from me. He understands money. So he controls mine.
GORDON:	So when he tells me he has found the money to build himself an artist's studio in the return of the house, I am delighted.
TOMMY:	He finishes with the art college. They have nothing more to teach him. He lives and works at home.
DAVID:	An elaborate extension is built. All glass. Nothing else like it in the town.

SUSIE:	The studio where he will produce his masterpiece.
SARAH:	"The sun, Mother," he says. "I need the sun".
LARRY:	If you want the nurse, how do you propose we pay for her?
BECKY:	I propose we sell this house and its contents, lock, stock and barrel. I propose we split the proceeds between us. I propose that we do the same with any stocks and shares or whatever else she has in that regard. And out of what we each get, we can share the cost of putting Mother in a nursing home.
LARRY:	You're talking rubbish. Mother fought all her life to hold on to this house. When Father was gambling money hand over fist, she managed to hold on. She's never going to agree to sell it.
BECKY:	Tell her she has to. You can persuade her to do anything. She even funded your ridiculous glass room.
LARRY:	Well that's the thing. You see I have no intention of leaving my studio either. You want to evict Mother and me as well. I'm telling you, you can't.
BECKY:	There must be a way. There has to be a way. I have to escape.
LARRY:	I may as well tell you the score. The house isn't ours to sell even if Mother and I wanted to leave as much as you do. I took out a mortgage to build my studio and to pay off some bills. I thought I'd be able to meet the repayments, but work has been slow.

146

BECKY:	You sit in your studio all day long drinking yourself into a stupor and you are surprised when you get nothing done.
LARRY:	You're missing the point. The house belongs to the bank.
BECKY:	You mean there's no getting out?
LARRY:	We have to trim our sails. Sell some of the furniture. Some of the silver and all those terrible china dinner services that Mother bought at auctions and pretended were heirlooms. They should fetch something. And we'll keep the old girl here. As long as she's in the house the bank manager won't throw us out. She's still well got in the town.
BECKY:	You're just as ruthless as he was.
LARRY:	A chip off the old block, my lovely.
BECKY:	I'm not your lovely. And I wasn't his.
LARRY:	Oh but you were.
SARAH:	Oh but she was. From the minute that child was born, my husband had eyes for no one else.
GORDON:	Besotted.
DAVID:	Never stopped cuddling and caressing her.
TOMMY:	Charming to see a father so in love with his little girl, people said.
CHARLENE:	And when the little girl grew up?

147

LOUISE:	I said to him, "You have an unholy love for the girl". I said I'd tell the priest. He knew I wouldn't. You don't tell things like that.
SUSIE:	So I turned a blind eye. Ignored the pawing. Ignored her white face.
NICOLE:	The little hypocrite. I've made her pay.
SARAH:	She knew well what she was doing. She stole my husband.
LARRY:	(To the audience.) My sister was a thief, all right. She stole everything. She waited until I was in my studio one day, sleeping, out cold. Exhausted from…this and that. She stole the silver. She stole the china. She stole Mother's mink coat. She packed the car and stole it and left. She has gone. We'll never see her again. The little hypocrite.
SARAH:	(As Mother) I'll track her down. There are people in this town who will do things for me. If I ever find out where she is I'll have her prosecuted and sent to jail.
BECKY:	Which, of course is what she did. This time her hatred overcame her fear of scandal. So here I am in my little cell with bars on the windows. The walking stick no longer thumps in my head. No one calls me, "my lovely", and reaches out, drunkenly to feel me. My father is dead. My mother will die soon. My brother will end his life in a stupor. The bank will take the precious house and carve it into bed-sitting rooms, where people will have parties and talk to each other.
LULU:	Where people will break the law in large numbers and laugh in large numbers.

148

BECKY:	And I am free. Even here in what people call a jail. I am out of doors.

SCENE THREE.

LULU:	1975. The year of the commune.

Music. Blood Sweat and Tears. Lucretia Mc Evil. NICOLE and LOUISE cuddle up under a sleeping bag. The chorus make the sound of a train passing in the distance. LOUISE extricates herself gently and sits up.

LULU:	When she came to Ireland, she was a student of Irish history and a virgin. She had never been drunk. She had never taken drugs. She went to church on Sundays and respected her parents. Homosexuals were perverts and stealing was wrong and dangerous if you got caught. Now she is sleeping with me. We shoplift every morning. We get stoned every afternoon and every night we get drunk. How's that for an education, Kiddo. She hasn't written home for a month.

She shakes NICOLE awake.

LULU:	Call your mother.

LULU *leaves the bed.*

NIKKI:	I made a reverse charge call to my mother and said I was in a remote place learning Irish. She wanted to believe me but I think she was afraid. At least she knows I'm alive. I love this woman, Lulu. I know it's not her real name. Her friends call her Trixie. They rent this house between them and they sublet this room to Lulu but I don't think the landlord knows about that. It's a

149

big room with two huge windows with old threadbare curtains. And a big marble fireplace. When you look out the window there's a row of big old trees. Some place this was once. The friends want rid of me. (The train rattles by again.)

The chorus come together to create the Galway train, Complicite-style. LOUISE *and* NICOLE *sit opposite each other on the train.*

NIKKI: I was on the train to Galway. My mother had asked me to see Connemara for her. I was sitting opposite a dark-haired woman.

LULU: Why don't we find the bar and have a drink?

NIKKI: Why, I don't drink. But thank you.

LULU: And she looked at me as though I had horns on my head and I thought, "This is one prim wee creature. She was just born to be scandalized!" Well let's go to the dining car anyway and you can have some coffee and tell me about yourself.

STEPHEN: But there wasn't any dining car on the Galway train so they had to stay where they were.

LULU: I suppose you can't believe how primitive this country is, coming from, where exactly do you come from?

NIKKI: Arizona.

LULU: You'd never have a train without a dining car in Arizona? And Pullman seats?

NIKKI: The trains are pretty good.

150

LULU:	What exactly are Pullman seats? They're always talking about them in the movies.
NIKKI:	They're big and wide and kinda soft.
LULU:	Sounds like you could have an interesting time in those seats on a long journey. In the tunnels.
NIKKI:	There arc no tunnels in Arizona.
LULU:	I love the way American trains in the movies always go "Whooo, Whooo", when they go into the tunnels.
STEPHEN:	There are no tunnels on the Galway line and the seats have no springs.
LULU:	I've been caught out on this train before so I always bring a flask of coffee. Will you have some?
NIKKI:	If it doesn't leave you short.
LULU:	(Pours coffee) Not a bit of it. But I must tell you that it has a wee brightener in it.
NIKKI:	You mean it's laced with something?
LULU:	Uisce Bheatha.
NIKKI:	Oh my God! You're speaking Gaelic! My mother told me to go meet people who spoke Gaelic.
LULU:	Then your mother would approve of me.
NIKKI:	So what's that stuff that's in the coffee?
LULU:	The Water of Life.

NIKKI:	That's the most romantic name for hooch that I've ever heard. So we had coffee with the Water of Life in it and the dark-haired woman told how she lived in a sort of commune in a place called Ballybothar and how they were going to subvert the Capitalist System, end the production of nuclear energy and the war in Vietnam, re-green the planet with justice for all and legalise cannabis and LSD.
LULU:	In a nutshell, put an end to Male Tyranny. And Organised Religion. Same thing.
NIKKI:	The campuses at home were full of this stuff. Which is why I had been sent to Ireland to meet people who spoke Gaelic, where my mother was sure there were no words for women's liberation or cannabis. What's the Gaelic for cannabis?
LULU:	Tine Bheatha. Sláinte.
NIKKI:	This Water of Life was great. I could go on this journey forever.
LULU:	I just love it when the train goes, "Whooo, Whooo." I wish this train would do it.
STEPHEN:	The Galway train had got as far as Ballybothar and it was worn out
SARAH:	An announcement was made.
DAVID:	(incomprehensibly muffled under static) Anyone who wants to go any further will have to go by bus.
NIKKI:	More Gaelic?
LULU:	Come on. This is our stop.

"The Train" ceases its motion and becomes the sleeping communards again. Music. Blood Sweat and Tears.

NIKKI: So Lulu persuaded me to come home with her and I remember walking with her from the station through the town and my rucksack being very heavy and eventually we arrived at a big house. And we came upstairs and I remember thinking I couldn't carry my rucksack another step and then we were in a room and it was full of smoke and music, and people were sitting around drinking beer.

LULU: This is my friend Nikki from Nebraska"

NIKKI: I'm from Arizona.

REBECCA: She's Alice from Arizona.

STEPHEN: Alice doesn't live here any more.

LULU: You stupid fuckers have no manners.

NIKKI: She closed over the doors in the middle of the room where were all lying around and suddenly we were in another room with big windows. This was her room.

LULU: Come on love. Get into bed. Wherever you're from, you're home now.

NIKKI: And that first night she said, "Don't be frightened. Just go to sleep. I'll watch over you." But when I woke up she was gone and all the people from the other room were sitting looking at me.

STEPHEN: Alice in Wonderland. How'd you get here, Alice?

NIKKI:	My name's Nikki. And I came with Lulu.
CHARLENE:	Nikki and Lulu. I have died and gone to France.
DAVID:	Trixie has been reading Colette.
REBECCA:	Is that why you scuttled off to bed so quick?
STEPHEN:	You missed a great party.
NIKKI:	Is there anything to eat? I mean, like breakfast? Eggs? Bacon? Coffee? I could fix us some if you show me the kitchen.
TOMMY:	Aren't you aware of how the workers on the coffee plantations in South America are exploited by ruthless multi-national exporters, based principally in the United States?
CHARLENE:	For you to enjoy that cup of coffee, someone has laboured like a slave to bring a pittance home to his family who live in a shanty town, with no sanitation.
GORDON:	And as for bacon and eggs. Well for a start, we don't eat meat. It isn't natural for human beings to do so, although I did hear a story about guys stuck out on the Antarctic who ate each other, which posed some really interesting ethical questions. (Lots of nodding.)
SARAH:	You're straying from the point. The pigs are kept in deplorable conditions, with no sanitation. And pigs are intrinsically clean creatures.
REBECCA:	As are the battery hens that produce your breakfast eggs. But they are cooped up in tiny cages.

SUSIE:	Total shit.
STEPHEN:	So you won't find your coffee and bacon and eggs here.
NIKKI:	That's OK. I'll eat anything.
GORDON:	It's not quite like that. You can't just help yourself. Everybody has to contribute. It's one for all and all for one.
NIKKI:	I'll contribute as soon as I get my next cheque from home. But in the meantime could I have something now?
SARAH:	The larder is bare until Trixie gets back.
NIKKI:	She's gone shopping?
DAVID:	"Shopping", "cheques from home"! Your vocabulary reflects an ingrained bourgeois mentality, which is inherently selfish, elevating and indulging the middle-class, nuclear family at the expense of the greater good.
NIKKI:	You sound pretty middle class yourself.
REBECCA:	Dave's father is a judge.
DAVID:	Bastard thinks he's God.
CHARLENE:	Dave's father has never spoken to him since he failed the leaving.
SARAH:	In rejecting his family, Dave has struck a significant blow to a cornerstone of the bourgeois establishment, at great personal cost.
SUSIE:	Far out, Sarah. I mean. Yea.

LULU re-enters the scene.

GORDON:	We are a living example of a new sociological phenomenon.
NIKKI:	Where does the money come from?
LULU:	They draw the dole.
NIKKI:	You mean you're living off the state.
LULU:	Precisely.
TOMMY:	What we are doing in fact, is exercising our right as citizens to divert the resources of the state into channels and individuals with the will to reform society.
LULU:	(Unpacks her basket.) Who wants breakfast?
NIKKI:	I'm starving.
LULU:	Well set the table then. Momma has provided.
GORDON:	Listen to Lady Bountiful.
LULU:	Who doesn't draw the dole and who provides?
GORDON:	Trixie.
LULU:	Trixie is defunct. It's Lulu from now on.
GORDON:	Lulu it is.
NIKKI:	What do the rest of you do?
SUSIE:	I am writing a book on ancient Celtic drug culture.

156

LULU:	Great book. No. I mean it.
REBECCA:	Gordon and me are organising a rock festival to take place at the summer solstice in the field with the Ballybothar standing stones.
CHARLENE:	That will be so beautiful.
LULU:	Rebecca used to be in a band and Gordon was her manager. Tell her to sing, Gordon.
GORDON:	Sing, Rebecca.
REBECCA:	Fuck off, Gordon.
NIKKI:	May I use the bathroom please?
CHARLENE:	There isn't one.
SUSIE:	We keep it locked up.
STEPHEN:	The Victorian obsession with cleanliness has had a damaging effect on the human psyche, especially in the area of sexual relations. It has re-emerged in the 20th Century in the image of the scrubbed and gleaming American, with too many white teeth and shiny hair.
SUSIE:	The Celts put lime in their hair to thicken it. Far out.
STEPHEN:	All this washing is bad. Sweat is good.
Everyone nods.	
NIKKI:	But I need to use the lavatory.
TOMMY:	Everyone should be responsible for their own waste. Should be made acknowledge it. Deal

with it. The water tables in the country are being polluted by the proliferation of septic tanks, due to the upsurge in building due to the untrammelled greed of the capitalist property developers.

LULU: Just go out in the stables. Bury any solids. There's a communal trowel.

The Chorus curls up in various couplings. Stoned.

NIKKI: That was my introduction to the Ballybothar commune. They would pontificate all day and get stoned all night. Lulu was the only one who went out to work. She never lectured. She didn't smoke as much as the others. She did drink a lot of whiskey though. She defended me when the others found out my father was in the army. I fell in love with Lulu.

LULU: I told her I worked at helping some desperate and derelict people in the town. I visited their homes. Nikki asked to go with me but I had to refuse.

NIKKI: Her "patients" as she called them were at a sensitive stage. Strangers frightened them.

LULU: We did encounter one guy once, a poet who proceeded to give me a graphic description, which he knew I would relish, of his sexual high jinks of the previous night. Nikki was shocked. I told her it was dangerous for her to know me. She loved that idea. I said I was employed by a charitable agency in Dublin and that was why I had to travel up every week to report to them.

NIKKI: She preferred to make that journey on her own too.

LULU:	And we screwed every chance we got. She was so innocent.
NIKKI:	I was so in love and so stoned all the time that it took a while for the penny to drop. But suddenly, one morning, I knew what Lulu really did.
LULU:	I would have told you sooner or later. I thought you weren't ready.
NIKKI:	You treat me like a child.
LULU:	I didn't want you to run away from me.
NIKKI:	It was patronising of you. I haven't run away from you in spite of your friends. They get at me all the time.
LULU:	Don't you see! I was right. You realised by yourself. That's much better than being told. That means you've grown up.
NIKKI:	In that case, take me with you next time you go to Dublin to collect the drugs. I want to see you in action.
LULU:	I can't possibly do that. My bosses would kill me.
NIKKI:	You're shutting me out. I can't stand that.
LULU:	We all need our own private space.
NIKKI:	What other lies have you told me? That you loved me? Was that a lie?
LULU:	Back off.

NIKKI:	Don't do that! Don't push me away.
LULU:	She started following me into town. Into shops where I would be lifting things. She unnerved me. Once I nearly got caught.
NIKKI:	And then she took to staying over in Dublin. Not coming back for a couple of days at a time. So I followed her there. As I thought there was someone else. A man.
LULU:	One week when I returned from Dublin, she seemed very subdued.
NIKKI:	I've had a letter from home.
LULU:	Nothing wrong, I hope?
NIKKI:	My mother wants me to come home. She sent me the fare.
LULU:	Great. What are you going to do with the money? Have a party?
NIKKI:	I'm going to buy a ticket to Phoenix.
LULU:	Really?
NIKKI:	Do you want me to stay?
LULU:	It's entirely up to you.
NIKKI.	I'll think about it.
LULU:	Next day I left her asleep as usual when I went out. Before I started dealing, I went into a clothes shop. I was seeing a new man. I wanted some new tops. Maybe a long flowing skirt. I had my big shopping bag. I was excited. Cocky.

160

Nobody saw me, I was sure. Going out the door I was stopped by a policeman. I looked back into the shop to see who had spotted me. And there she was. She was crying.

GORDON: So Trixie was arrested and they found the clothes and all the hash and LSD she had for sale.

SUSIE: And then they raided the house and we were all busted.

DAVID: And we were all had up before my father.

STEPHEN: Bastard refused to allow bail.

CHARLENE: We were all given three months for possession.

DAVID: He threw the book at Trixie. She got 18 months.

REBECCA: The Ballybothar Standing Stones Rock festival had to be abandoned. And we had done the posters and all.

SARAH: All because of that snake in the grass. If I could get my hands on her.

TOMMY: What else would you expect from a child of the American Military Industrial complex. An imperialist lackey.

NIKKI: I went from the shop straight to the train and the plane home. It broke my heart that I would never see Lulu again. After all, she had taught me so much.

LULU: I left jail straight for the airport. I was determined to see Nikki again. She didn't know

161

it yet but she was due a few more Irish lessons, in Phoenix.

Music

SCENE FOUR.

SUSIE: 1987.

The chorus are the Irish paparazzi/media, complete with trench coats, cameras, sound booms and Charlie Bird).

STEPHEN: The story so far. We're standing outside the house of local councillor Christian Fitzgerald, waiting for comment from him on recent allegations of planning corruption within the Ballybothar urban district council, allegations which include his name.

DAVID: The story dates back to when a local developer and millionaire, namely Matthew Chisholm, applied to the council for permission to develop part of his 300 acre estate at Chisholm Hall, as a holiday home complex, which was to be developed in conjunction with the tourist board to promote elite tourism in the Ballybothar area. An area famous for its standing stones, which are also on the Chisholm estate.

STEPHEN: Mr. Chisholm also proposed building a heritage centre at the stones and charging an admission fee to anyone wishing to visit it.

DAVID: The proposal met with local opposition from those who argued that there has been a right of way to the stones during the time of Mr.

Chisholm's predecessors and that now he was simply privatising them to make money. The Council refused planning permission.

STEPHEN: But within a year, Council reversed its decision and the building project went ahead.

CHARLENE: Around the time of the completion of the Chisholm Hall Holiday Homes and Interpretive Centre, Matthew Chisholm's daughter, Clare, married Christie, or Christian as he prefers to be known, Fitzgerald.

REBECCA: It was the wedding of the year and was featured on the front cover of Irish Society, the magazine for the discerning reader.

SUSIE: The happy couple bought the ramshackle remains of Warwick House. They restored it in loving detail to live in themselves.

NICOLE: The restoration was featured in Irish Society magazine.

LOUISE: Clare told the magazine,

CLARE: "It is our intention to fill this house with children and dogs!"

LOUISE: She also revealed in a frank and exclusive moment,

CLARE: "We would like to open a section of the house for public viewing at certain times of the year. It is after all a place of great historic interest not just because of its architectural beauty, but because it was the stopping place of Daniel O'Connell. My husband is very conscious of his civic duty. One family cannot claim to own our national heritage."

STEPHEN: Now Christian Fitzgerald's reputation is under scrutiny.

NICOLE: Tabloid newspapers start muckraking. Friction has been reported between the golden couple.

LOUISE.   Clare, dignified as always, maintains a discrete silence. Friends say she is never stronger than when in a crisis.

CHARLENE BIRD: To-night, the family is under siege as the nation's media camps on their doorstep. It remains to be seen how this scandal will pan out. Charlene Bird, O'Connell Terrace, Ballybothar.

Inside the house, CLARE *is doubled over, gasping for breath.* CHRISTY *is glancing through papers and discarding them.*

CLARE: You mean it is Sonia the papers are talking about?

CHRISTIE: Sonia. Yes.

CLARE: How long has it been going on?

CHRISTIE: A while.

CLARE: God. You're ruthless.

CHRISTIE: You said you wanted the truth.

CLARE: Since she was working for us as an au pair?

CHRISTIE: What does it matter?

CLARE:	Do the children know?
CHRISTIE:	What the hell do you mean?
CLARE:	I mean did you do things in front of them? Did they see you at it?
CHRISTIE:	What do you take me for?
CLARE:	An adulterer.
CHRISTIE:	I have never done anything to harm the children.
CLARE:	You don't think their father being involved in bribery and corruption on a grand scale will harm them? You don't think having the gutter press expose their parents' marriage will harm them?
CHRISTIE:	They're too young to be aware of any of this. By the time they're old enough to understand, it will all have blown over.
CLARE:	And where will you be? In St. Petersburg, with Sonia, living in a garret? Making love on the Nevsky Prospect?
CHRISTIE:	To be honest with you I don't know where I'll be. I'm just concentrating at the moment on staying out of jail. But if I did have time to daydream, the Nevsky Prospect sounds damn good.
CLARE:	Are you telling me that you're really serious about this girl?
CHRISTIE:	I suppose I am.
CLARE:	When were you going to tell me about her?

165

CHRISTIE:	I wasn't.
CLARE:	You would just have gone on deceiving me.
CHRISTIE:	Yes. You wouldn't have found out if the press hadn't started digging up this other business.
CLARE:	What about her? She's an intelligent girl. Would she be happy to go on indefinitely as your bit on the side?
CHRISTIE:	It suits her fine. She's pragmatic.
CLARE:	Where is she now? In the flat in Dublin?
CHRISTIE:	I sent her to France. She's in the villa.
CLARE:	Oh good! She can work on her tan in my house, lounging by my swimming pool, probably wear my clothes, run up bills at my expense, while you organise our divorce.
CHRISTIE:	Clare, this is silly.
CLARE:	Why have you done this to us?
CHRISTIE:	She makes me feel alive.
CLARE:	I think I'm going to be sick.
CHRISTIE:	Please, Clare! Stop this interrogation. I didn't set out to be cruel. You're forcing me to tell you things.
CLARE:	You just accidentally sent your mistress to my house in France to wait for you.

CHRISTIE:	What Sonia is doing in France at this moment is not important. What we say to those guys outside the door, is.
CLARE:	What would you like me to say?

She calls the press pack to her. They dash over cameras clicking.

I would like to dispel any rumours of a rift between Mr. Fitzgerald and myself. If anything, we are closer together than ever before. There are times in every marriage when it is in need of refreshment and we are both grateful to our wonderful au pair, Sonia, for enlivening and restoring our devotion to each other. In a frank and exclusive and intimate interview, I will admit to anyone who cares to listen that Mr. Fitzgerald has always been a tiger in bed. Now it's like sleeping with the zoo. Thank you, Sonia. And our thanks also to all you kind people in the press for your interest and genuine concern for us and our family. Mr. Fitzgerald and I would like to invite you all to the Warwickshire Arms in the town square, where a buffet supper has been provided for you at our expense. Goodnight to you all. (The press scurry away, yelping.) In your dreams, Christy. Tell the world whatever you like about yourself and your tart. I'm going and I'm taking the boys with me.

CHRISTIE:	You don't need to do that. Stay here with the children. Don't disrupt them. This house is your home and their home no matter what. I'll leave if you want me to.
CLARE:	That's noble of you. Where are you going? France, I suppose?

CHRISTIE:	For God's sake, Clare, let it rest. There's a far more important issue at stake here. Don't you realise that if I'm investigated for having bribed councillors to overturn the planning decision on the holiday homes and the heritage centre, we could stand to lose everything.
CLARE:	You mean you're guilty?
CHRISTIE:	What do you think? Wait. Don't give me a knee jerk reaction. What do you think?
CLARE:	I had no reason to doubt you before.
CHRISTIE:	Do you doubt your father?
CLARE:	My father's not being investigated.
CHRISTIE:	No! I'm the fall guy.
CLARE:	Did you or did you not bribe the council?
CHRISTIE:	I came to an accommodation with some of them. Pointed out that the building of the holiday village on the lake would be a great new amenity, as would the heritage centre. Pointed out that the town would benefit overall. In short I clarified the mutual advantages to it's going ahead.
CLARE:	And money changed hands while you made these clarifications?
CHRISTIE:	Sometimes it helps to open people's eyes.
CLARE:	Have you any idea how cynical you sound?

CHRISTIE:	Have you any idea how fucking naïve you sound, Miss Holier-Than-Thou, fucking Goody Two Shoes?
CLARE:	Excuse me?
CHRISTIE:	Where do you think I got the fucking money? Under a cabbage at the bottom of the garden?
CLARE:	I see.
CHRISTIE:	About time the penny dropped for Daddy's girl.
CLARE:	Which of you cooked up the idea that you bribe them?
CHRISTIE:	You might say the idea descended on us like the Holy Ghost on the Apostles on Whit Sunday, all at once. It was a mutual decision. I would test the water, to see if there was anyone open to persuasion. Your father would provide the persuasion.
CLARE:	So everyone got what they wanted.
CHRISTIE:	Exactly! And no harm done to anyone. A win/win situation if ever there was one. Everyone is delighted with the heritage centre. It's just the media making a fuss about nothing.
CLARE:	I'm baffled by you.
CHRISTIE:	Don't give me a sermon on standards in public office. This was a different situation. We weren't exporting rotten beef. We were adding to the town.
CLARE:	No. I mean I don't understand what was in it for you. What was your kickback?

CHRISTIE:	I wanted to run for the Dáil. I still want to run for the Dáil. As well you know. And your father said that with the money he would make out of the new scheme, he would be able to afford to sponsor my campaign.
CLARE:	And where did I come in?
CHRISTIE:	You didn't. It was a business deal.
CLARE:	Are you sure I wasn't thrown in for good measure as a, what did they call it long ago, a handsel? Did my father handsel you? With me? I can hear him. "There's Clare, now, and she's a fine looking girl, if she is a bit horsey an' doggy, and she'd make a politician a fine wife, for she can speak up and she's good with the words and you could do worse than take her off my hands and I'd never see you stuck."
CHRISTIE:	I did love you. Then.
CLARE:	I thought so. Now I wonder if you ever thought beyond your reflection in the mirror.
CHRISTIE:	Stop it, Sarah. Enough is enough.
CLARE:	You can't stop it now, Christie. The wheels are in motion. The tumbrels will roll on to the bitter end.
CHRISTIE:	You and your bloody rhetoric. That's the great thing about Sonia. She knows when to shut up.
CLARE:	You won't hear either of us when you're in Mountjoy.

GORDON:	That's no kind of talk, Clare. We've got to prevent that happening. And your father has got to help us.
CLARE:	You said it yourself. You are the patsy in this situation. He'll hang you out to dry.
CHRISTIE:	Not if you ask him not to. And you have to. For the sake of the children.

The Media pack come to the front of the stage, (apart from SUSIE *and* TOMMY *who go to prepare for their scene.) The others send reports to their various media.*

STEPHEN:	As investigation into the Chisholm Hall Holiday Village and Heritage Centre planning scandal continues, reports are widespread that Councillor Christian Fitzgerald, the Ballybothar solicitor has fled the country.
DAVID.	Unavailable for comment was his wife, Clare, who has taken their two children to an undisclosed address.
LOUISE:	When questioned, Mr. Matthew Chisholm, the millionaire business man, whose multi-million pound development is at the centre of the controversy claimed to have no knowledge whatsoever of the claims of bribery that have been levelled at his son in law.
NICOLE:	"If he is guilty", said Mr. Chisholm, "then he must be made to pay, as must all who subscribed to his corruption. He has betrayed his country, his town and also his family. If he is found guilty I do not think that I will find it in my heart to forgive him."

CHARLENE:	When traced to St. Tropez, former au pair Sonia Stanislavski, in an intimate and exclusive interview, told of her heartbreak on hearing of the Fitzgerald scandal. "I was so shocked," revealed the sultry sex bomb as she wept on board the yacht belonging to multi-millionaire business man Gregory Acropolis, with whom she shyly admits to being madly in love. "Greg is a tiger in bed," confessed Sonia. "I never thought I could find happiness after Christie, but now at last, after three weeks, I have".

SCENE FIVE.

REBECCA:	Clare Fitzgerald put her house up for sale. It was bought by the Council, who boarded it up and who took down the blue plaque.
STEPHEN:	There was a road-widening scheme in the pipeline and if the house was going to be in the way, it was better not to draw too much attention to it. It lay like that for ten years.
LOUISE:	The turn of the century.

The chorus leaves the stage. The GIRLEEN *and The* BOYO, SUSIE *and* TOMMY *emerge out of the shadows. They are emaciated and shaking. The* GIRLEEN *is dying.*

GIRLEEN:	But two people found their way in.
BOYO:	They crept into the big house like shadows.
GIRLEEN:	No one could detect them. They were almost transparent.

172

BOYO:	They move into the attic of The O'Connell house, where they definitely could not be seen by the outside world.
GIRLEEN:	The attic had skylights. No one was going to climb up and look in the skylights. I like it here. Can we stay here forever?
BOYO:	This is your house now. If only you weren't so cold.
GIRLEEN:	That's part of it. The cold. But we're not going back now, are we? You haven't changed your mind?
BOYO:	Not unless you want me to.
GIRLEEN:	I want to go on with it.
BOYO:	I'll go with you, so.
GIRLEEN:	Only the birds can look in at us. Sea birds flying over the town. Why are they so far inland?
BOYO:	They're getting away from a storm at sea.
GIRLEEN:	Tell me about the storm at sea.
BOYO:	It will only frighten you.
GIRLEEN:	Nothing frightens me now. I love the storm at sea story. Go on.
BOYO:	The clouds start piling up on the horizon.
GIRLEEN:	What colours are the clouds?
BOYO:	The clouds are purple and red and green.

GIRLEEN:	What colour is the horizon?
BOYO:	The horizon is black. And the sea starts to rise up to meet the sky.
GIRLEEN:	I know the sea. The sea is turquoise at Clogher Head. With white froth spouting out of it.
BOYO:	The sea is turquoise with white froth. And it rises up over the black horizon to meet the purple and red and green of the sky. The sea and the sky explode together. The sea birds are flung inland and that's why they're here.
GIRLEEN:	Are they hurt, would you say?
BOYO:	They are tired.
GIRLEEN:	Like me. What happens to the sea after the explosion? Does the sea have a convulsion?
BOYO:	After the explosion, the sky shudders and goes white. The sea goes black.
GIRLEEN:	Except for the white foam.
BOYO:	The sea sets off for the land at a great gallop like a thousand black horses.
GIRLEEN:	Like a thousand black horses at the fair at Ballinasloe.
BOYO:	Far, far bigger than any horses we ever saw at Ballinasloe. And far more of them.
GIRLEEN:	I can't imagine that.

174

BOYO:	Imagine the sea. It's really thousands of black horses and the white foam is their manes. That's what Da used to tell us. And the horses are galloping to the land, with their backs all rising and falling at different times and that's what makes it heave and toss. That's what Da used to tell us.
GIRLEEN:	I can't imagine Da.
BOYO:	Look at me. Can you see me?
GIRLEEN:	A little bit. Let me feel your face.
BOYO:	Now can you remember? I'm the same as Da only he was older and he had a scar on his cheek. (He draws a line across his cheek with her finger.) Here. From a kick he got. From a horse. Or from another man.
GIRLEEN:	Do you think Da is under the sea?
BOYO:	Ma is under the sea.
GIRLEEN:	Do you think that's where he went too? Did he follow her, do you think? The way you're following me?
BOYO:	We're going together.
GIRLEEN:	I saw her going in. At Clogher Head I saw her. I saw her going.
BOYO:	I can't remember Ma.
SUSIE:	At Clogher Head the sea is turquoise and that means there are mermaids there. Ma said that her Grandmother had seen mermaids there, combing their hair on the rocks. And their

combs were twinkling with jewels, her Grandmother said. And she shouted down to them from the cliff and waved and they threw their combs into the sea and jumped in after them. And her Grandmother could see them swimming under the water with their big silver tails and they swam into the cave at the far end of the beach. So she ran down as fast as her legs could carry her and she took off her dress and swam into the cave and she was very frightened, for her mother, Ma's Grandmother's mother had told her never to go in there in case the tide turned and she would be trapped. Well she swam on and on and she had never realised that the cave was so deep into the rock. And eventually she came to a beach. But it was so dark she could see nothing. And then there was a twinkling light and then two twinkling lights and she could just make out the shape of the two mermaids combing away again. And then she felt the tide coming in and she started to panic and she turned to swim back but she could make no headway and she cried out for help and the next thing she was lifted up by two big fish on either side of her and she fainted and when she came to she was on the strand and it was night time. And her mother nearly killed her when she got home. And that very night all her hair fell out and she had to wear a wig for the rest of her life.

BOYO:	Do you want anything, Girleen? Do you want to eat? I'll go and get you something if you say the word. Eat something for me.
GIRLEEN:	It won't be long now. Stay with me.
BOYO:	Maybe Ma has turned into a mermaid.

GIRLEEN:	She could never swim, Da said.
BOYO:	I think Da is in the sky. I think he was blown up into the clouds, after the fire...
GIRLEEN:	Look up through the skylight, at the clouds. Can you see his face in the clouds? Can you see his face with the scar?
BOYO:	No. It's got dark. Can you not see that it's dark?
GIRLEEN:	I can't see anything.
BOYO:	Do you want me to light a fire?
GIRLEEN:	That would only slow it down. No. No fire. Tell me about the sea.
BOYO:	Over in the west the sun is just going down. The sky is blue and streaked with orange. The sea is darker than the sky but it is blue also and calm and there are big streaks of orange and red in it too, like the scarves mother always wore. And the sea and the sky are together. You can't tell where one begins and the other ends.
GIRLEEN:	They are singing to each other.
BOYO:	The sea birds are back there now. They are sitting on the water. All together. All together at last.
GIRLEEN:	I can see them. I can see Da. I can see Ma.
BOYO:	Are they speaking to you?
GIRLEEN:	They're holding out their arms.

She sinks down against BOYO'S *chest. He lays her gently on the floor.*

177

BOYO: Take it easy now, Girleen. Easy. I'll lie down beside you. And in a while I'll be with you and we'll all be together again. All together. (He lilts the tinkers' song from the top of the play, "Under the stars by the light of the moon"…etc.)

DAVID: The Council sent a sanitation officer on a routine visit to inspect the vacant house.

STEPHEN: It was Council property and they couldn't risk being accused of bringing an infestation of rats.

REBECCA: They found the remains of the bodies of two young people, one male one female, both of whom had died, it transpired from starvation.

GORDON: There was a big fuss and bother, which eventually died down when it appeared that the children were travellers, whose parents had both died tragically within a year of each other and the settled community couldn't be held responsible.

NICOLE: The house became the focus of ghost stories and ghost hunters.

LOUISE: A gang of youngsters broke in one night to spend the night and to meet the ghosts. They brought a Primus stove.

CHARLENE: One group succeeded in terrifying the other to the point that the stove was kicked over and the house badly burned.

SARAH: Which played into the hands of road builders who thought their way was now cleared to pull it down.

178

GORDON: It was after all only a re-constructed house, no matter how many illustrious patriots had slept there.

SCENE SIX.

REBECCA: The Real Story of Daniel O'Connell's visit to Ballybothar.

LOUISE: Times had passed since the garrison was withdrawn and the house had been bought by a butcher, who had done rather well, thank you very much, by providing those enemy soldiers with their meat and victuals.

SARAH: When his wife learned that Daniel O'Connell would be passing through the town on his way to address a rally in Dublin she insisted that her husband use his position on the town council to invite him to stay in their house overnight.

GORDON: The invitation was issued and accepted.

Cheers from the company. SARAH swoons and is attended to by the servants.

REBECCA: Everybody in the house got new clothes from Dublin.

TOMMY: The servants had to wear a uniform. Livery, she called it. Silk breeches and white stockings and patent leather shoes, for the men. And a lace shirt and a cut away coat. Like something out of a pantomime.

SARAH: Maybe they should have wigs.

CHARLENE:	The female servants got black dresses with starched white collars and cuffs and white linen aprons with broiderie anglaise frills.
LOUISE:	They bought a piano and it took six men to get it up the stairs to the drawing room and the Mistress got the sheet music of a song and practised how to play it and the Master sang it, for it was known that Daniel O'Connell loved foreign music.
GORDON:	(singing) Panis Angelicus, Dat panis hominum etc.
SARAH:	They hoped that The Liberator would be prevailed upon to sing himself.
SUSIE:	And as for the food. Never before had the town heard of such a banquet, with settings for 20 people. Game hanging in the scullery. Jellies and aspics in the larder.
REBECCA:	The table was groaning with the weight of china and silver and crystal glasses. And the sideboards were groaning with the weight of the decanters and the drink.
LOUISE:	It was well- known that The Liberator liked his food and his French wines.
STEPHEN:	You could see that by looking at him. Tall. Imposing.
DAVID:	A figure that could carry a cape and a cane.
STEPHEN:	A stentorian, mellifluous voice that travelled for miles.

180

LOUISE:	It was well known that he liked the ladies too. In fact where I come from it was said that you couldn't throw a stick over a wall without...
SARAH:	That's quite enough from you. We don't want to hear what's said where you come from.
TOMMY:	So the moment arrived and everything was ready, floors gleaming, fires burning, candles twinkling, servants all lined up in the hall.
REBECCA:	Starch melting with the sweat.
SARAH:	Terrified of fainting again.
GORDON:	You'll be fine. This is the most important day of our lives.
TOMMY:	One servant posted outside at the gate, to signal when the carriage turned into the terrace.
GORDON:	The front door open and welcoming.
CHARLENE:	You couldn't throw a stick over a wall without what?
LOUISE:	I'll tell you later.
TOMMY.	He's coming. Here he is! Here he is!

TOMMY *joins the welcoming line up.* NICOLE *enters in cape, big hat and cane.* GORDON *leads everyone in applause.* NICOLE *bows and walks along the line until she reaches* SARAH.

SARAH:	You are most, most welcome.
NICOLE:	Delighted, I'm sure.

GORDON:	(speaking in Irish) On behalf of the citizens of our town, I want to extend the warmest of welcomes to you the most distinguished citizen of this country...
NICOLE:	Hold it right there with the Gaelic.
SARAH:	I beg your pardon-but it is Mr. O'Connell isn't it?
NICOLE:	Mort Weisbaum at your service Ma'am. Mr. Daniel O'Connell's American agent for his forthcoming lecture tour of Europe and America.
SARAH:	I see. You are welcome to our house. (to servants) Get another place set at the table. Open up another bedroom.
NICOLE:	Thank you Ma'am, but that won't be necessary. You see I have just called to say that my client will not be able to stop off at your dear little house today.
SARAH:	Not able to…
NICOLE:	Mounting pressure of the forthcoming tour and a pressing need to go to Westminster before he sets off for Europe...You will understand I'm sure.
GORDON:	Of course we understand. Perhaps when he returns…
NICOLE:	Sure. Sure. Mr. O'Connell asked me to present you with this miniature portrait of himself as a token of…Well as a token. He has signed it. Personally.

182

Hands over box containing miniature portrait to SARAH.

DAVID: That was it.

STEPHEN: The American left.

SUSIE: The Mistress fainted.

REBECCA: The picture of Daniel O'Connell was hung up over the fireplace in the dining room. But it was so small you had to really peer at it to make it out.

LOUISE: The family and their guests entered into a pact.

CHARLENE: The servants were sworn to secrecy.

GORDON: It never got out that the visit did not take place.

DAVID: In time the household began to believe that in fact the visit had taken place.

STEPHEN: If anyone asked any awkward questions, the signed portrait was there for all to behold.

SUSIE: A proof that something had happened.

CHARLENE: The family and the servants all wrapped themselves up sweetly in their little fantasy for the rest of their lives.

SARAH: And their secret died peacefully with them, in their beds.

GORDON: So when over a century later, at last the Ballybrophy ring road was ready to be built, the conservationists started protesting and no one could gainsay   them. A heritage site was still a heritage site. The house would have to stay.

STEPHEN:	So the council made it habitable again and opened it as a hostel for the migrant workers who were flooding into the town.

REBECCA and DAVID enter with cases. REBECCA is about five months pregnant.

REBECCA:	*(In Polish)* It's a big house. Do you think there will be many people living in it?
DAVID:	*(In Polish)* Probably. But they said we'd have a bedroom to ourselves.
REBECCA:	*(In Polish)* Many people must have lived here.

EPILOGUE.

LENA:	Everyone is coming here to our house. To let themselves go. To pretend.
CHRISTIE:	For God's sake, Clare! What do you take me for?
LARRY:	The point is the house belongs to the bank.
CLARE:	An adulterer.
CHRISTIE:	This house is your home and the children's home.
LENA:	Sometimes just sitting in the dark.
BOYO:	This is your house now. If only you weren't so cold.

GIRLEEN:	The sea at Clogher Head is turquoise. Tell me about the storm at sea.
NIKKI:	I could go on this journey forever.
BOYO:	We're going together.
LULU:	Wherever you're from, you're home now.
DAVID:	*(In Polish)* From Kracow.
REBECCA.	*(In Polish)* From Gdansk
STEPHEN:	*(In Lithuanian)* From Vilnius.
CHARLENE:	*(In Czech)* From Prague.
SARAH:	*(In Hungarian)* From Budapest.
NICOLE:	*(In Russian)* From Moscow.
GORDON:	*(In Turkish)* From Ankara.
TOMMY:	*(In Romanian)* From Bucharest.
LULU:	Don't be frightened. I'll watch over you.
GIRLEEN:	I can see Ma and Da.

END.

A/S/L

AGE/SEX/LOCATION

A NEW THING

BY

PAUL O'BRIEN

CHARACTERS.

BI-VI

VELVET

MAN

LEN

SUE

RON

LISA

ROSE

LOUBY

PIPER

VERNE

SET.

A/S/L IS SET IN A SITTING ROOM, A SITTING ROOM, A
BEDROOM AND A CAFÉ.

SETTING.

DECEMBER 1999. Y2K IS COMING.

SCENE ONE.

Lights rise slowly on two normal looking women sitting at a table in a café which is draped with Christmas decorations.

VELVET: So tell me more.

BI-VI *stirs her tall drink and takes a sip.*

BI-VI: Well, I see you staring at me through the office window. It's after work so there's only two of us left. I notice you looking at me so I make sure and open my top button. I want you see me. I feel your eyes running up and down my body. It's a summer evening so I turn towards the window and let the sun shine through my white top. I'm not wearing any bra. I'm not wearing any underwear at all.

VELVET: Do you like me looking at you?

BI-VI: Ya. I've noticed it before. But this time it's just me and you. My skin feels more sensitive. Everything is heightened. It's the anticipation of how all of this is going to play out.

BI-VI *tastes some cream off* VELVET'S *finger.*

VELVET: I call you into my office. You keep sending my letters to the wrong people. You're making me and my company look bad. I need to have a word with you.

BI-VI: I hitch up my skirt a few inches before I open your door. I hope you'll notice it. I want you to spank me.

VELVET: I'm not into that.

BI-VI: What?

VELVET: No hitting.

BI-VI: OK.

VELVET: Get in here.

BI-VI: I lay my papers out in front of you and lean in
                    over your shoulder. I know you can see a little
                    bit. Do you want to see more? I've never been
                    with   another woman before.

VELVET: Yes, I want to see more.

*A man approaches the table with a table cloth over his forearm. He
leans into* BI-VI.

MAN: Save up to 25 percent off today. We can get you
                    any prescription...

VELVET: Are you still there?

MAN: Save up to 25 percent off today. We can get you
                    any prescription…

BI-VI: Hang on I can't get rid of this fucking nuisance.

MAN: Save up to 25 percent off today. We can get you
                    any prescription…

VELVET: Here, I found this last night. Thirty day free
                    trial.

BI-VI *opens her handbag and takes out a hammer.*

VELVET: Did you get it?

BI-VI *eyes up the size of the hammer.*

BI-VI: Ya, thanks.

BI-VI *grabs the man and throws him against the wall.*

MAN: Save up to 25 percent off today. We can get you
                        any prescription…

BI-VI *hits the man in the face with the hammer. He falls behind the
small coffee bar upstage.*

MAN: Save up to 25 percent off today. We can get you
                        any prescription…

*BI-VI beats him repeatedly. She raises from behind the sofa covered in
blood but with a look of satisfaction on her face. VELVET sits back down
facing BI-VI.*

VELVET: Fucking pop ups.

Both Ladies take a drink of their coffee.

BI-VI: SSSSSSSSSSSSSSSSSSSSSSSSSSSorry about
                        that.

VELVET: What was that?

BI-VI: My S button keeps jamming.

Lights down. We hear internet connections over internet connections.

SCENE TWO.

Lights up on a bedroom. There is a small toy Christmas tree on the bed side locker. LEN struggles to zip up his jeans and put on his shoes.

LEN: I'll see you next week Sue.

SUE *replies from the closed bathroom door.*

SUE: Don't you go anywhere.

LEN: (*to himself*) Ah shut the fuck up.

SUE: What?

LEN: Nothing muffin.

LEN fixes his hair in the mirror. SUE sings 'Crash' in the shower. RON enters and quietly observes the messed up bed etc. LEN doesn't see him. RON sits on the bed. LEN spots RON in the mirror. He tries to act casual in his conversation.

LEN: Hello Ron.

LEN *shifts uncomfortably and looks at his watch.*

RON: Hello Len.

RON *takes off his shoes with a groan.*

RON: Could you pass me my slippers Len?

LEN: Of course Ron.

LEN *hands RON his slippers.*

RON:	I got a cold.
LEN:	Have you? That's a fucking disgrace that is. Terrible. I'm livid I am…for ya. Like you know, a good friend you are.
RON:	I had to leave work.
LEN:	You're early alright. Not that I know what time you're coming home from work at or anything. I'm just guessing, you look early you do.

RON *puts on his slippers.*

RON:	Is Sue in the shower?
LEN:	Who? I haven't seen her. I was just trying to find…that crack…in the wall. I couldn't walk by here after seeing that. It'd have me awake and everything.
RON:	What crack in the wall?
LEN:	You can't see it from the inside. A hair line fracture structure they calls it. Dangerous. Your windows could fall out or anything Ron. I'll go and get some plaster and wood. It's lucky I spotted it. I'd have nightmares and everything about that.
RON:	I'll go with you. I'll just put me shoes back on.
LEN:	Ya, ya, grand.

LEN *checks the perfectly fine wall. Running his hand up and down.*

LEN:	You know something Ron. Ah no, it's not that bad, you should get another twenty years out of it. It not worth you getting pneumonia for. Leave your slippers on you. Did you get anything for yourself?
RON:	I got me a Lemsip.
LEN:	Ya? What flavour?

RON *looks in bewilderment at* LEN.

RON:	Lemon.
LEN:	Oh ya, lemon.
RON:	I hope they do the trick.
LEN:	I hope so.
RON:	Why aren't they called Lemsips? There's more than one in the box.
LEN:	I think it's just a name like Panadol. They don't call them Panadols and Anadins.
RON:	I suppose.

RON *stands up.*

RON:	Are you thirsty?
LEN:	What have you got?
RON:	I think there's a beer in the fridge.
LEN:	There's none…thing more nicer than a beer, ya if you have one.

RON *changes his tee shirt while* LEN *hides the empty beer can that was on the locker.*

RON: I see another accident up by the hospital.

LEN: Ah sure it's a terrible road, terrible.

Long pause.

LEN: I nearly crashed up there meself.

RON: Did you.

LEN: Ya.

Long pause.

RON: When was that.

LEN: Last week there. Christmas eve.

RON: That's a bad time to die.

LEN: I didn't…obviously.

RON: Obviously.

Pause.

LEN: Nearly did though. Die.

RON: I'll get that drink.

LEN: Ya, right. Drink.

LEN *follows* RON.

RON: You wait here sure. I'll bring it up to you.

LEN:	I'll get it. You're not feeling well.
RON:	I got the sniffles.
LEN:	My dog, Madra died of that same thing.
RON:	The sniffles?
LEN:	Dog sniffles are worse, they're supposed to be like acidy or something. They've big noses you know.
RON:	I'm not a dog Len.
LEN:	So you're not Ron.
RON:	I'll get the drink. You wait here.
LEN:	There mightn't even be one down there.
RON:	How would you know that?
LEN:	I wouldn't. Just, there'd be no drink in my house of a Monday. I presume you're the same.
RON:	I always buy meself a can for New Years. Something to toast with at midnight.
LEN:	Sure then I couldn't possibly drink it on you then. Don't even bother looking for it. It'd be bad luck or something ruining your…thing, your ritual. Not ritual but…eh…tradition.
RON:	It's alright. It's just something that I came up with this year.
LEN:	Ron. I drank your beer Ron.

RON: Did you Len?

LEN: I did. And I feels terrible.

RON: What about fucking me girlfriend? How's that playing on your mind?

LEN: The same, ya, terrible.

RON: That's funny cause I feels terrible meself.

Exit RON. LEN *stands quietly in thought.* RON *enters with some towels over his arm.*

RON: Leave them there for Sue. She likes the hot towels.

LEN: Are you not mad at me or anything Ron?

RON: You see that girl in there?

LEN: Ya.

RON: How can you and the door closed?

LEN: I suppose I can't then.

RON: No you can't. Only I can.

LEN: Even with the door closed?

RON: I have the key. That's called a metaphor, what we just said.

RON *takes the key from his pocket and locks the bathroom door.*

SUE: What are you doing Len?

LEN: Nothing. Ron's home.

SUE:	Ron?

RON *closes the bedroom door.* LEN *backs off.*

SUE:	Ron? Open this door.
LEN:	I didn't get no pleasure out of it one bit now Ron.
SUE:	Open this fucking door before I break your head for you. Ron. Now.

RON *stops.* LEN *slides out of his path.*

SUE:	Locking me in the bathroom. That's it Ron. That's all I can handle.

RON *opens the door.* SUE *pushes him out of the way and enters in a morning gown. Her hair is wrapped in a towel.*

SUE:	Who do you think you are? Do I look like some piece of fucking meat that you can lock away whenever you feel like it?
LEN:	I'm going.
SUE:	No Len, he is.
RON:	I've got a cold.
SUE:	I don't care what you have. You're a numbskull and I'm finished with you.
RON:	I've got the sniffles.
LEN:	You can stay at my house for a while Ron. There's no shower like here in it but…

198

SUE:	Shut up Len.
RON:	I don't want to stay nowhere. This is my house.
SUE:	Who's name is it in?
RON:	Who pays the rent?
SUE:	Doesn't matter. Who's name is it in?
RON:	Who pays the rent?
SUE:	It doesn't matter. It's in my name
RON:	Ya, but who pays the rent?
LEN:	Does Ron pay the rent?
RON:	Ya I pays the rent.
SUE:	But whose name is it in?
RON:	It doesn't matter, I pays the rent.
LEN:	Well then Ron should stay here if he pays the rent.
SUE:	Shut up you.
RON:	I'm not leaving Sue. I didn't do anything wrong. You did.
LEN:	Why don't Ron stay here and you kip with me for a few days till he gets better?
RON:	Me and Sue are staying here Len. You're going.
SUE:	He's staying.
RON:	He's going.

LEN:	I'm going.
SUE:	You're not.
RON:	He is.
LEN:	I am.
SUE:	This is my house.
RON:	Who pays the rent?
SUE:	Will you shut up about the fucking rent? I can pay me own way. I've been telling you for days that we're done. Finished Ron. Over. Fin-e-to. Gone. Goodbye. See ya. Get your stuff.
RON:	You can't kick me out in my condition.

RON *forces out a cough.*

SUE:	It's been one thing or another for the last week or so. It's time to go Ron.
RON:	There's only a couple of days to the New Year Sue. We can start a fresh.
SUE:	And I wants to bring in the New Year a happy woman Ron. Not the way I am now.
LEN:	Can I give you a lift anywhere Ron?
RON:	I'm staying.
SUE:	Ron? Ron? Look at me. I loves him now. Not you.
RON:	I'm staying.

RON *grabs a blanket from the bed and closes the door.* SUE *throws her shoe at the closed door.*

SUE: Ah fuck you then Ron.

SCENE THREE.

ROSE *and* LISA *sit opposite each other in the café. They both wear tee shirts with their names on them.*

LISA: What's he doing now?

ROSE: Making a sandwich.

LISA: Is he still going to go through with this comedy thing tonight?

ROSE: There's no talking to him.

LISA: Lock him in the bathroom or something before he makes a show of you.

ROSE: Wait. He's gone quiet.

Lights up on PIPER'S *sitting room.* PIPER *sits on a sofa with a laptop resting in her lap.* LOUBY *is making a sandwich off stage.*

LOUBY: Are you sure you don't want one?

PIPER: Na, I'm not really hungry.

LOUBY: The corned beef smells lovely. It doesn't sound lovely though, does it? Corned...beef. The beef

is corned. Like an old woman's foot. Are you
sure you don't want some?

PIPER: Na.

LOUBY: That's what the jelly bits are in it. Slices of
                    blisters and puss.

Return to ROSE *and* LISA.

LISA: You there?

ROSE: Corned beef.

LISA: Just when you thought things couldn't get any
                    more exciting, he brings out the beef.

ROSE: Wrong kind though.

LISA: Would you never think of jumping out of a
                    fucking plane or something? Do you never get
                    pissed off at home all the time?

ROSE: I go out, I'm hardly ever here. I'm working.

LISA: It's not much of an existence though, is it?

ROSE: Are we talking about me now or you?

LISA: Ya, sorry. I'm just pissed off that's all. If I have
                    to watch another fucking Disney movie today
                    I'm going to throw the fucking telly through the
                    window.

ROSE: Where is he?

LISA: He's asleep. Nap time. He'll be awake all night
                    now though.

ROSE:	I'll talk to you later.
LISA:	Ya, I'll be back after nine. I have to kick the shit out of a bottle of wine first. BTW, I think something is going to happen between me and Len.
ROSE:	What do you mean?
LISA:	He's acting funny. He asked me to get me Ma to mind the baby on New Years. He said he has something important he wants to ask me.
ROSE:	Holy fuck.
LISA:	I know.
ROSE:	I have to go, talk to you later.

PIPER closes her laptop and flicks through the stations on the TV. Enter LOUBY. He places his sandwich down, takes off his shoes, wipes his soles along the floor to take off his socks, removes his jumper, fixes the cushions, straightens his balls, picks up his sandwich and sits down. He puts the cushion on his lap, straightens his balls, picks something from his teeth at the back of his mouth, slaps his hands together, picks up the sandwich raises it to his lips and...

PIPER:	Can I have a bite?

LOUBY *looks mortally offended at* PIPER.

LOUBY:	No.
PIPER:	What?
LOUBY:	Are you serious?
PIPER:	I only wants a little bit.

LOUBY:	You said you weren't hungry.
PIPER:	I'm not, it just looks nice, that's all.
LOUBY:	It looks nice? That's no reason. That painting looks nice, go and eat that.
PIPER:	Don't be stupid.
LOUBY:	If you're hungry I'll make you one.
PIPER:	I don't want one, I just wants a bit of yours.
LOUBY:	For fucks sake.
PIPER:	What?
LOUBY:	I asked you, I asked you like. Do you want something and you said no.
PIPER:	I wasn't hungry then.
LOUBY:	It was two fucking seconds ago. Pressure, it's always pressure in here. There's a large sliced and a turn over out there.
PIPER:	What are you talking about pressure for? It's a bit of corned beef.
LOUBY:	But it's fucking my corned beef.
PIPER:	Why, did you buy it?
LOUBY:	Ya.
PIPER:	Oh, so it's your money now.
LOUBY:	What are you talking about?

PIPER:	Last time I checked both of our wages went into that account.
LOUBY:	I never said they didn't.
PIPER:	Well how do you know you bought it then?
LOUBY:	I'm not even going to answer that now.

PIPER *starts to flick rapidly through the channels.* LOUBY *can't bite his sandwich.*

LOUBY:	Will you stop?
PIPER :	Stop what?
LOUBY:	Flicking.

PIPER *purposely drops the remote on the floor.*

LOUBY:	What did you do that for?
PIPER:	You told me to stop.

LOUBY *picks up the remote and lays it beside him. He pauses and begrudgingly gives in.*

LOUBY:	You can have some if you want some.
PIPER:	Na.
LOUBY:	Here just take a bite will you?
PIPER:	I don't want none.
LOUBY:	Eat it.
PIPER:	Shove it up your hole. All I wanted was a bit of crust off the corner of it and you were too

	miserable to give it to me. Now you can choke on it if you want.
LOUBY:	I'm giving it to you now ain't I?
PIPER:	Only after begrudging me it. It won't taste the same.
LOUBY:	What do you mean it won't taste the same? You can't taste begrudgery.
PIPER:	That's lucky or I'd be after starving to death.

LOUBY *slaps the sandwich onto the plate.*

LOUBY:	Are you happy now?
PIPER:	What?
LOUBY:	I don't want it now either. You can't even let me have a bit of corned fucking beef without sucking the will to eat it out of me.
PIPER:	Sharing is caring Louby.
LOUBY:	What did you say? Sharing is caring? What the fuck is wrong with you?
PIPER:	What does it say about us when you won't even give me the crust off your bread?
LOUBY:	There is it. Have the fucking thing.
PIPER:	No. Me Ma reared me better than that. I don't eat no ones scraps.

Long silence. PIPER *begins to flick again. She stops.*

LOUBY: I'm not looking at that shite.

PIPER: Why? No bang-bang?

LOUBY: Are you serious or what? I wants to know. All
                    this because I wanted a poxy fucking sandwich
                    all to meself.

PIPER: I likes this.

LOUBY: It's the God channel.

PIPER: I'm looking here to see what they say about
                    Gluttony.

LOUBY: Ya, oh hang on now, maybe we can all learn
                    something. Hopefully he'll read that passage on
                    stupid bitchery.

PIPER: Oh that's funny, why don't you put that in your
                    little comedy thing tonight?

LOUBY *gets up and walks for the door.*

LOUBY: What do you mean little comedy thing? It's a
                    gig. A real life honest to God gig. Do you not
                    think I'm funny?

PIPER: Did I say that?

LOUBY: You didn't not say it.

PIPER: I've not idea what that last sentence means.

LOUBY: You didn't not say that I wasn't good.

PIPER: I didn't not say that you weren't good? What?

LOUBY:	Nothing.

PIPER:	Well what are we talking about then?

Pause.

LOUBY:	I am funny.

PIPER:	Ya.

LOUBY:	Was that a sarcastic ya?

PIPER:	(*Sarcastically*) Ya.

LOUBY *walks from the door and back to* PIPER.

LOUBY:	This is serious Piper. Am I funny? You don't think I am, do you?

PIPER:	No.

LOUBY:	Well, you're fat.

PIPER:	Don't be such a fucking child.

LOUBY:	Well I didn't want to say anything but since we're being so honest with each other today. You eat too much. I was actually doing you a favour not giving you a sandwich.

PIPER:	Get out.

LOUBY:	Why? Are you wanting to talk to your little fake friends on the net are you? I, space bar, hate, back slash, coma, exclamation point, real life. Why don't you put on some make up and a nice dress and go and meet some real people?

PIPER:	Fuck off.

| LOUBY: | Go on, risk it. A real conversation. |

| PIPER: | Get out I said. |

LOUBY grabs his jacket and bangs the door. PIPER jumps up and checks the window.

| PIPER: | Take your time. |

PIPER *eats the sandwich and switches on her laptop.*

SCENE FOUR.

RON shuffles around in a dressing gown and slippers. He cups a mug in his hand and walks for the sofa. SUE and LEN are going at it like rabbits upstairs. RON acknowledges them with a glance up. He blows his nose and wraps himself up in a blanket. RON looks absolutely miserable. He sits silently listening to SUE moaning above his head. RON sits at an already powered on computer.

SCENE FIVE.

PIPER sits at her laptop. Lights up on the café. Enter ROSE. She walks past VERNE. We keep jumping from the café to 'reality.'

| RON: | Hello. |

ROSE *stops.*

| PIPER: | No, I don't want to know how big your cock is. |

ROSE *sits down at another table and lights a fag.* VERNE *waits a second and walks over to her.*

VERNE: Excuse me?

PIPER *doesn't answer.*

VERNE: I didn't mean anything. I just said hello.

ROSE: That's what they all say.

VERNE: That's the tradition isn't it?

RON sits beside PIPER. She looks motionless. RON waves his hand in front of her face.

RON: I have a cold.

PIPER: Good for you.

RON: I have to stay away from my computer or I
                   could give it a virus. Get it? Virus.

PIPER *struggles out a polite laugh.*

VERNE: What does lol mean?

ROSE: It means laugh out loud.

VERNE: So I made you laugh?

ROSE: No, you made me snigger but they don't have
                   any abbreviations for that yet.

VERNE: What are you doing in here?

ROSE: Waiting for a friend. Look, no offence but I
                   don't really talk to fellas in here. They can only

210

think of one thing when they're in front of a computer, IMO?

ROSE *realises that* VERNE *doesn't understand IMO.*

ROSE: In my opinion.

VERNE: That's OK, I don't like talking to men either.

VERNE *walks away.*

RON: Anyway, real mean wear skirts.

PIPER: What was that?

RON: Ah nothing, it's just a thing someone used to say.

PIPER: Rowdy Roddy Piper.

RON: Say that again.

ROSE: Rowdy Roddy Piper.

VERNE: How do you know that?

ROSE: Because I've been a wrestling fan since I was a kid.

VERNE: No way. Me too. I was at Wrestlemania last year.

ROSE: No fucking way. You saw Benoit win the title?

VERNE: Ya, I only live down the road.

ROSE: Holy shit. That was the best main event I have ever seen at Wrestlemania. What was it like to be standing in the middle of twenty thousand people when all the confetti was falling and his music was playing. Did you see him crying when they gave him the belt?

VERNE: I have to tell you that it's not every day a fella meets a girl who likes wrestling. Well none that will admit it anyway.

ROSE: I'm always getting jeered for it. But I don't care.

There is a smiley silence. RON *shapes to leave.*

VERNE: Well…

ROSE: Do you want to sit down?

VERNE: I thought you were meeting someone?

PIPER: She won't be in for a while.

RON: Who would have thought that wrestling would have scored me points with a woman?

PIPER: Don't get ahead of yourself.

RON: I'm only joking.

VERNE *sits down.*

PIPER: A/S/L?

RON: What?

ROSE: You're a newbie I take it?

VERNE: Stumbled in here yesterday. I'm lost to tell you the truth.

ROSE: A/S/L means Age/Sex/Location. People like to know who they are talking to.

VERNE:	I'm 25/Male/Boston, and you?
ROSE:	I thought you were from New York?
RON:	Why?
PIPER:	Wrestlemania was at Madison Square Garden last year.
VERNE:	I'm from Boston but I've been living in New York for nearly seven years now.
ROSE:	I want to go someday.
VERNE:	Why don't you?
ROSE:	I don't move easily between places.
VERNE:	Over here you can be whoever you want. Nobody will even remember you.
ROSE:	I don't know whether that's a good or a bad thing.
VERNE:	It can work both ways.
PIPER:	What do you do for a living?
RON:	Well, I'm a business man. I mostly sell property and land sometimes. What about you?
PIPER:	I'm in the…music business. Producing mainly.
RON:	Oh ya? Anyone that I'd know?
ROSE:	Ya. Loads of them. Confidentiality.
VERNE:	I understand.
ROSE:	What do you look like Mr. business man?

RON describes himself as VERNE. He dressed in a nice suit, carries a briefcase and talks in a New York accent. His name is stitched into the back of his jacket.

VERNE: And you

PIPER describes herself as 'ROSE'. Her name is evident on her dress. ROSE sits opposite VERNE at a table. Lights down on RON and PIPER.

VERNE: This is all new to me.

ROSE sits frozen in front of VERNE.

VERNE: Hello?

VERNE *looks into* ROSE'S *eyes.*

VERNE: Are you there?

ROSE: There was someone at my door.

VERNE: I thought you were gone.

ROSE: I will be shortly.

VERNE: What could be more important than this lol?

ROSE: My boyfriend has a gig tonight.

VERNE: Didn't know you were involved with someone.

ROSE: Neither does he apparently.

VERNE: Is he in a band?

ROSE: No, stand up. He's about as funny as a spoon.

VERNE: Lol. Well it was nice to meet you

| ROSE: | Listen, I'm sure you'll find whatever it is you're looking for in here. Just don't go around here trying to slam people. BB. |

VERNE looks blankly at ROSE.

| ROSE: | It just means 'Bye Bye'. |
| VERNE: | OK, BB yourself lol. |

Lights come down on ROSE. ROSE doesn't move. VERNE looks slowly around him. He reaches out very slowly and touches ROSE'S breast.

SCENE SIX.

LOUBY stands under a spot light with microphone in hand. He looks terrified.

| LOUBY: | It's nice to be here tonight. I was walking down the street the other day and I saw a sign in the window of a restaurant saying 'reserved'. Now I don't know about you but I wouldn't like anything in a restaurant to be re-served to me, would you? Reserved, that's a stupid word. You know what else is a stupid word? Unintelligent. Or is that another word for stupid? |

LOUBY points to the side of his head pointing out 'intelligence'. LOUBY takes the mic away to swallow. We hear feedback from the sound system.

| LOUBY: | I'm in a relationship now too. Fucking hard work that is. I have to pour beans all down my front and pretend to be unconscious drunk just to get her to undress me. They say that if you want to know what your girlfriend would like when she's old all you have to is look at her |

mother. Well at least she'll be skinnier, her mother is dead about seven months now. That should be enough time for decomposition.

A girl ran up to me when I was twelve and kicked me in the balls. I still didn't want to punch her in the face as much as I want to punch my girlfriend in the face pretty much all the time. As a matter of fact if I had the sack I would have left her years ago. All I needs is a spine. Don't love her no more. Haven't for years. I just could never tell her for some reason. There's always been something and then again I've always been a cowardly bastard too. The things that used to make me smile just makes me want to choke her. And I would choke her only for I know I'd probably wouldn't let go. And then I'd have a new girlfriend in prison named Mike. I'd love to just grab her and say... What's your obsession with making sure the fridge is closed? You closes it, then checks it. How do you check it? By opening it to make sure it isn't open. On what fucking planet does that make sense? I'm upstairs trying to write new material and you keep slamming as hard as you fucking can every door in the house including the doors on that stupid pink coo coo clock your bitch of a mother got us for Christmas. That's why I have no funny fucking lines tonight. That's why people are leaving. Cause you're a crooked little fuck when you don't get your way. You're a twenty six year old child. Mean-fucking-while I'm dying a death here back at the ranch. You sir (*off stage*) why are you leaving? (*Pause*) Cause I'm crap. Lovely. You're right too. It's not my fucking fault though. I tried I did. I could have been fucking brilliant if I never clapped eyes on that

216

blood sucking, energy draining, dry, frigid, cold, heartless fucking...

The mic is cut off. LOUBY *drops the mic and continues to shout.*

LOUBY: I wanted to do my best…

Lights down.

LOUBY: Turn on them lights, turn them on before I go up to that box and rip your fucking heads off. Do you hear me?
Music.

LOUBY: Now there's music trying to drown me out too. What wrong with these fucking people?

SCENE SEVEN.

RON *enters the sitting room.* SUE *is sitting on the sofa.* RON *takes off his coat and tries to kiss* SUE *on the top of the head. She pushes him away.* RON *sits down. Long pause.*

RON: Is there something the matter?

SUE: Len had a shower this morning and there was nowhere to hang his towel. Do you know why there was nowhere to hang his towel? Because yours was still on the rail.

RON: He can use mine if he likes.

SUE: I love him Ron. And he loves me. He's just weirded out at the moment cause you're still here. He's thinking about leaving me already.

RON:	What did he say to you?
SUE:	Nothing. I can just tell.
RON:	This is our house.
SUE:	Not no more. My brothers are coming over after tea. I think you should leave before then. It's for your own good.
RON:	Where is he now?
SUE:	Who?
RON:	Len.
SUE:	In work.
RON:	Len doesn't work, never has.
SUE:	I got him a job with me.
RON:	Arranging flowers?
SUE:	Deliveries. Why does this even matter?
RON:	Cause I'm better for you than he is.
SUE:	No you're not. I need a man Ron. Someone who'll stand up to me. Tell me to fuck off, go on.
RON:	Why would I do that?

SUE *hits* RON *in the chest.*

SUE:	Spit in my face, tell me you hate me. Something.
RON:	I don't hate sure. I loves you I'm telling you.

SUE:	You never shows me. Where's the passion Ron? You never gets angry, you're never happy. You're always…too.
SUE:	I'm with Len.
RON:	Don't forget, he's my friend. I seen him do stuff that you haven't.

Pause.

SUE:	He loves me Ron. Simple as that.
RON:	I do too. More than him.
SUE:	Can you prove it?
RON:	Course I can.

SUE *looks hard at* RON *but walks to the door.*

RON:	What is it?
SUE:	Nothing, it's OK.

RON *stops her and gently turns her by the arm.*

RON:	Is there something the matter Sue?
SUE:	It's nothing.
RON:	What is it.
SUE:	Nothing, it's just me Ma. She'll be grand I'd say.
RON:	What happened her?

SUE:	She was in a crash this morning. They're after bringing her to Dublin.
RON:	Was she on her own?
SUE:	Ya, slid off the road. She might have a broken back.
RON:	What can I do?
SUE:	I need some money. I haven't got anything to get up to her. Christmas cleaned me out.
RON:	How much?
SUE:	Just enough for petrol and flowers and stuff like that. Maybe four hundred?
RON:	Four…eh, I haven't got that on me.
SUE:	I'll get it for you. Gimme your card.
RON:	You have it.
SUE:	That one hasn't been paid. Your bank card.
RON:	Why hasn't it been paid?
SUE:	Are you going to nag me about money now Ron?
RON:	No, here.

RON *gives* SUE *his bank card.*

RON:	Can you get a tenner out for me? I've no dinner.

SUE:	I'll get you sausage rolls, just like you likes them.
RON:	Did I prove to you that I loves you then? Cause I do.
SUE:	This isn't the right time though Ron. Just make sure you're gone before me brothers call round.
RON:	I was thinking about getting me a new girlfriend. What do you think of that?
SUE:	I'd be delighted for you.
RON:	Someone better than you.
SUE:	Don't start Ron.
RON:	Someone much better.

SUE *exits. Lights down.*

SCENE EIGHT.

PIPER *is pressed against her door.* LOUBY *bangs off stage.*

LOUBY:	It was all just part of the act.
PIPER:	Well you can act like fucking off now.
LOUBY:	Did you think I was funny?

PIPER:	Hilarious you wanker.
LOUBY:	No need for the name calling.
PIPER:	And what about all the names you called me?
LOUBY:	If I jumped off the bridge would you do the same?
PIPER:	No, I'd let you drowned.
LOUBY:	I didn't think you were going to be there.
PIPER:	And does that make it alright?
LOUBY:	I've said worse stuff about you and you never knew.
PIPER:	Are you trying to piss me off even more?
LOUBY:	No, me point is that you get hurt about something if you can hear it.

PIPER *looks totally puzzled by* LOUBY'S *last statement.*

LOUBY:	Sure what if I was saying stuff about you all the time but you never heard it? It wouldn't bother you. I thought we were in that stage in our relationship were I could bring you to a gig and show you exactly what I was saying about you.
PIPER:	Are you stoned or something? You makes me feel stupid cause I haven't a clue what you're fucking saying half the time and it's not me, it's you. You make no sense whatsoever to me. I'm constantly walking around confused by more than half the stupid shit you come out with. I don't even like you that much to be honest. So fuck off. Go and confuse some other poor fucker

222

into thinking that they're stupid. Goodbye
Louby, you stupid fuck.

LOUBY: Is there any chance you'd let me in for a piss?

SCENE NINE.

Lights up on ROSE *sitting at a table.* VERNE *enters. He passes* ROSE
and stops between waving and not.

ROSE: Are you not going to say hello?

VERNE: I was hoping to talk to you again.

ROSE: Why?

VERNE: What?

ROSE: What is it about us that's interested in the
stranger?

VERNE: So you're curious about me.

ROSE: I didn't say that.

VERNE: But you meant it. I don't blame you. I'm
fucking gorgeous I am.

ROSE: Me too.

VERNE: Isn't everyone in here?

ROSE: Yep, not one average or ugly person in here.

VERNE:	Coincidence that, especially since we get to describe ourselves.
ROSE:	Being interested in someone and being curious about someone are completely different things.
VERNE:	I prefer if you were curious about me.
ROSE:	Why's that?
VERNE:	Interested is the middle of the day. Curious is a night time sport if you ask me.

VERNE *clicks his fingers and* VELVET *brings over some drinks.*

ROSE:	And what if I was neither?
VERNE:	You'd be talking to someone else.
ROSE:	Maybe I'm waiting for someone else. Maybe you'll do until my real curiosity arrives.
VERNE:	One way or the other you're talking to me now. Chances are you'll want to keep talking to me.
ROSE:	You're a cocky little fucker aren't you?
VERNE:	Not really, I'm just aware of what my good points are.
ROSE:	And what would they be?
VERNE:	I have a good imagination and I can type with one hand.
VELVET:	Have you seen Bi-Vi?
ROSE:	There she is.

224

BI-VI *is standing by the counter.*

VELVET: She's logged on so she's in here somewhere but she's not answering.

VERNE: We're kinda busy here.

VELVET: Fuck you Verne.

VERNE: I'm sure you would.

VELVET *walks away.*

ROSE: I don't cyber.

VERNE: Everyone cybers. Drink?

ROSE: Not me, if that's what you're into you can move on. I don't drink.

VERNE: I was offering lemonade, freshly squeezed, and hang on there. Who said I would cyber with you anyway?

VERNE *begins to pour.*

ROSE: Well you won't be so what's the point in talking about it? Just a drop will do.

VERNE: There's only two types of women who come in here but won't have cybersex.

ROSE: Is that right?

VERNE: Biscuit?

ROSE: No thank you.

VERNE:	Those that are lesbians and those that don't have computers. Now I know you have a computer so…
ROSE:	No, I don't need to pretend. I'm the one who is having sex in the real world and doesn't need to type it all out with a stranger.
VERNE:	Most people pretend to do it in the real world as well. How many people are actually thinking about their partners when they're having sex? Everyone is into the fantasy. Even you I bet.
ROSE:	Fantasy is a world away from the creepy perverts you get on here. I'm not into heaving breasts and love truncheons. Not my thing.
VERNE:	Love truncheon? Lol.
ROSE:	Or man meat.

VERNE *laughs harder.*

ROSE:	The bald headed champ, the purple urchin. I've heard them all.
VERNE:	You seem to know an awful lot of names for the one eyed monster.
ROSE:	I used to go out with a namer.
VERNE:	What's that?
ROSE:	He used to name everything. You know belongin to him and me.
VERNE:	And what did he name your heaving breasts?

226

ROSE: Well my cleavage was mammary lane.

VERNE: Did he stroll down it often?

ROSE: He tried, yellow pages, his fingers did the walking mostly.

VERNE: And how did he get on with that?

ROSE: None of your business.

VERNE: My apologies.

ROSE: Is that all you come in here for?

VERNE: I have a busy life. I like meeting people on here.

ROSE: You've met people face to face?

VERNE: A few.

Pause.

ROSE: And?

VERNE: None of your business.

ROSE: Touche.

VERNE: What does Touche mean?

ROSE: No, lol, read it with an accent.

VERNE: Oh, touché.

ROSE: Exactly.

Pause.

VERNE: So what are you doing for the big countdown?

ROSE:	I usually spend New Year's at home.
VERNE:	I'll be away on business myself.
ROSE:	On your own?

VERNE:	Ya, I travel a lot. It can be lonely sometimes.
ROSE:	Where are you heading?
VERNE:	Dublin.

Long pause.

VERNE:	It's in Ireland.
ROSE:	Ya, I know where it is.
VERNE:	Listen, I have to go. Important client. BB.
ROSE:	Verne, wait.
VERNE:	Ya?
ROSE:	Why do you like wrestling? I was just wondering.

Pause.

| VERNE: | Everyone likes an illusion Rose. That's why we like magic shows and fat people wear black. Here is just the illusion for the twenty first century. BB. |

Lights up on RON'S sitting room. The doorbell rings continuously. RON looks out the window. We can hear kicking and banging at the door.

| RON: | Time to say hello to the family. |

RON *takes a poker from beside his seat and rolls up his sleeves.*

SCENE TEN.

SUE *sits typing on the computer.* LEN *lies on the bed.* LEN *smokes.*

LEN: What's that big fish on the wall for?

SUE: That's Billy the Bass. It sings. I got that on holidays in Tunisia. I don't know why. It reminded me of Ron.

SUE *switches off the computer. She slides on the bed beside* LEN.

LEN: Who do you talk to on that yoke?

SUE: It's just a friend. It's like a pen pal.

LEN: What about this Y2K?

SUE: All the banks and the traffic lights and all are going to blow up tomorrow night apparently.

LEN: That won't happen.

SUE: Hopefully it will wipe out my credit cards.

SUE *kisses* LEN.

LEN: Finally the place to ourselves.

SUE: It's nice, ain't it?

LEN: I hope your brothers weren't too hard on Ron.

SUE:	Forget about him. He's gone now anyway.

SUE *runs her fingers through* LEN'S *hair. He passes her the fag.*

SUE:	Do you ever wonder.
LEN:	What?
SUE:	About us.
LEN:	What about us?
SUE:	Just about us.
LEN:	No.
SUE:	Never?
LEN:	Na, it's going fine, isn't it?
SUE:	I thought it was going better than fine.
LEN:	Ah ya, me too. It's…
SUE:	I love you Len.
LEN:	I loves you too muffin. What's the matter with you?
SUE:	Love me like a pat on the back or love me like marry me one day.
LEN:	There is only one kind ain't there?
SUE:	No.
LEN:	Ah marriage is old fashioned anyway. No one does that anymore.
SUE:	I want to. Someday.

SUE *passes the fag back. Pause.*

SUE: I want kids and the whole deal.

LEN: Maybe one day.

SUE: Do you mean that?

LEN: I would, only for I had the snip.

SUE: What?

LEN: Ya, complications down there. I was lucky I didn't lose a leg.

SUE: What happened to you?

LEN: Meningitis. I got it in me sack.

SUE: Fuck off.

LEN: I did, it was the Chinese version. Nearly killed me when I was a young fella.

SUE: You got it in the sack?

LEN: Ya, it was either nip it in the bud so to speak or lose it all.

SUE: That's bullshit.

LEN *sits up.*

LEN: What?

SUE: You can't get Meningitis in your sack.

LEN: Are you calling me a liar Sue?

SUE: No.

LEN:	Well you fucking are obviously.
SUE:	You do have a habit of stretching the truth Len.
LEN:	Is that what you think of me?
SUE:	Well you do, don't you? Why don't you just be a man and say that you don't want to have kids. Or you don't want to have them with me anyway.
LEN:	We've only being going out with each other for a week Sue.
SUE:	I know. I said someday.
LEN:	Well give me a chance to warm up to the situation. You're ruining everything now you are with your fucking mouth.

LEN *gets off the bed and starts to dress himself.*

SUE:	Where are you going?
LEN:	Home.
SUE:	Are you sulking now?
LEN:	No.
SUE:	You are.
LEN:	I hates pressure.
SUE:	Where's the pressure?
LEN:	Fucking kids and marriage. No, I don't see pressure anywhere sure.

SUE:	We'll forget about it then. Stay here. It's raining outside.

LEN *sits on the bed but still facing away from* SUE. *There is a long pause.*

SUE:	Are you staying?
LEN:	I didn't bring an umbrella.

SUE *hugs* LEN *from behind.*

SUE:	Why don't we go out later? Me and you as a couple?
LEN:	We can't.

SUE *pulls out the bank card that* RON *gave her.*

SUE:	It's on me.
LEN:	Where did you get that?
SUE:	Ron.
LEN:	No way.
SUE:	What?
LEN:	That's not right.
SUE:	What? You can fuck his woman but you won't spend his money. Is that it?
LEN:	No, it's just that I already owes him a tenner from last week.

SUE starts laughing. LEN soon follows. They kiss and fall back on the bed. Lights down. Lights up on RON *in the sitting room. He is icing his knuckles and listening to SUE and LEN laughing upstairs. His face is swollen. RON fires the ice pack across the room.*

SCENE ELEVEN.

ROSE *and* LISA *sit on a bench.*

LISA: I told you he was a fucking loon. A comedian. He wouldn't make…fucking…eh, eh laugh, like. I'm that upset I could shit meself now.

ROSE: You've never even met him.

LISA: Still don't make him not a wanker, does it?

ROSE *bursts out laughing.* LISA *soon follows.* ROSE *lights up a joint.*

ROSE: Me numb, no, me…numbs are gum…

ROSE *laughs.*

LISA: What are you trying to say?

ROSE: Me gums are numb.

LISA *laughs.*

ROSE: Me numbs are gum. What the fuck am I saying eh?

LISA: I don't know. Stoned out of your face I am though.

ROSE:	How in the name of Jesus are we going to go back to work in this state?
LISA:	I think we need a break anyway.
	LISA *takes a bottle of wine from her bag.*
ROSE:	This is good now. LISA *unscrews the top.*
ROSE:	Do you think I'd be this relaxed if he was at home now?
LISA:	Forget about him.
ROSE:	Already done.

LISA *takes out two crystal glasses. She pours and they both clink.*

LISA:	It's a pity about this weather though.

ROSE *fleetingly looks up and the 'sun' comes out and birds begin to sing.*

LISA:	Who would work on a day like today?
ROSE:	Do we have any music?
LISA:	Who do you like?
ROSE:	Anyone but Sting. He could depress Prozac that fella could.
LISA:	How does this sound?

LISA *plays 'Perfect Day.'*

ROSE:	What's that word? Apt?

LISA:	Len is definitely acting strange.
ROSE:	How do you know. Know for sure I mean.
LISA:	Know what for sure?
ROSE:	When it's all over?
LISA:	Do you close your eyes when you kiss him?
ROSE:	I don't…no, don't think so.
LISA:	Then it's over.
ROSE:	Just like that.
LISA:	Na, it's over long before that. The open eyes thing it's just it all coming to the surface.
ROSE:	He had his eyes closed, always did.
LISA:	Len kisses me gentle. Even when we're doing it.
ROSE:	Does he?
LISA:	Ya. Have another drink.

ROSE *and* LISA *drink.*

LISA:	So what about this new guy that you met in the café today?
ROSE:	Who told you about that?
LISA:	I hear everything.
ROSE:	He's alright.
LISA:	Have you cybered with him yet?

ROSE:	No.
LISA:	Len would kill me if he knew I was on this all the time talking to strangers.
ROSE:	I'm not a stranger.
LISA:	I know that, you know what I mean though. We never met or anything.
ROSE:	You know more about me that me own mother does.
LISA:	True.
ROSE:	I got your photo's last night btw.
LISA:	I didn't get yours though.
ROSE:	My scanner's broke.
LISA:	Don't lie to a liar. You're going to have to show me your face sometime. I beginning to think you're an ugly bitch now.
ROSE:	Maybe I am.
LISA:	It just boils down to trust. We've been chatting in here for year. All I want to know is what you look like. I was shitting myself sending you a picture too you know.
ROSE:	I'll send some tonight.
LISA:	Promise?
ROSE:	Promise.
LISA:	So what do you think of mine?

ROSE:	I love the giant fish.
LISA:	I got that on holidays in Tunisia. It sings. Billy the Bass is his name.
ROSE:	What does he sing?
LISA:	Do you want to find out?

Long pause.

ROSE:	What do you mean?
LISA:	How would you like to be a bridesmaid?

Pause.

ROSE:	I...wouldn't know what to say in the middle of your family. You'd be off chatting to people.
LISA:	I don't trust many people in this world Rose but I trusts you. Think about it is all I'm asking.
ROSE:	I will. And I'm flattered.
LISA:	Well you're going to have to make up your mind soon.
ROSE:	Why's that?
LISA:	They reckon everything is going to crash at the stroke of midnight on New Year's. Y2K they're calling it.
ROSE:	That won't happen.
LISA:	What if it did? We'd never be able to talk to each other again.
ROSE:	Have you never heard of the phone?

LISA:	That might work if you'd ever give me your phone number.

Pause.

LISA:	Didn't think so. You can't hide behind your keyboard forever Rose. A friend is a friend no matter how you met them.
ROSE:	Is it the same with men?
LISA:	What do you mean?
ROSE:	It doesn't matter where you met them, does it?
LISA:	Are we talking about the new fella now? Verne, is that what he calls himself?
ROSE:	I'm just talking in general.
LISA:	He's a fraud.
ROSE:	How do you know?

Pause.

ROSE:	Well?
LISA:	I was only looking out for you now. I want you to know that. So I...eh, well I was pretending to flirt with him earlier on and I said I wanted to meet up with him.
ROSE:	What did he say?
LISA:	Well at first he tried to tell me that he was a yank business man. But when I told him I'd be heading to Dublin for the millennium he wanted to met me. All of a sudden he was from Ireland

and worked in a factory. I only did this for your own good now mind you.

ROSE: I was wondering what an American was doing in an Irish chat room anyway.

LISA: He was a bit of a weirdo actually. He said his girlfriend was sleeping with his best friend and they were riding upstairs all the time but he wouldn't leave the house.

ROSE: Fuck sake.

LISA: I know. And then he was going on about his hand was sore or something. He was fighting her brothers. He wasn't making much sense. It was a lucky miss, I'll put it to you that way.

ROSE: The story of my life.

LISA: You weren't thinking of meeting this nutcase were you?

ROSE: You know me I would have probably backed out anyway. It just seemed…different, exciting or something.

LISA: I'm all for exciting but you should watch out. There's a lot of freaks and weirdos that come on here.

ROSE: I know. I wouldn't have met him anyway. It's just not me.

LISA: I know you wouldn't have. You have to trust someone first.

ROSE: Exactly.

LISA: Exactly.

240

SCENE TWELVE.

VELVET *is tied by her wrists from a rope hanging from the ceiling. She is dressed in leather.* BI-VI *stalks her with a whip in her hand.*

VELVET: Describe to me where we are.

BI-VI: We're in a field. It a golden field. We're sitting in the long grass just off the pathways. I brought us a picnic.

VELVET *looks around smiling like she can see exactly what* BI-VI *is describing.*

VELVET: Do we have the red napkins and the wicker picnic basket?

BI-VI: Of course.

VELVET: What kind of day is it?

BI-VI: The sun is making a shadow on your face and putting a shine on your hair.

VELVET: And what am I wearing?

BI-VI: You're wearing a summer dress. It's blue. It's flimsy around your legs but tight around your body. Your breasts bounce slightly when you walk.

VELVET: Am I not wearing a bra?

BI-VI: Let me check.

BI-VI *slowly and seductively slides her hands under* VELVET's *top. They both obviously enjoy it.*

241

BI-VI: I guess not.

VELVET: I'm not sure, maybe you should check again.

BI-VI: Patience.

VELVET: OK, tell me more.

BI-VI: Well there's other people here but they seem to be sticking to the pathways. We can hear them but can't see them. There's a gentle breeze that blows colder when the wind changes. I can begin to make out your nipples.

VELVET: Did you say the people are near us?

BI-VI: Yes. They could walk in on our little picnic anytime.

VELVET: Kiss me.

BI-VI *kisses* VELVET.

VELVET: I will do anything you want me to do to you.

BI-VI *walks around* VELVET *smiling.*

BI-VI: SSSSSSSSSSSSSSSSSSSSSSSSSSSSSSS…

VELVET: Haven't you gotten that fucking keyboard fixed yet?

VELVET *easily slips her wrists out of the rope.*

BI-VI: I think I'll just get a new one.

VELVET: It's a fucking nuisance.

BI-VI: I know, I know.

Both ladies pause.

VELVET: Where were we?

BI-VI: I sssssssssssssssssslid over to…

VELVET: See ya.

BI-VI: Where are you going?

VELVET: This is shit. I need someone with a decent keyboard.

BI-VI: It just comes and goes. It mightn't happen again for weeks. I can't run out and get a new one now.

VELVET: I don't ask for much. A decent keyboard is pretty standard when you are cybering with someone though.

BI-VI: Fuck off then.

VELVET: There's no need to talk to me like that.

BI-VI: I'll talk to you anyway you like you little bitch.

BI-VI *pushes* VELVET.

VELVET: That's better. So are you finally going to fuck me?

BI-VI: Not only am I going to fuck you. I'm going to play Marvin Gaye as I'm doing it.

'Sexual Healing' plays.

VELVET: Who's that?

BI-VI: Marvin Gaye.

VELVET:	Who?

Long pause.

BI-VI:	What age are you?
VELVET:	Thirteen, and you?

Pause.

VELVET:	What age are you?

Pause.

BI-VI:	I'm just fourteen. I hope you like older women.
VELVET:	I would if you were a woman.
BI-VI:	What do you mean?
VELVET:	Every fella on here pretends to be a lesbian so he can cyber with girls. Don't think you're the first to come up with that idea.
BI-VI:	So you think I'm a boy?
VELVET:	I know you are. You type like a boy. You're rough with me. I don't like that.
BI-VI:	Why not?
VELVET:	Because I was raped before.
BI-VI:	By who?
VELVET:	My boyfriend at the time. He held me down and put his cock in my ass. I asked him to stop but he wouldn't.
BI-VI:	Where did this happen?
VELVET:	In here.

244

BI-VI:	What? Did you use a webcam or something?
VELVET:	No. It happens to me often. Boys can be too rough in here. I want to make them cum but they're too impatient. They just type whatever the like about me. Even if I ask them to stop.
BI-VI:	So he never touched you in real life?
VELVET:	I've never even met him before. Don't want to either. Some guys are nice when you met them but I don't think he would be.
BI-VI:	How many boyfriends have you got in here?
VELVET:	A few, five or six.
BI-VI:	How do they become your boyfriend?
VELVET:	Why, are you asking?
BI-VI:	It all depends, what do you look like?
VELVET:	I only send pics to my boyfriends.
BI-VI:	Describe yourself to me. I want to know everything.
VELVET:	I'm about 5' 3". I've got green eyes and black hair. People say I'm chubby but I like to think I'm cuddly. I've got a nice ass and small tits. But I suppose they'll get bigger. Anything else you want to know?
BI-VI:	Do you shave your pussy?
VELVET:	I've tried. Not much happening down there for me yet.
BI-VI:	Are you a virgin?
VELVET:	No.

BI-VI:	What's the dirtiest thing you've ever done?
VELVET:	Lots of stuff. I played with a guy's dick in a restaurant once.
BI-VI:	Why?
VELVET:	Cause he asked me to. He was a friend of this guy I knew. He was cool, older.
BI-VI:	Have you ever sucked a cock before?
VELVET:	Ya, I don't really like doing that so much but boys like it so I do.
BI-VI:	What kind of pictures do I get if I become your boyfriend?
VELVET:	Special pictures. Lol. If you're nice to me after that there could be more things in it for you.
BI-VI:	How can I be your boyfriend?
VELVET:	Just ask.

SCENE THIRTEEN.

PIPER *sits on the sofa at her place. She clicks on her mouse.* LISA *appears beside her.*

| LISA: | I don't know why…I have friends here but I kinda need to talk to you. Len didn't propose, well he's not going to tonight I mean. He left me. I'm hurting bad here. He said he found a |

new woman. He didn't let me down gently or anything. Said she was better than me at everything. I love him. I really love him. And he doesn't love me. I don't know what to do. What am I supposed to tell the child? Her heart is going to be broken. He's moving out of town and everything. You know where he met her? Line fucking dancing. That's hilarious, isn't it? I can just see the two of them with their check shirt and their tassels. I was only hoping for the best anyway. It didn't happen. Anyway, fuck him. I'm going out tonight. I'm going to get fucking gorgeous, I don't know where I'm going to go but I'm going somewhere. I'm not counting down those seconds on my own tonight. No way. Anyway email me when you get this.

LOUBY *stands in the door with a bag in his hand.*

LOUBY: I've been doing a lot of thinking and I've been thinking obviously cause I've   been doing a lot of it and we shouldn't, probably see each other anymore.

PIPER: Grand.

LOUBY: I'll always remember you in a good light. You were good to me. I'll think of   you at twelve tonight.

PIPER: What time is it?

LOUBY: Two. What are you doing tonight anyway?

PIPER: I was thinking of staying here…

LOUBY: Probably…

PIPER:	But I'm not going to. I'm going to into town with a friend of mine.
LOUBY:	Who would that be?
PIPER:	You wouldn't know her.
LOUBY:	Oh, it's a her.
PIPER:	Ya, Lisa. She's a good friend.
LOUBY:	Can I come?
PIPER:	I thought that we finished?
LOUBY:	Well I'm feeling sorry for you.
PIPER:	No need to feel sorry for me.
LOUBY:	It's the least I owe you. To give it one more shot I mean. I don't want you crying about me or anything. I couldn't handle that.
PIPER:	Kiss me.
LOUBY:	I don't think I'm ready for that yet.
PIPER:	Just shut up and kiss me you fucking eejit.

LOUBY *drop his bag and kisses* PIPER. *She keeps her eyes open. So does he.*

LOUBY:	What are you looking at?
PIPER:	You kept your eyes open.
LOUBY:	So did you.
PIPER:	I know.

SCENE FOURTEEN.

RON sits at his computer. Moaning and a squeaky bed can be heard upstairs louder than normal. RON just sits there quiet, too quiet. Lights up on the café. ROSE enters. VERNE sits at a table.

ROSE: Have you seen Lisa in here?

VERNE: She just left.

ROSE: Thanks.

ROSE *walks away.*

VERNE: Where are you going?

ROSE: I know you lied to me.

VERNE: About what?

ROSE: Everything.

VERNE: I don't understand.

ROSE: You never said one true thing in here the whole time we talked.

VERNE: And what's wrong with that?

ROSE: What's wrong with that?

VERNE: Don't be a hypocrite Rose. What about you and the music industry? And do you really think I believe that you're (describe actress in front of him). Everyone lies in here. That's the whole point of this fucking place. If we were all as gorgeous as we say we are why the fuck are we

249

in here all night every night? We're like packs
of hungry dogs. Searching each other out.

ROSE: Some of us have friends in here.

VERNE: Friends? You're lonely Rose. You're heading
into the twenty first century with nothing or no
one. Have you ever really just let fly in your
life? Have you ever just dropped your
knickers…

Lights up on RON'S *house. The noise upstairs has become louder and
louder. It raises and raises.*

RON: …and just bent over? Say nothing like and you
don't know what to expect. Just close your eyes
and wait to be fucked.

Quiet. ROSE *exits.* RON *tries to calm himself. We hear loud music
upstairs and footsteps.* LEN *enters in a green dressing gown. He seems
startled to see* RON.

LEN: I was just going to get a light.

LEN *walks.*

LEN: I thought you were supposed be gone?

RON: This is my house.

LEN: You do pay the rent.

LEN *lights his fag. He sits at* RON*'s computer and fiddles around with
the keyboard, mouse etc.*

LEN: You'll have to show me how to use one of these
things one day Ron. I think there's a message
here for you. Someone called Rose.

250

RON: That's me new girlfriend.

LEN: That's great news. We should have a couple's
                        night out.

LEN *begins to type something.* RON *grabs his arm.*

LEN: Hang on, your S button is stuck.

LEN *clicks the mouse to stop it.* LEN *and* RON *are face to face.*

LEN: Maybe you should get a new keyboard.

RON *looks down.*

RON: Are those my slippers?

LEN: I got a lend of them. I knew you wouldn't mind.

RON *hits* LEN *a head butt and stamps on his head numerous times.*

SCENE FIFTEEN.

ROSE *is back in the café.* LISA *sits motionless in front of her.*

ROSE: Lisa? I can see your name. Can you see me?
                        Hello answer me.

LISA: Sorry. I'm here. I was just getting a drink.

ROSE: Stephen's green. Tonight. Can you make it?

LISA: Are you serious?

ROSE: Ya, fuck it.

LISA: I'll be there.

ROSE:	I'm sorry to hear about you and Len.
LISA:	Fuck him. He's not worth talking about. I would have only been settling for him anyway. We don't close our eyes either.
ROSE:	I'll meet you at the Grafton Street entrance. Do you know where that is? Wear something so I know it's you.
LISA:	I'll find it. You know what I look like. Send me a picture of you.
ROSE:	Check your email.

Pause.

LISA:	You sent me one.
ROSE:	Told you I would.
LISA:	We're going to have a ball tonight. Me and you. Fucking men, they're all fucking wimps.
ROSE:	Thanks for warning me about that fella in here. He turned out to be a fucking looper after.
LISA:	They all are.
ROSE:	I'll be wearing a red coat.
LISA:	OK, BTW, Happy New Year lol.
ROSE:	Happy New Year. See you tonight.
LISA:	Yasssssssssssssssssssssssssssee you later.

PIPER *turns off her computer.* RON *turns off his computer.*

BLACKOUT.

BLOOD

BY

CLARE DOWLING

CHARACTERS.

ELAINE SANDS	-	bride, twenty
CIARAN		groom, mid-twenties
KATE		video recordist, twenty-two
WILMA		wedding organiser, mid-twenties
CHRIS SANDS		mother of the bride, late thirties
MICK		best man, mid-twenties
NOEL		church caretaker, mid-twenties
NICOLA SANDS	-	sixteen
FR. JACK		twenty-eight
DEIRDRE		bridesmaid, mid-twenties
AMY		butchers' assistant, eighteen
ALICE		Chris's sister, twenty-nine
VALERIE		Chris's sister, twenty-eight
VINNIE SANDS		father of the bride, a butcher, late thirties
PHIL		civil servant, mid- to late-twenties
LINDA		Amy's sister, mid-twenties
GINA		kissogram, nineteen

SETTING.
A PARK
A CHURCH
A BUTCHERS'
THE SANDS' FAMILY HOME
A PUB

TIME.
NOW

Lights up, a park. Wind blows and birds chirp. Several chairs form benches. Regular park-goers (WILMA, NOEL, MICK) sit reading and relaxing. CIARAN enters, wearing chef's checked pants under his coat. He takes a jeweller's box from his pocket and nervously examines it, hiding it behind his back as ELAINE runs on. She kisses him passionately, oblivious to the onlookers.

ELAINE: Tell me.

CIARAN: What.

ELAINE: Oh come on! The big mystery. The summons to the park.

CIARAN: Ah, just wanted to ask you somethin'. That's all.

ELAINE: Oh. I thought it was important.

She flops dramatically onto her back on the grass, arms outstretched.

ELAINE: God. This is gorgeous. Lie down! The grass is like a duvet, it's that thick. Come on, lie down with me.

She drags him down with her, laughing. He attempts to keep his composure in the face of the obvious interest of the park-goers. He struggles to his feet again.

CIARAN: I have to be standin'. To do it properly.

ELAINE: Do what properly?

CIARAN: Elaine. I asked you here today because this is where we met. 1st June 1993. You were lyin' out here on the grass readin' a book. And you were readin' quietly for ages and ages and then you must've read somethin' funny because you laughed. I never told you this, but I was watchin' you from over there for a week before I could get up the courage to talk to you.

ELAINE: I know. Here, what are you hiding behind your back?

He drops to one knee.

CIARAN: Elaine. Will you marry me?

The birds hush. The wind stops. The park-goers watch surreptitiously. The silence stretches.

ELAINE: Yes! I will marry you, yes.

CIARAN: Yeh will?

ELAINE: Yes. I'd love to.

They kiss. After an age, a park-goer coughs in disapproval. They quickly part. Belatedly, he produces the ring.

CIARAN: I hope you like it. But I still have the receipt.

ELAINE: No, no, it's beautiful, Thank you.

CIARAN: I can't believe this...when? When will we do it?

ELAINE: I don't know. The summer? June.

CIARAN: Yeh. And I thought we might make it small. You know, personal. But if you want a big day, just say the word –

ELAINE: Of course I don't. After all, it's for us, isn't it?

They kiss again. KATE enters with a camcorder and moves tentatively around them. Gradually, they become aware of her and look at her in confusion.

256

KATE:	This is where I'm supposed to be, isn't it? Our Lady of Sorrows Church?

Lights up on the church, which becomes a hive of activity. AMY enters and starts to tune her cello, NOEL sweep the floor and MICK rearranges chairs. CHRIS enters as WILMA sweeps breathlessly forward with her clipboard.

WILMA:	You haven't put on any weight, have you Elaine?
ELAINE:	What?
WILMA:	It's just that I did a wedding last year – Dalkey Island Hotel – gorgeous – but didn't the bride suffer an attack of nerves the week before and went on a binge – whole sliced pans, pounds of chocolate, Kentucky Fried Chicken family dinners – you name it. Dress didn't fit the poor thing on the day. Oh, the tears. Of course, they blamed the wedding organiser – me – for the whole thing. Never again, I said. You haven't been eating sliced pans have you?
ELAINE:	No.
CIARAN:	I might have put on –
WILMA:	Oh, a suit looks fine even if there's extra weight, Ciaran. Now. where's the father of the bride?
CHRIS:	Vinnie should be here any minute.
WILMA:	Good. Now all I'm missing is the priest. Would you..?

She thrusts the ends of the ribbons in CIARAN's hands and swans vaguely off to the back wall, trailing ribbons as she goes.

CHRIS:	Sorry Ciaran. She's lost the run of herself a little. And to tell you the truth, I've only encouraged her.
ELAINE:	Mam, you're not over-doing it now, are you?
CHRIS:	I'm not doing anything, that's just it. I've sat back and chosen at leisure from her catalogue and then she goes and does all the work. It's great.
ELAINE:	How about a cup of tea.
CHRIS:	Now stop fussing, I don't want a cup of tea. I'm dying to read these telegrams. I know we should save them until tomorrow but just one or two won't hurt. (*tears open one*)
ELAINE:	(*reading over her shoulder*) "Elaine and Ciaran, sorry we'll miss your wedding. Best wishes from Bernie and Tom."

ELAINE *and* CHRIS *companionably huddle together over another.*

CIARAN:	I'll leave you to it then.
CHRIS:	But they're for you too...

He swiftly moves off. ELAINE *shrugs apologetically.*

CHRIS:	He told me yesterday that he didn't want me to give you a lift to the train on Saturday morning. That he was capable of getting you there all by himself.
ELAINE:	I think he feels a bit out of it since the hotel closed.
CHRIS:	But he was working today, wasn't he?

ELAINE:	Yeh. Making Rice Krispie cakes for a kids' party in Malahide. One day in two weeks.
CHRIS:	Still, you're working, aren't you? Here, we'd better leave the rest of these till tomorrow. I've to go through make-up arrangements for you and Deirdre. Where *is* she?

KATE fiddles in quiet desperation with her camcorder. She searches in her bag, where she finds an envelope. She tears it open.

KATE:	Kate. Sorry to land you in this at such short notice, but in a way, it's your own fault. It was just a turn, that was all, there was no need for you to rush me to out-patients. Anyway, all you have to do is to hold the fort for an hour or two, until I get out of here –
WILMA:	There's a socket over there if you need to recharge.
KATE:	Recharge what.
WILMA:	The battery?
KATE:	Oh yes, that's probably what's wrong.
WILMA:	Your father mentioned that he'd do some background footage. To intercut with the actual wedding.
KATE:	You mean – you want me to shoot now? I thought I was just here for a practise run –
WILMA:	Might as well get the whole lot, shall we?
KATE:	Right. Sure.
WILMA:	And how is your father?

KATE:	I've just rang and they said they're going to do some tests. He's really sorry that he let you down at the last minute.
WILMA:	Oh nonsense, it couldn't be helped. Very talented man. Still, I'm sure you're just as good.

KATE *escapes towards the socket.* MICK *joins* CIARAN.

MICK:	(*to* CIARAN) I've left the car running out the back if yeh want to make a quick escape.
CIARAN:	Don't think anybody'd notice if I did. We said a small wedding. We agreed.
MICK:	Sure what do you care? Aren't they payin' for it?
CIARAN:	I don't need remindin' Mick!
MICK:	Should have listened to me.
CIARAN:	Here we go.
MICK:	Fact is, yer born alone and yeh die alone. Yeh can try and fool yerself by fillin' in the middle bit with someone else, but yeh can't change the facts.
CIARAN:	Now there speaks a man who hasn't met the right woman yet.
MICK:	No such thing. It's a good chat-up line though, they think they've got a challenge on their hands.

He takes the ribbons from CIARAN *and makes for* WILMA.

MICK:	So, tell us, do you do many weddin's?

WILMA:	Why, are you looking for a wedding organiser?
MICK:	What? Me? You must be jokin'. Naw, haven't met the right woman yet, not like himself. But did you know, a surprisin' number of people meet their future spouses at a weddin'?
NOEL:	I'm closing up at eight. Not a minute later.
WILMA:	I know, and we're just about to start.
NOEL:	And there's to be no confetti tomorrow.
WILMA:	Yes yes, you've reminded me four times already. What on earth...can we get rid of this?

She holds up a thick white cable she's discovered on the wall.

NOEL:	No! I mean, you can't. It's a satellite cable. Fr. Walsh's. He likes to watch a bit of TV before Mass.
WILMA:	Yes alright. Chris? Which would you go for? (*ribbons*)
CHRIS:	Hmmm. The white, I think.
WILMA:	Yes, I adore the white. Virginal. And it *is* the cheaper of the two. That's because most people go for the pink.
CHRIS:	Well, the pink then?
WILMA:	You could always have both. That's what most people do.
CHRIS:	(*dryly*) Do they. I'd have to ask Vinnie. The cost.

WILMA: Oh, but he told me weeks ago that you were to
                    have whatever you wanted, Chris. He was quite
                    firm about that.

CHRIS: Oh. Well in that case, let's have both.

WILMA: Lovely. (*calling*) Could everybody go outside
                    please? Fr. Jack's instructions.

CHRIS: Hold on. We're missing somebody.

*The wedding party freeze. A murmur grows louder. Lights up downstage
where NICOLA is hunched at the feet of the front-row audience, a
textbook on her knees. She puts the book down and starts to pace.*

NICOLA: For it cannot be but I am pigeon-hearted and
                    lack gall to make oppression bitter, or ere this I
                    should have fatted all the region kites with this
                    slave's offal. Bloody bawdy villain!
                    Remorseless, treacherous, lecherous...(*memory
                    failing her*)...treacherous, lecherous...(*gives up
                    and looks at book*)...kindless fucking villain!

*She flings the book down in frustration. It lands at NOEL'S feet, who is
poised with his dustpan.*

NOEL: You Nicola? Because if you are, your mother's
                    looking for you inside.

NICOLA: Christ. What is it now? Can't she leave me in
                    peace and quiet for one minute?

NOEL: She says you're supposed to be in the
                    procession. You're supposed to be part of your
                    sister's wedding. You're supposed to be a little
                    flower-girl.

NICOLA: And I'm supposed to have an English exam
                    tomorrow afternoon!

NOEL:	Just passing on a message.
NICOLA:	Don't suppose you did "Hamlet" for the Leaving, did you?
NOEL:	No.
NICOLA:	Oh. What did you do instead?
NOEL:	Can't remember.
NICOLA:	Couldn't have been that long ago.
NOEL:	I'm just passing on a message, that's all. And by the way. It's pigeon-livered. Not pigeon-hearted.

He carefully empties his dustpan. She exits. Lights back to the church. The wedding party exits, save for CHRIS, WILMA and KATE. FR. JACK bounds on, in 501's and an out-dated leather jacket. He looks around.

FR JACK:	This should do just fine for our purposes, Chris.
CHRIS:	Quaint, isn't it? This is where Vinnie and I got married.
FR JACK:	Yes? Still, it really doesn't matter, does it?
CHRIS:	What.
FR JACK:	The church. In New York, we have Mass in the most peculiar places. School halls. Parks. Private homes. I once said Mass on a basketball court. We all had a game of basketball afterwards, great fun.
WILMA:	Oh, you'll probably find all this very old-fashioned, after New York and all. I'm afraid

we're going for a traditional white wedding, Father Jack. No sports of any kind.

FR JACK: Absolutely Wilma. It's good to see you looking so well, Chris. I didn't get a chance to say it earlier. Had my entire congregation on its knees for two weeks for you.

CHRIS: Thanks. And it's good to see you Jack. It's nice to have someone from the family saying the mass.

FR JACK: Even if we are only third cousins removed.

CHRIS: Still. Alice and Valerie are looking forward to seeing you. (*pause*) You do remember them, don't you? My sisters?

FR JACK: Oh, vaguely. I've been away a long time...

CHRIS: You must remember Valerie. Didn't you two hang around together quite a lot before you left?

FR JACK: Yes, now we're a little out of time...(*to* WILMA) do you think we might get started?

WILMA: Yes, well we were waiting on you, Father.

CHRIS: Vinnie too. He's working late. Thursday night opening.

WILMA: We'll have to start without him. Do you want to go ahead and get changed Father? I know it's only a rehearsal –

FR JACK: Sure.

He peels off the leather jacket to reveal a skimpy t-shirt. He becomes aware of KATE filming him, and preens slightly, before thrusting the jacket into WILMA's hands.

FR JACK: Sexy, eh?

KATE: Sorry?

FR JACK: Isn't that what you say in the film business? A sexy shot. Nothing to do with sex, of course.

WILMA: Jack? Do you think we might start?

FR JACK: Absolutely. Now, Chris, if you want to go outside and join the others...

CHRIS: But won't I be in the church? As mother of the bride?

FR JACK: Oh no, I never allow the mother of the bride to sit in the church. Separated? Isolated from the couple? Oh no. It's a communal affair, a bonding of people, a cohesion...well, you'll see what I mean as we go along. (*to* WILMA) Now. Do you think we could get rid of these chairs?

WILMA: But – where do we sit?

FR JACK: Ah. That's the beauty of it. We don't.

He enthusiastically moves a chair, coming up hard against NOEL.

NOEL: Fr. Walsh never said anything about chairs being moved.

FR JACK: Well why don't we ask him?

NOEL: He's still in bed.

FR JACK:	What did the doctor say? Will he be able to con-celebrate the wedding mass tomorrow morning?
NOEL:	He might. Then again, he might not. Depends.
FR JACK:	Thank you Noel.
WILMA:	(*calling*) Hello? Can we have a hand to move these chairs? (*murmuring*) Kate? I think as little as possible of Jack, if that's okay. Now. Has anyone seen the bridesmaid?

Lights up downstage. ELAINE leads DEIRDRE on. DEIRDRE is crying.

DEIRDRE:	Sorry, Elaine. Sorry.
ELAINE:	Oh stop Deirdre, there's nothing to be sorry about. I shouldn't have asked you to be bridesmaid, not so soon.
DEIRDRE:	I should be over it by now. I really did think we were going to get married. When he was slow about proposing, I thought I'd take the bull by the horns, it being leap year and all. And he said yes, Elaine, and that he was just popping down to the corner shop to get a bottle of wine to celebrate. I haven't seen him since.
ELAINE:	I never liked him anyway. You're better off on your own.
DEIRDRE:	I have the job, the car, the apartment, the savings account in the First National. What else is there but a relationship? What's left? We all need someone, Elaine.
ELAINE:	You just haven't found the right person yet.

266

DEIRDRE:	It's more than that. What is it about some women, no matter how hard they try, they seem to attract nothing but the losers and the creeps and the married guys and if they're lucky, the occasional closet homosexual. I really liked him too.
ELAINE:	Maybe you shouldn't try so hard, maybe that's what's wrong –
DEIRDRE:	Is there something wrong with me? Is it something I do? Please tell me if it is, Elaine. You'd tell me if I was doing something wrong, wouldn't you?
ELAINE:	But you're not! Just relax a bit, that's all.

They turn upstage, where the rest have straggled on and are moving chairs. KATE is filming CHRIS when MICK moves into her line of vision.

KATE:	Am, I already have you on tape, so if you could just sort of scoot over there –
MICK:	Someone was telling me this interestin' fact the other day. Did you know that a surprisin' number of people meet their future spouses at a weddin'?
KATE:	Imagine that. Could you...to the left a little..?
WILMA:	Kate? Could you manage to get the mother of the bride on tape?
KATE:	Well I was trying to...yes, yes of course.
NOEL:	I'm closing up at eight.
WILMA:	I know, but do you think you could let us stay a little longer? I'll pay you. Double time.

267

NOEL: No. Sorry. There are things I have to do on a
                   Thursday. Important things. Can't put them off.

ELAINE *joins* CIARAN.

ELAINE: Sorry about the madness.

CIARAN: It's true what they say. It's the bride's day.

ELAINE: Well, just think of Saturday. A whole week
                   together.

CIARAN: Yeh. In Galway. I wanted to take you
                   somewhere special. I wanted to do it properly
                   Elaine.

ELAINE: What does it matter where we go? So long as
                   we're alone?

CIARAN: (*unenthusiastically*) Yeh.

ELAINE: Don't sound so excited. It's weeks since I've been
                   invited to your flat, you know. I'm starting to
                   think you're saving yourself.

CIARAN: Ah, Mick's had people stayin', been a bit mad.
                   Galway, eh?

She leans in, about to kiss him.

FR JACK: (*calls*) Elaine? For the register tomorrow. What
                   name are you taking?

ELAINE: Oh, I'm just keeping my own, I think.

*She turns back; CIARAN has bolted. WILMA attempts to take AMY's
cello.*

WILMA:	I'm sorry, but we're going to have to move you, okay?
AMY:	This is my seat. I was told to sit here.
WILMA:	I know, but we're all going outside you see.
AMY:	But I'm playin' the music for the weddin'. Vinnie said.
WILMA:	Well perhaps we'll put you standing over there –
AMY:	(*sudden temper*) I'm playin' the music! For the weddin'! And I can't play the music if I'm standin'!

She grabs her cello back and sits down, then ignores the lot of them.

WILMA:	She wasn't a good idea.
CHRIS:	She was Vinnie's idea. She's actually very good Wilma.
WILMA:	Still. Everyone outside again please! Hurry hurry!

They exit. FR. JACK *skips back to* AMY *with some sheet music.*

FR JACK:	Almost forgot. I don't know if you'll be able to manage this, but have a try. Now, I'll give you a cue to start, when the bride comes in. Like this (*sweep of arm*). Have you got that? Will I do it again for you?
AMY:	I got it the first time. Father.

He hurriedly backs off and watches as AMY *plays a few notes. He freezes. Lights up downstage on the road.* VALERIE *enters, lugging a suitcase which she plonks down. She looks around expectantly, discovers that she's alone.*

ALICE: (*off*) Shit. Shit!

ALICE enters, dragging a half-open suitcase. She flings it on the ground, hurls it open and starts to rifle through it. Glamorous clothes and lingerie fly through the air.

ALICE: I'm after forgetting it...shit shit Chris'll murder me.

VALERIE: What have you forgotten.

ALICE: We're already late, this'll be the last straw if I've forgotten the bloody...oh wow look, I thought I'd lost that skirt...and there's that damned reading, mind it for me will you? What did she ask me to do a reading for anyway –

VALERIE: Probably because you're Elaine's godmother.

ALICE: Am I? Shit, I should have gotten her a bigger present in that case, shouldn't I? Being godmother. Still, I'm hardly expected to remember, I was only eight at the time. Chris just did it to spite Mother.

VALERIE blesses herself. ALICE belatedly follows suit, then rummages more.

ALICE: I've very definitely forgotten it.

VALERIE: What! What have you forgotten Alice?

ALICE: The veil! The bloody veil.

VALERIE plucks a veil from the case and hands it to ALICE.

VALERIE:	I packed it last night. In case you forgot.
ALICE:	You mean I couldn't remember my own name last night. (*pause*) I really don't know if I can handle this wedding.
VALERIE:	Now don't start that again please. You're here and you're going and that's that. And Alice? About tomorrow –
ALICE:	I won't touch a drop, cross my heart and hope to die. Anyway. Now we have the veil. The sacred veil passed on from generation to generation.
VALERIE:	It's beautiful, isn't it? I remember Chris wearing it.
ALICE:	Bloody thing is cursed.
VALERIE:	Just because you didn't have any luck with it doesn't mean nobody else will! (*pause*) Sorry Alice. That just came out. I didn't mean...

ALICE abruptly and haphazardly stuffs the clothing back into the suitcase and exits, the veil trailing full length from the suitcase. VALERIE looks towards FR. JACK, then exits quickly. Lights back to the church. FR. JACK bounds to the exit.

FR JACK:	Listen up! We're going around by the side of the church, through the grounds, then in and up to the altar, alright? Music Amy!

He cues her and exits. She plays the music. It is dark and sombre. VINNIE skulks in, wearing butchers' clothes, breathing hard. Unnoticed, he watches AMY for a while. In frustration, she flings down the sheet music.

VINNIE:	Don't.

271

AMY:	It's supposed to be "Here Comes The Bride".

VINNIE:	I told all the customers who were askin' after you that you were tunin' up to knock those stuffy guests out of their seats tomorrow with that thing.

AMY:	Yeh? Who was askin' after me Vinnie?

VINNIE:	Mrs. Ryan, Gerry, Sandra Walsh, they all were. I told 'em I had to cope on me own for the evenin', because you were needed here.

AMY:	(*pleased*) I was. But I'm glad you missed me.

He picks up the music and places it back on the stand with a flourish. He pretends to be a conductor.

VINNIE:	Go on. Give us a blast.

Charmed, she plays. VINNIE closes his eyes; she watches him, enraptured.

VINNIE:	How is she? Chris?

AMY'*s music comes discordantly to a halt.*

VINNIE:	Did she look tired?

AMY:	No. She looked fine.

VINNIE:	You're not just sayin' that because it's what I want to hear?

AMY:	She looked fine I said!

VINNIE:	Alright Amy. Go on back and open up for me, will you?

AMY:	But do you not want to hear me play?

VINNIE:	I'd love to, but I don't want to keep the customers waitin'. And Amy?

AMY:	I won't. I won't go near the slicer or the knives. You don't have to keep tellin' me that Vinnie!

VINNIE:	I wasn't goin' to say that. It's just that if someone calls in, well, just tell him I'm out. Won't be back.

She exits. He moves downstage and kneels. He starts to mumble; it sounds like praying. Footsteps approach. PHIL enters and stands behind VINNIE.

PHIL:	There's no sense dragging me half-way across the town when I'm only doing my job, Mr. Sands.

He holds a document out to VINNIE.

PHIL:	Registered in the Circuit Court on the 2nd of March 1996.

VINNIE *tears up the document and throws it in the air like confetti.*

PHIL:	Look Mr Sands, they tell me to give you a copy so I have to give you a copy. You can do what you want with it after that. Anyway, you've already got the original. From the Sheriff. He delivered it on...let me see, 10th of March.

VINNIE:	Don't spout dates at me, you fucking glorified civil servant.

PHIL:	I'm actually not a civil servant. I'm –

VINNIE:	A lackey, that's what you are.

PHIL:	Yes, well, whatever you want to think.
VINNIE:	Comin' into my shop in front of the locals – in front of my neighbours, people I've known all my life! – and producin' that thing. How dare you. They're all sittin' over their shepherd's pie right now, "did you hear that Vinnie Sands is goin' under?" "Oh, I know, last person in the world you would have expected. Shockin'!" Shockin'.
PHIL:	Well you didn't meet me yesterday like you were supposed to. Am I right there? (*no response from* VINNIE) I've come to arrange a time with you. I don't have to, you know. I'm not obliged to, a lot of them wouldn't bother.
VINNIE:	Caring sort, aren't you?
PHIL:	Not really. But I thought I'd make it easy on you, with the wedding. Still, if you don't want to, that's fine by me. It's easier if I can do it on my own time.
VINNIE:	Wait. Can you leave it till next week. Till the weddin's over. Please.
PHIL:	Sorry. Can't. I'm going on holidays on Saturday morning.
VINNIE:	(*laughs*) Holidays. Well, don't let me put you out.
PHIL:	Would you like me to make a start on it tonight or what? Otherwise I'll have to do it all tomorrow. Up to you.

VINNIE *manages a nod.* PHIL *exits.* VINNIE *starts to chant again.*

274

VINNIE: (*jingle from Crazy Prices ad*) "That's great, that's ace, that sets the pace, that's great that's Crazy Prices." (*chants it until finally, he sings it*). Imagine listenin' to that all day every day. I do. For a year now, since the supermarket went up down the town. You can hear it over the intercom, clear as day. They play it every five minutes Monday to Friday, every two minutes on a Saturday. That's 108 times a day, 810 times a week, that's 42,120 times in the last year I've listened to that fuckin' jingle – I'm expectin' it to be played when me daughter walks up the aisle in the morning. And that's not countin' the times I sing it to meself. You know the kind of tune that follows you around, that gets right inside your head until you can't get away from it, you can't shut it out. You're lyin' in bed and you're singin' it – you're in the pub and your brain is tappin' it out – sitting in traffic – watching the TV – waiting in a queue for the bank and that tune is goin' round and round your head until you think you might be going mad. You try and block it out, make it go away. Sing something else (*sings loudly off-key in a burst*) – no use – think another thought – can't – will your mind to go blank – impossible. Finally you jam your hands over your ears hard – harder – hard till it hurts – but you can still hear that fuckin' tune!

He exits. Lighting change to butchers. AMY enters with a lump of meat and a meat hammer. NICOLA hunches in a corner, buried in a book. KATE enters.

AMY: (*by rote, with a sales pitch*) Our special tonight is tender Irish lamb, five chops for six pounds and we'll give you four chicken legs with that. Excellent value all around.

KATE: Well, that certainly is cheap –

AMY:	Too cheap. But we're tryin' to undercut the supermarket.
KATE:	Listen, would you mind if I got a bit of background footage of you? Here? Working?
AMY:	But we' re closing soon. Nine sharp on a Thursday. No later, because I have to get back. otherwise she'll worry.
KATE:	Who?
AMY:	Sister Joan. She got me the job here. She tried the whole street, but nobody would give me a job except for Vinnie.
KATE:	Two seconds, that's all it'll take, okay?

She trains the camcorder on AMY. AMY drops the hammer and smiles shyly.

| KATE: | That's lovely, but maybe if you could keep working? |

AMY thumps the meat again, but remains beaming into the camera. KATE considers, then moves around to the back of AMY, shooting from behind.

| KATE: | I'll give you a signal and you just go on like normal, okay? Just pretend I'm not here. Four, three, two, one, action! |

AMY hammers as normal, but then ruins it by stealing a shy look backwards.

| KATE: | Right...thanks Amy, that was great. |

KATE consults her notebook. NICOLA looks up from her textbook.

NICOLA:	Do you know what rhenish is. The king drinks it.

KATE:	No, sorry. Do you know what a focus puller is?

NICOLA:	No, sorry.

FR. JACK *sweeps through, laden with bottles of champagne.*

FR JACK:	Ah. Kate. Coming upstairs? There's a bit of a reunion.

NICOLA:	Not gonna ask me?

FR JACK:	Ah, well, you live here Nicola. Kate's a stranger. We must look after her. That right Kate?

KATE:	But I –

He whisks her off with him. AMY *continues to lambaste the meat.*

VINNIE:	(*from OFF*) Take it a bit easier Amy. You're not trying to kill it.

He enters a moment later, pulling on a clean apron. He moves behind her, putting his hand over hers and guiding it.

VINNIE:	Now. First thing is stance. Legs set good and solid and far apart. Stand tall, and loosen your shoulder, that's it, and let your elbow swing. Just let it swing. That's it.

He arranges her stance, then guides her hand again. She gives the meat a tentative thump, then another. VINNIE sets a rhythm by slapping his hand on the table. NICOLA, furious, ups the volume of her mumbling.

NICOLA:	Can you keep it down please!

VINNIE:	Sorry. Perfect, Amy! We'll make a butcher out of you yet.
AMY:	It was easy. Will I get the slicer? Remember, you promised to show me how to use the slicer? Vinnie?

But VINNIE's *attention has immediately strayed to* CHRIS, *who enters.*

VINNIE:	Hello love. Thought you were upstairs.
CHRIS:	I decided to walk home from the church.
VINNIE:	Walk.
CHRIS:	(*laughs*) Yes. Walk, Vinnie. I can still manage a short walk. Hello Amy! Have you been busy?
AMY:	(*curtly*) No. It was slow all evenin'.
VINNIE:	Yeh, well it's dinner time. They'll be in later.
CHRIS:	I'm having a bit of a drinks party upstairs soon, before the final dress fittings. Would you like to come up Amy?
AMY:	No. Vinnie's going to teach me how to use the slicer.
CHRIS:	Maybe some other time, eh? I need him upstairs.
AMY:	But he promised! You promised Vinnie.
VINNIE:	Some other time Amy, okay? Now go and start putting the stuff away into the fridge please.

AMY *reluctantly leaves.*

CHRIS:	Funny little thing. You should have seen her face the day I walked in here from the hospital. I thought she was going to cry.
VINNIE:	She was just worried about you. Her way of showin' it.
CHRIS:	Elaine said she found her in our bedroom while I was away. Just sitting on the bed. Wearing my slippers and nightgown.
VINNIE:	Ah, no harm in her Chris.
CHRIS:	Vinnie, you don't always have to excuse her you know. I don't want her in our bedroom again.
VINNIE:	I'll tell her. Now go on upstairs and have a rest.
CHRIS:	Vinnie. Stop. I'm in the clear. I'm alright.
VINNIE:	I'm just afraid Chris. Afraid that it'll come back.
CHRIS:	It won't. You know, they're right, what they said in the hospital. They said that once I had something to do, once I had something to get out of the bed in the morning for, I'd feel better much quicker. And I do.
VINNIE:	That's great love. That's really great.

AMY *stands half-hidden in the entrance, watching.*

CHRIS:	That man. Coming out of the church. Did you know him?
VINNIE:	No.
CHRIS:	It's the supermarket, isn't it. It's affecting us.

VINNIE:	Affectin' everybody. But we're fine, Chris. We're doin' just as good as ever. Really.
CHRIS:	I've gone a bit mad with this wedding, haven't I? You should have stopped me, you know, if we can't afford it –
VINNIE:	I want a big weddin' as much as you. I want to send me first daughter off in a bit of style. None of them nosy neighbours will be able to say that we couldn't give her a good send-off.
CHRIS:	Who cares what they think.
VINNIE:	I care. Now, I'll be up as soon as I've cleaned meself up.
CHRIS:	Alright. Nicola? Nicola love?
NICOLA:	WHAT! Oh. Sorry Ma.
CHRIS:	It's time for drinks and a final dress fitting.

NICOLA *slaps her book closed and marches out with a martyred air.*

VINNIE:	That young one. She wants manners put on her.
CHRIS:	She's just under pressure Vinnie. Don't be long, alright? Oh, and Wilma told me to remind you about your wedding speech. No tasteless jokes, she said.

She exits. AMY *re-enters cautiously.*

VINNIE:	Amy? Now I'm not givin' out to you, but don't be sayin' in front of Chris that business is not doin' well.
AMY:	But it's not.

280

VINNIE: (*unconvincingly*) It'll pick up. We just need to target the market, slash prices, be competitive. Run more specials.

AMY: Is she goin' to die.

VINNIE: What? No. No of course she isn't.

AMY: They sometimes let them home from hospital if they're goin' to die. Sr. Paul was let home and she died the same night.

VINNIE: She's been let home because she's alright.

AMY: I was just thinkin' that you're too busy with her home to teach me anythin' anymore. It's been weeks since we stayed here late at night, just the two of us, with you showin' me things and teachin' me about the shop.

VINNIE: I've been busy Amy. Next week, alright? And another thing. Don't be goin' through Chris's stuff again. She told me.

AMY: Sorry. I was just wonderin' what it was like. To be married. To you. (*quickly*) To someone like you I mean.

VINNIE laughs and pats her affectionately. He starts to hammer the meat.

AMY: That man is out the back.

The hammer slips and he smashes his own hand. He slumps in the chair NICOLA has vacated and sits. AMY exits. The soft chant of the supermarket jingle sounds from OFF. AMY re-enters with a plaster and ointment. She kneels at VINNIE's feet and starts to tend to his hand.

AMY:	I heard him in the church. But I wasn't spyin', honest! That priest told me to give him back his music and I heard.
VINNIE:	Listen to me Amy. Not a word, understand? Not a word to Chris or Elaine or Sr. Joan for that matter, alright. But especially not to Chris. I don't want her to know. This is just between us. You and me. Alright?
AMY:	You and me. Alright Vinnie. Won't tell her a thing.
VINNIE:	I just have to get it sorted, that's all. I just need some time to get it sorted... that's all..
AMY:	We'll sort it Vinnie. We will. You and me. You and me.

She tentatively pats his hand, growing bolder when he accepts her comfort. LINDA runs in, carrying a shopping bag. She envelopes AMY in a bear hug.

LINDA:	Oh, look at you! All dirty and hot! I was up at the convent and they told me you were still working. Well I hope this man here is paying you well, eh? Hello Vinnie.
VINNIE:	Linda. Good to see yeh again. (*pause*) Amy? Are you not goin' to say hello to your sister?
AMY:	Hello.
LINDA:	And look what I got for you! Spent hours looking for just the right thing, Paul too. He's outside in the car waiting.

She takes an expensive but childish cardigan out of the bag. She pulls it on an unresisting and mortified AMY.

LINDA:	Oh, it really suits you, doesn't it Vinnie?
VINNIE:	You're a stunner in that Amy.

AMY *frantically tears the cardigan off and flings it down.*

AMY:	They wear those in the convent. The ten year olds, Linda. Why do you always buy me those stupid clothes!

VINNIE *nods to* LINDA *and makes a discreet exit upstage.*

AMY:	In front of him! You gave that to me in front of him!
LINDA:	Vinnie? But he thought it was nice.
AMY:	I give them away. All the things you buy me. To the younger ones.
LINDA:	We'll change it. And you get the choose. How about that?
AMY:	Why didn't you come and visit me at Easter. I sat there waitin' for you all day and you never came.
LINDA:	(*effusiveness gone now*) Sometimes, Amy, I don't know whether you want me to visit or not. Sometimes you act like you'd prefer to be on your own. I ring all the time, you know, and you never come to the phone. Never.
AMY:	Don't like talkin' on the phone. But don't miss another Easter, Linda. Please.
LINDA:	I won't, I promise. In fact, from now on, we'll see each other a lot more often. (*pause*) I've a surprise for you.

AMY:	(*excited*) What surprise. Tell me.
LINDA:	(*teasing*) I might.
AMY:	Linda!
LINDA:	Oh Amy, I'm finally able to do it! What with the mail order business taking off from home and the new house and everything settled between me and Paul ...Listen, I couldn't do it before now, you do know that, don't you Amy? I tried my best, but I'm only managing it now.
AMY:	I don't know what you mean.
LINDA:	I'm taking you home. Tonight. To live with Paul and me in Wexford. How about that?

She hugs AMY *again. Lights up downstage.* KATE *enters, with her camcorder on a tripod, as the wedding party enter upstage. She reads another letter.*

KATE:	Kate. They're keeping me in overnight, even though I've told them a thousand times that I'm alright. I'll be there in the morning, but I'm afraid you're on your own tonight. Now. Be careful about the windows when you're shooting indoors. The light will close down the aperture and you'll get only silhouettes. Aperture. Oh, that's great Dad. Bloody great. How am I supposed to know what aperture is.

She examines her camcorder. FX a champagne cork popping loudly, then raucous laughter and chatting. Lights up on VALERIE, FR. JACK, WILMA, ELAINE, CIARAN, MICK *and* DEIRDRE. VINNIE *holds an open champagne bottle, the rest glasses.* KATE *swings her camcorder upstage.*

KATE:	Sorry. I missed that. Would you mind just..?

284

VINNIE *does an awkward re-run of shaking the bottle and popping it as the rest look on in silence.*

KATE: Thank you. And could everybody move away from the windows?

She brings ELAINE, CIARAN and VINNIE downstage, where a light comes up. (All conversations take place in this light, where KATE drags group after group) All three look stiffly and silently into the camera.

KATE: Just pretend I'm not here. Could you pour the champagne?

VINNIE: (*awkwardly*) Right. Ah, the bride first.

ELAINE: Oh? You were so late into the rehearsal I thought it had slipped your mind altogether that I was getting married tomorrow.

VINNIE: Fat chance, dyin' to get rid of you. Passin' the torch to this man here, eh Ciaran? (*to* ELAINE) How's herself?

ELAINE: Great. I've never seen her so excited. I really think this wedding is the best thing that could have happened to her.

VINNIE: Good, good. Well, I'd better not keep her waitin'. (*to* CIARAN, *in passing*) Oh, did yeh get a new job? He'll be able to keep yeh in style now Elaine.

ELAINE: (*quickly*) He was just workin' for the day Da. But he's been for two interviews.

VINNIE: Oh. Just thought with the chef's garb and all...Sorry.

He quickly moves on to CHRIS and VALERIE.

ELAINE: Listen, he didn't mean anything by that –

CIARAN: I know what he meant. And he's right.

ELAINE: He's just funny like that – old-fashioned. (*pause*)
                 But maybe you could fill in the time somewhere
                 else –

CIARAN: We've been over this, and I'm not workin' in a
                 burger joint. I'm qualified. Anyway, something'll
                 turn up. (*pause*) I was just thinkin', if you're not
                 gonna take my name tomorrow, maybe I should
                 just take yours.

ELAINE: Stop.

CIARAN: Ah, I was only jokin'.

ELAINE *pulls him out of the camcorder's view.*

KATE: Sorry, but you' re out of focus. Hello?

ELAINE: Let's get out of here, will we? Hardly seen you
                 all day, and anyway, I hate all this relative stuff.
                 Why don't we go over to your place. Mick hasn't
                 anyone staying tonight.

CIARAN: But...but it's unlucky Elaine. To spend the night
                 before the wedding with each other.

ELAINE: You don't believe that rubbish. I know you don't.

He disentangles himself from her and gulps his drink.

CIARAN: Oh I do. Strongly. Another drink?

*He hurries off, leaving her confused. DEIRDRE is next in the light as
MICK gallantly hands her a cup of champagne. His strut wavers as
KATE hands him a large circular deflector.*

286

KATE:	Could you just hold that up? Over your head? Perfect.
MICK:	Ah Jesus. (*to* DEIRDRE) You're the bridesmaid, aren't you? I'm Mick. Best man. It's me first time, doin' best man.
DEIRDRE:	Yeah? I've been through it seven times before. Always the bridesmaid, never the bride, as they say.
MICK:	Betcha didn't know this, but they say a surprising number of people meet their future spouses at a wedding.
DEIRDRE:	Really?
MICK:	Yep. How about meetin' up later tonight? Just so you can show me the ropes for tomorrow.
DEIRDRE:	Yeh, alright, I'd love to. In fact, if you wanted, we could go for something to eat now and then meet up again later, I know this really nice restaurant, it's sort of intimate –
MICK:	I think maybe just later. Casual like, a drink or two.
DEIRDRE:	Oh, OK. Great. Nine-ish?
MICK:	Eleven-ish?

VALERIE *and* CHRIS *are next.* VINNIE *pours champagne with a flourish.*

VALERIE:	You're certainly in a good mood.
VINNIE:	And why wouldn't I be? Isn't me daughter gettin' married in the mornin'?

He's gone again, humming loudly, patting backs and laughing.

VALERIE: You don't look too convinced Chris.

CHRIS: There's something going on and he's not telling
me. But the minute this wedding is over, I'm
going to get it out of him.

VALERIE: I wouldn't like to get on the wrong side of you
these days.

CHRIS: Those pills they gave me, they're incredible. I
think I'm going around half-stoned.

VALERIE: But it wasn't that serious, was it Chris?

CHRIS: No, no. They got it in time. Never been better.
Anyway. I haven't even had a chance to ask you
how you are, or how is work going, or was the
flight decent.

VALERIE: I'm okay, I'm still in the bookshop and the flight
was fine.

CHRIS: And?

VALERIE: And what?

CHRIS: I don't know, it's just that you never say whether
you're happy or you're miserable or you're dying
to come home out of it. You just never know
with you.

VALERIE: Well I suppose I am happy, whatever that
means. And London *is* my home now Chris.

CHRIS: I just always thought you'd be back. (*pause*)
Whenever you'd worked out what was eating
you.

288

KATE:	Sorry, a little to the left, thank you. And you're..?
VALERIE:	(*relieved*) Valerie. On the bride's side.
ALICE:	(*off*) Shit. Shit!
CHRIS:	And that'll be Alice. Get ready for a grand entrance. (*to* VALERIE) How are you coping with her?
VALERIE:	Mostly I want to flatten her. But I cope.
CHRIS:	It's your house. You could ask her to leave. It's high time she stood on her own two feet again.
VALERIE:	She'll go in her own time.

ALICE *totters on with a gift-wrapped present and the veil.*

ALICE:	Talking about me behind my back? I hope so. Here, Chris, this is for Elaine and Seamus.
CHRIS:	Ciaran. His name is Ciaran.
ALICE:	Is it? I've been callin him Seamus all evening and he hasn't corrected me.

She whips off the wrapping to reveal a tasteless figurine lamp.

ALICE:	You know, now that I look at it, it's a bit tacky, isn't it?
CHRIS:	I gave you that for your wedding four years ago.
ALICE:	Oh. Shit. Oh my God. Oh I'm so sorry Chris, I didn't know, you see I forgot to get a present and I just grabbed something from my own stuff –

CHRIS:	Actually Alice, somebody gave me that thing for my wedding and I palmed it off on you.

ALICE *becomes aware of the camcorder and manages a forced bray.*

ALICE:	Oh. Well, that's fine then, isn't it? And here's the veil. I'm afraid there's a tyre track on it. Long story. Is that champagne?
VALERIE:	It is, but we have mineral water too. I'll get you some.

VALERIE *goes to the table, as* PHIL *enters and looks around discreetly.*

ALICE:	Poor Valerie. I don't know what she'd do if she hadn't someone to fuss over. I'm dying to move out of her house, but I just couldn't do it to her.
KATE:	(*waving to left*) Could you just...a tad more...
ALICE:	But then I won't be in view.
KATE:	I know, but I have to get the rest of the guests. I don't want to offend anybody.

Offended, ALICE *marches off.* KATE *pulls* PHIL *into the light.*

KATE:	The bride or the groom?
PHIL:	I'm neither actually.
KATE:	What? Oh yes, I get it now, very funny. Could you stand just a smidgeon to the right? And look into the distance?

VINNIE *dashes across and pulls* PHIL *away.*

VINNIE:	What are you doin' up here?

PHIL:	That young one you have working for you below more or less threw me out of the shop, said she had to mop or something. I've to value the contents of your house too, you know.
VINNIE:	Get out and wait for me downstairs.
PHIL:	No problem. Oh, and Mr. Sands? Don't touch me again.

He exits. VINNIE stands watch by the exit, drinking heavily. ALICE manages to manoeuvre herself and CHRIS back in front of the camcorder.

ALICE:	I've just had a good chat with Elaine.
CHRIS:	Sorry?
ALICE:	Well, with me being her godmother and all, I'm responsible for her spiritually and morally and all that stuff, I read that somewhere. It's my duty to advise her about the marriage. There's a few pitfalls I've warned her about.
CHRIS:	I think it's a bit late to be warning her of pitfalls.
ALICE:	Well someone needs to.

ELAINE *and* NICOLA *are next.*

ELAINE:	Nicola? I thought you might have been upset. In the church, when we couldn't find you. You know, about not being a bridesmaid.
NICOLA:	I'm not upset. I'm dying to be a little flower-girl..
ELAINE:	I just thought it'd be less pressure on you. With the exam. Listen, you'll do fine. Brains to burn.

	Nobody has ever done the Leaving at sixteen in this family –
NICOLA:	Nobody's ever failed it either! Why did you have to go and set your wedding date for the very day my exams start?
ELAINE:	What? It just turned out that way, it wasn't on purpose –
ALICE:	Elaine! I didn't finish what I was saying earlier.
ELAINE:	Oh God.

She hurries off. FR. JACK makes for KATE, WILMA on his heels.

WILMA:	I hope I didn't come on too heavy earlier, Father.
FR JACK:	No, no, you're absolutely right. "Here Comes The Bride" it will be. And I have a version that'll knock your eyes out. Picked it up in the bible belt. Real authentic stuff.

He holds out a glass of champagne to KATE, who looks nervously at WILMA.

KATE:	I'm working. No thanks.
FR JACK:	Nonsense, this is a social occasion. Tell me now Kate, what's that circular thing that Mick's holding. It's on the tip of my tongue, but I can't remember what it's called.

WILMA grows suspicious as KATE searches for the right answer.

KATE:	It's a...it's a...it's a deflector?
WILMA:	Kate? I've noticed that you've most of the men on tape. Which is great, but perhaps you might

292

get the women too. We don't want to ruffle feathers. You know how guests are, like children. Come on Jack, we'll let her work.

FR JACK: Oh, no rush Wilma.

WILMA: (*reluctantly moving off*) Vinnie? Vinnie have you written your wedding speech yet?

FR. JACK *looks shrewdly at* KATE.

FR JACK: I remember now. It's a reflector. Not a deflector.

KATE: (*defeated*) My Da took a bad turn and I stepped in so that he wouldn't have to worry.

FR JACK: (*leaning in too close*) Your secret is safe with me, Kate. But I know a bit about video, so I'll give you a hand.

He grabs ALICE in passing and pulls her into the light. VALERIE has been making for ALICE with a mineral water. FR. JACK tries to make a quick escape.

ALICE: Oh don't rush off, Jack, we've hardly seen you since we arrived. We're starting to think you're avoiding us, aren't we Valerie? Our director here is getting all your attention.

FR JACK: I was just helping her.

ALICE: Of course. Where's she's gone...I was just advising Elaine about marriage, Jack. As Godmother.

FR JACK: I'm sure she'd benefit from your vast marital experience. How is Tommy anyway?

ALICE:	That was a bit below the belt, even if I did deserve it.

She blunders off as the rest fall silent. CHRIS *goes to them.*

FR JACK:	What? What did I say?
VALERIE:	They're separated. He's with someone else.
FR JACK:	Oh. Oh I didn't know. I'm sorry. That was awful.
CHRIS:	I wouldn't lose any sleep over it Jack. She's well able to dish it out but she can't take it.

NICOLA *passes, books in hand.*

NICOLA:	I'm going upstairs to study, and then I'm going to bed.
FR JACK:	I'll be saying a special prayer for you tomorrow Nicola.
NICOLA:	Well that certainly would put me mind at rest, Father.
CHRIS:	Nicola, you'll be sleeping in here tonight, you do know that, don't you?
NICOLA:	What?
CHRIS:	I'm sorry, it's just that we've so many people staying –
NICOLA:	Oh, great! Well, don't let me upset Elaine's wedding. Oh no. I've only got an exam tomorrow afternoon!

She exits. VINNIE *makes to go after her, but* ELAINE *stops him.*

ELAINE:	She's just under a lot of stress, Da. And I think she wanted to be a bridesmaid too. Just leave her.

But VINNIE thunders out, followed by CHRIS. Another silence descends.

WILMA:	Right then! Time for a final fitting everyone! And don't take any clothes until I give them to you. I did a wedding two years ago – Mount Juliet Hotel – fabulous – but didn't the valet service send the wrong clothes to the wrong rooms. Unfortunately, the mix-up concerned the bride and the groom. You can imagine.

The rest start to trail off. ELAINE catches up with CIARAN.

ELAINE:	Listen, I'm going down the pub later on, Mam said I had to cheer Alice up, she's upset or something. But I'm going to try and get away early, might call over to you at the flat.
CIARAN:	But Mick has a few of the lads organised for a couple of pints.
ELAINE:	Well, just get away early, like me.
CIARAN:	Did yeh want to meet for something special?
ELAINE:	Jesus, we're getting married in the morning Ciaran, do we have to have a special reason to meet any more?
CIARAN:	No, no course not. It's just that I'll be in late.
ELAINE:	I'll wait up for you. How about that.
CIARAN:	Ah, maybe we'll just leave it. We've both an early start, you know? Night love, see you in the mornin'.

He exits. After a moment, she follows. FR. JACK and VALERIE are left. KATE busily fixes them right next to each other. They stand rigidly.

KATE: Just you two then. Now, do you just want to chat away amongst yourselves?

VALERIE: Not really.

KATE: Oh. Right. Well, I'm sure I'm needed elsewhere. Oh and thanks Father. For your help.

She smiles at him, takes her equipment and exits. VALERIE looks after her.

VALERIE: Nice to know that some things never change.

FR JACK: I have no idea what you mean.

VALERIE: Oh relax Jack. No onlookers now.

FR JACK: You obviously never told them about us. Your family.

VALERIE: We were going to wait until we announced our engagement, remember? When that didn't happen, why bother?

FR JACK: (*evasively*) So. How have you been, Valerie?

VALERIE: Fine.

FR JACK: Seriously, Valerie.

VALERIE: What, you don't believe that I can possibly be alright? That I have the audacity to be absolutely fine without you?

FR JACK: I didn't mean that. Valerie, maybe we should talk.

VALERIE: What on earth would we talk about Jack?
                  Goodnight.

She exits. FR. JACK drains his glass and contemplates the half full bottle
of champagne. He grabs it and exits. Lights up downstage on VINNIE
sitting in a chair. During his monologue, the jingle starts up offstage,
throwing him off balance.

VINNIE: She looked at me like she didn't know me.
                  Nicola, upstairs. Public face slipped again. (*to*
                  right) Howya Missus Kelly ah sure we're blessed
                  altogether with the weather can I interest you in
                  a nice bit of round steak. (*to left*) A drawer out
                  the back bulging with unopened bills which one
                  will get paid this month? Was easy in the
                  beginnin'. No thought. Automatic. (*to left*) Shop.
                  Family. Weddin'. (*to right*) Bills. Solicitors
                  letters. Sheriff poundin' at the door. Just think
                  before you speak, count to ten, hold your tongue,
                  concentrate. (*to right*) Howya Missus Kelly oh
                  filthy day altogether can I interest you in a court
                  appearance. Fuck. No. Wrong. Getting hard now
                  pressure buildin' slippin' up more and more. (*to*
                  left) Another letter shit did she see the return
                  address ssssh not a word tear it up quick in the
                  fire Dr. Jekyll Mr. Hyde. Tight wire thin line
                  slippery slope concentrate concentrate.

Lights up in the butchers. He stays unmoving. LINDA enters, wearing
AMY's jeans and the new cardigan. PHIL. enters from the back with a
list.

LINDA: Ah, hello. Is Vinnie back there?

PHIL: No. I'm waiting on him myself. (*pause*) Funny,
                  isn't it, the smell in butchers. No matter how
                  hard they clean the place, there's still that smell.

LINDA: Funny all right.

PHIL: My girlfriend doesn't eat meat. Strict vegetarian.
               Won't go near me for two hours after I have a
               burger or something, imagine that? Mad.

LINDA: Mad.

VINNIE *stands tiredly and turns into the action.*

PHIL: Ah, Mr. Sands. Just wanted to check. Is that
               freezer – the new one – that in your name? Your
               sole name?

VINNIE: Yes.

PHIL *ticks his list and exits again out the back.* VINNIE *goes to* LINDA.

VINNIE: Stock-take. So, listen, Amy told me. Brave thing
               you're doin' Linda, not many would.

LINDA: Oh, I'm not such a martyr. Sr. Joan has been
               pushing me about her for the last year. There's
               not much more they can do for her since she
               turned eighteen. Biggest problem was
               convincing Paul. And now she says she doesn't
               want to come.

PHIL *enters again.*

PHIL: Excuse me. Mr. Sands, is that slicer registered in
               your name? It's not on lease?

VINNIE: No! I own it.

PHIL *exits again, watched suspiciously by* LINDA.

VINNIE: Between ourselves Linda, there isn't going to be
               a job here for Amy tomorrow. They're closin' me
               down.

LINDA:	What? Oh, that's terrible Vinnie –

VINNIE:	Yeh. But I'd like to see her settled.

LINDA:	You've been very good to her this past two years. All she ever talks about is you and this place. You've done a lot more for her than I ever did...

She trails off as AMY enters, wearing LINDA's dress which swamps her.

LINDA:	(*forced*) Oh, you look lovely! We did a swap, Vinnie.

AMY:	You said I had to think about it properly, Linda. I have. And I don't think I'll go, if that's alright.

LINDA:	Amy, you can visit. Can't she Vinnie? We'll be in Dublin all the time and you can visit Vinnie and Sr. Joan and –

AMY:	I know, but Vinnie needs me here Linda. I don't want to just walk out and leave him. Isn't that right Vinnie?

VINNIE:	Yeh, but there's no harm thinkin' about it.

AMY:	I have. I'm going to put away the meat into the fridge. It's time to close up. Bye Linda. Don't forget Easter.

She exits out the back, fluffing out the dress as she goes.

LINDA:	(*low*) The local boys. They're sniffing around and she's encouraging them. Sr. Joan doesn't know what she's been up to. She came in one night with scratches all over her hands and she smelt of drink. I have to get her away from them.

VINNIE:	I'll talk to her.
LINDA:	Would you? Just tell her I've everything set up for her at home, remedial classes and drama classes and –
MALE VOICE:	(*off*) Linda!
LINDA:	I'd better go. I've to break it to him that we'll be staying overnight. I'll call back early, alright?

She hurries out. PHIL *re-enters behind* VINNIE, AMY *on his heels.*

AMY:	He was back there Vinnie!
PHIL:	I told you he said I could be here. Now. The trolleys. Are they registered in your sole name –
VINNIE:	Yes. Yes. Yes. The trolleys, the fridges, the slicers, the knives, the sawdust on the floor, me daughter upstairs, they're all registered in my sole name. Idiot that I am, I paid upfront for everythin' I could, because I didn't want to owe any more than was necessary. If I'd got it all on lease, then you couldn't make off with it, could you?
PHIL:	But Mr. Sands, it's not on lease and that's not my fault, is it? Would I be right in saying that now? Just trying to do my job here. That's all.
VINNIE:	And I suppose the builder was only doing his job when he renovated this place and him with a contract to work on the supermarket. I suppose the bank was only doing its job when they threw money at me without so much as a word of advice. And I suppose the plannin' office was only doing their job when they let that big

300

fuckin' monstrosity go up down the road and ruin us all. And all I wanted was to do MY job!

PHIL: That walk-in cooler. That in your name?

VINNIE: You don't give a shit, do you.

PHIL: Just need to get finished up here tonight.

VINNIE: Oh yeah. Forgot. Yer goin' on holidays. Where you goin'?

PHIL: I'm afraid that's none of your business.

VINNIE: I'd say it's somewhere like Majorca, is it? Or Tenerife. Some cheap flashy resort full of people on twelve grand a year, all lettin' on they've made it.

PHIL briefly betrays his aggravation, but then goes back to his list with resignation.

PHIL: The walk-in cooler. That in your name or not?

NICOLA *blithely enters, absorbed in a textbook.*

NICOLA: My love is like a red red rose –

VINNIE: NICOLA! I mean, Nicola love, would you mind goin' upstairs?

NICOLA: Jesus Christ! I can't study upstairs! I can't study here! Where the fuck am I supposed to study? And don't you try bein' nice to me now Da! You pay more attention to HER than you ever do to me!

She points at AMY, then exits by the road. VINNIE takes PHIL by the shoulder and steers him firmly to the door.

VINNIE:	I won't have my family upset the night before the weddin'.

PHIL:	Right so. I'll be here early in the morning in that case. And Mr. Sands, what did I tell you about touching me.

VINNIE:	Don't you show your face here in the morning.

PHIL is pushed firmly out and exits. VINNIE brusquely exits upstage, AMY scurrying after him. Lighting change to church, dim. KATE enters with her notebook and a roll of masking tape. She looks around with trepidation. She reads a new letter.

KATE:	Kate. They took millions of tests and the results aren't back yet, but I know I'm fine, a little tired maybe. So just hold on until I get there tomorrow. Now. Try and get a quiet moment in the church to plan out your shots. Just follow the list below. First. Establishing shot of the church interior.

She busily tapes large X's to the floor, referring to the letter.

KATE:	Okay. LS groom and best man at the altar, close up groom...long shot of guests. Altar. Okay. (*reads again*) And remember, test the acoustics for echoes like I showed you.

She claps her hands several times and listens, satisfied. Then, a clap comes back. She tentatively claps again; another answering clap and a mournful moan. Terrified, she grabs her masking tape, her notes and flees. NOEL steps out of the shadows. He carries a small portable TV which he hooks up to the satellite cable. At a noise, he quickly steps back into the shadows. NICOLA enters with a textbook. She gets onto her knees.

NICOLA:	Hail Mary full of Grace the Lord is with thee blessed art though among women and all that.

Mary, this is difficult. You see, me studies lead me to believe that you don't actually exist, but I'm prepared to put that aside in me time of need. It's about this exam. Now, I'm not tryin' to say that it's more important to me than to anybody else. Sandra, a girl in my class, says she's gonna commit suicide if she doesn't get an A or a B plus – she has an old skippin' rope tied to her bedroom door for when the results come out, imagine that. But if I fail this exam tomorrow Mary, I know I'm gonna end up workin' in me Da's filthy butchers and marryin' some eejit like me sister and that'll be that, won't it? Please Mary. Cos I really really want to be a physicist and if you grant me this favour, I'll devote my entire career to provin' your existence.

She opens her textbook and shuts her eyes.

NICOLA: (*rapidly*) Get thee to a nunnery. Why, wouldst though be a breeder of sinners? I am myself indifferent honest, but yet I could accuse me of such things, that it were better my mother had not borne me.

She peeks at the book and is relieved.

NICOLA: Cheers Mary. Now, if only I knew what it fuckin' meant.

NOEL: It's the exchange between Hamlet and Ophelia, isn't it? It simply means that Hamlet is telling her to enter a convent, where she'll be in no danger of breeding sinners.

NICOLA: Thought you didn't do this for the Leavin'.

NOEL:	I didn't. But that doesn't automatically ban me from reading it, does it? And what are you doing here? It's late and the church is closed.
NICOLA:	Yeh? Well what are you doin' here so? Skulkin' around?
NOEL:	I can come and go as I please.
NICOLA:	The king and his castle. You're really uptight about this place, aren't you? Listen, mind if I stay here for a bit and study? Forced out of me own bedroom cos of HER weddin'.
NOEL:	Your sister's wedding you mean.
NICOLA:	Look, I've nothin' against her, alright? She's grand, she's fine, she's good crack sometimes. But nobody gives a damn that I've an exam tomorrow afternoon!
NOEL:	Well you can't stay here. I've things to do.
NICOLA:	So do 'em. I won't make any noise, I promise.
NOEL:	There's a programme I want to watch. Alone. So please...
NICOLA:	Alone? What is it, one of them nature things where they all run around naked?
NOEL:	Certainly not. Now would you mind leaving?
NICOLA:	Why don't you watch it at home?
NOEL:	I don't watch it at home because I can't put a satellite dish on the block I'm in and the cable people won't connect me until next year. Satisfied?

NICOLA: Jesus. Sorry.

She huffs back to her book. NOEL hesitates, but temptation gets the better of him. He turns on the TV, puts on a pair of headphones, and unearths a packet of popcorn. He watches intently, forgetting about NICOLA.

NOEL: Tanzania. (*Pause*) 2nd June 1945. (*Pause*) Gandhi. (*Pause*) Formerly known as Persia. (*Pause*) Watergate.

NICOLA: (*tentatively*) What does "calumny" mean? When he tells her if she marries someone else, she won't escape calumny?

NOEL: 1963. (*Pause*) Calumny. Means slander. (*Pause*) Winston Churchill. (*Pause*) He's putting a curse on her.

NICOLA: He was a right pig when you think about it, wasn't he? Lettin' on to be mad and then insultin' people.

NOEL: The whole point is that we don't know whether his madness is feigned or not.

NICOLA: It'd be much easier if we knew one way or the other.

NOEL: But then it wouldn't half as interesting, would it?

NICOLA: Here, d'you mind me askin', but what're yeh doin' in a dead end job like this when you know all about Shakespeare and have all the answers to them quizzes and you could be anythin' you want.

NOEL: Did it occur to you that this is what I might want?

NICOLA: Well, no –

NOEL: No! I wonder whether anything occurs to you
                     unless it directly concerns yourself.

NICOLA: I'm sorry, I didn't actually mean –

NOEL: If you actually meant it, then we'd all know
                     where we stood, wouldn't we? But it's the
                     throwaway comments, the careless remarks, the
                     casual quips, that's what cuts us to the quick,
                     isn't it? Because we don't understand where that
                     cruelty comes from, we didn't consciously do
                     anything to provoke it. Try telling your half-
                     sister that you're sorry you made her feel bad
                     because you moped and whined your way
                     through her wedding day, but that you Didn't
                     Actually Mean To!

NICOLA *grabs her book and runs for the exit.*

NOEL: Wait. I'm sorry. I apologise. Please. Stay and
                     study.

She stands frozen. He goes to her and takes the book from her hand.

NOEL: They'll want one of Hamlet's famous soliloquies.
                     You'll need to know that. Now. To die, to sleep –
                     no more, and by a sleep to say we end the
                     heartache... come on Nicola.

NICOLA: And the thousand natural shocks that flesh is
                     heir to; 'tis a consummation devoutly to be
                     wished.

NOEL: What does that mean.

NICOLA: Death is no more than a sleep.

NOEL:	Good. Go on.

NOEL sits down in front of the TV and starts to watch it. NICOLA inches to another chair and sits.

NICOLA:	To sleep, perchance to dream: ay there's the rub, for in that sleep of death what dreams may come when we have shuffled off this mortal coil must give us pause...give us pause...I can't remember...
NOEL:	Mitterand. Think, Nicola. You know it, you know you do.
NICOLA:	There's the respect that makes calamity of so long a life.
NOEL:	See, I told you. Chirac? Yes, Chirac. See Nicola? It's all in your head, it's just a question of digging it out.

She's asleep. He turns back to his TV. To black. As NICOLA goes off, raucous laughter in the black. Pub lights up. VINNIE sits centre stage. CIARAN, MICK and Friend 1 (FR. JACK) and Friend 2 (NOEL) loudly command a corner position, Friends with backs to audience. DEIRDRE, dressed to the nines, waits in another corner, ELAINE and ALICE in another. Action splits between CIARAN's group and ELAINE and ALICE.

VINNIE:	Whiskey please.
MICK:	(*to* CIARAN) Cheers. Soon I won't have a mate left to drink with, yer all gettin' married on me.
CIARAN:	It's natural, yeh know? People get married at our age.
MICK:	What're yeh tryin' to do here, exclude me from some sorta private club? Make me feel there's

	something wrong with me cos I haven't found me Ophelia yet and you have?
CIARAN:	Thought yeh weren't lookin'.
MICK:	I'm not! I am not! Alright? Here, d 'you want another –
CIARAN:	It's my round! I can still manage a round you know!

He thunders to the bar. After a moment, MICK *follows.*

ALICE:	It's one thing being left for a younger woman. I could have handled that. In twenty years' time, I would have expected it.
ELAINE:	(*wearily*) I know.
ALICE:	But being left for an older woman? A woman with greying hair and wrinkles, a woman with a daughter older than me, a woman he met in the park where she was playing with her grand-children – a grandmother for God's sake! He left me for a grandmother.
ELAINE:	I know.
ALICE:	Here. Have another drink. *I'm* not allowed one. Did you know that Valerie has put me off the drink?
ELAINE:	I know.
MICK:	So tell us. About this marriage thing. Sure she's the one?
CIARAN:	She's the one alright.

308

MICK:	Yeh, but how do you know? Like, in general.
CIARAN:	You just know.
MICK:	But how. How do you know that maybe you haven't already met The One but you didn't realise it and you let her go. How do you know if The One is out there for you at all. How do you know that the existence of The One is nothin' more than a big scam, and you should just settle for someone as disillusioned as yourself and get down to the business of endurin' each other because you can't bear to spend another second on yer own!
ALICE:	The note was pinned to the fridge with blu-tack. Blu-tack!
ELAINE:	I KNOW! Sorry. Aunt Alice? The break-up wasn't anything to do with...sex, was it?
ALICE:	No. I don't think so, I don't know for sure. The minute he said there was someone else, I just ran out the door.
ELAINE:	(*morosely tipsy*) I shouldn't be telling you this, but I think Ciaran's avoiding it. Sex, I mean. I don't know if it's me or if it's something else.
ALICE:	Want my advice? Confront him. Ask him why. That's where I went wrong. Here, have another drink.
CIARAN:	You alright?
MICK:	I just want to make sure I'm not missing out on The One, that's all. So, like, how did you know. With Elaine.

CIARAN:	(*fervently*) Well, I just knew, deep in me gut. Instinct, if yeh like. I knew from the first moment I laid eyes on her in the park. It was like...coming home. Felt like a great big part of me had been empty before I met her and now –
MICK:	Yeh yeh alright, I get the idea. Beyond me, I think. C'mon. We're wastin' valuable drinkin' time on this rubbish.
CIARAN:	Wait. Can I ask you somethin', like in general? About, you know, sex. Were you ever not able...if you were depressed about somethin' else, did you ever not feel like it?
MICK:	Naw, not me, no way. Oh, you mean you?
CIARAN:	No! Just talkin' in general.
ALICE:	Go on Elaine. Have it out with him. Better now than later.
ELAINE:	I don't know if that's such a good idea...
ALICE:	Nonsense. Give as good as you get, it's the only way. Don't slink off like I did. Do you want another drink?
ELAINE:	No!

ALICE pulls ELAINE to her feet and pushes in the direction of CIARAN's table. ALICE then exits.

ELAINE:	Hi. Sorry to interrupt. Need to talk to you Ciaran.
CIARAN:	Sit down there, you look a bit shaky.

310

ELAINE: (*loudly whispers*) Ciaran. D'you remember in the beginning, we used to be really really passionate?

CIARAN: (*mortified*) Ah, let's talk about that later, will we?

ELAINE: What later? You never want me in your flat any more.

The other three pretend to busily drink. CIARAN gets ELAINE to her feet.

CIARAN: Time to get you home I think.

ELAINE: (*loudly*) Stop patronising me! I need to know before tomorrow. It's important to me. Do I not do anything for you any more Ciaran? Is that it?

The other three and VINNIE look up in unison at CIARAN, then quickly away.

CIARAN: Know what your problem is? You always want it! You never leave me alone! Dunno how any man could keep up with you!

Horrified, she runs out. CIARAN slumps at the bar. GINA enters upstage in an outfit consisting entirely of leather and chains. She holds a whip and a scroll. Two helium balloons are tied by long strings to both her wrists. She halts, gathering her courage, then advances with bravado. All present look up. A great crude roar from the men's table stops her in her tracks.

MICK: Over here, love! Ciaran! Come back here.

GINA unfolds her scroll and gingerly lifts her leg onto MICK's chair.

GINA: Ciaran, I hear you've found a girl –

CIARAN *rejoins the group with a display of macho abandon and enthusiasm.*

CIARAN: It's not for him. It's for me!

GINA: What? Oh. Sorry. Sorry...

She scurries over to CIARAN, *searching for her place in the scroll.*

GINA: Hear you've found a girl...oh yeah...you're gonna give marriage a whirl –

More catcalls and whoops. GINA *shakily raises her voice.*

GINA: Soon you'll be chained to the kitchen sink – No more late nights or high
jinks –

She half-heartedly cracks her whip, to more wild cheers.

GINA: (*rapidly*) To give you a taste of what's to come –
When married and under the thumb –
I'm going to do Eileen – Elaine, sorry – a favour –
By breakin' you in, a job I'll really savour.
So get down on your knees and cower,
A good floggin' will keep you on the straight and narrow.

FRIEND 1:   Me next.

GINA: Could you – would you get down on your knees please?

CIARAN: That sounds good. What for?

GINA: I have to flog you.

More cheers and obscene comments. CIARAN slugs back his pint leisurely.

GINA: Can you get down please? It says here at the bottom of the poem "flog five times." Please. I have to do it.

MICK: Ah come on Ciaran, give her a break.

CIARAN: Hey, no problem. Give us another round here please!

GINA: Look, let's just get this over with, alright?

But CIARAN makes a complete production of it. Finally, GINA drops the scroll and flees to extreme downstage, where she attempts to flag a taxi. An embarrassed silence falls over the four men. The two friends leave.

MICK: (*curtly*) You could've done it a bit quicker than that. I've to go. Deirdre's waitin'.

He goes to DEIRDRE. CIARAN *sits alone, trying to keep up his act.*

MICK: (*to* DEIRDRE) I'm not late, am I? We did say eleven.

DEIRDRE: No, no, I'm a few minutes early. (*checks her watch*) Oh. A few hours actually.

She solemnly presents him with a white rose.

DEIRDRE: I once did bridesmaid for a friend of mine, she was from Africa, Zambia or somewhere like that. And they have a tradition where the bridesmaid gives the best man a gift. I ran to Interflora and I got this specially for you.

MICK: Oh. Right. Cheers. I, ah, haven't got you anything.

DEIRDRE: No, no, that's fine. You can give it to me tomorrow.

She sails out, MICK *trailing behind in trepidation.* CIARAN *exits slowly, coming face to face with* GINA.

CIARAN: Sorry. About that.

GINA: All you had to do was get on your knees! You could have made it easy for me! But no, you had to make me beg and grovel and plead with you, like I was some kind of...well I hope you got off on it! Taxi! Taxi! Bastards. They never stop when I'm in this gear. Taxi!

She shivers. CIARAN *takes off his coat and holds it out. Suspiciously, she slides in her arms. The helium balloons, still tied to her wrists protrude from the top of the coat either side of her head.*

CIARAN: Don't you usually have a minder?

GINA: He's off sick. And if a taxi doesn't stop, I've no way of gettin' home.

CIARAN: Can't have that. I'll get you home.

GINA: No, really, I'm fine –

CIARAN: Least I can do. Come on.

Protectively, he leads her off. Lights flicker warningly in the pub.

VOICE: Come on please! We must clear the house.

VINNIE gets unsteadily to his feet. A single bright light comes up downstage and pub lights go to black. Gaze fixed high above, he moves slowly downstage. He bends and picks up imaginary pebbles and hurls them in the direction of his gaze.

VINNIE: That's great that's ace that sets the pace that's
                great that's crazy prices. That's great that's ace
                that sets the pace THAT'S GREAT THAT'S
                CRAZY PRICES. Why aren't you playin' it
                now? Why are you quiet for once? Probably
                home in yer beds, whoever you are, safe and
                sound and snug, bloated from your hefty annual
                reports and your fat audited accounts. Come on
                out! Come on! Show yerselves, have the
                decency to let the rest of us see what you look
                like. We deserve that much, what d'you think?
                Ah, faceless bastards hiding behind yer suits and
                yer shiny shoes and yer young squeaky clean
                store managers and yer stupid slogans.

*He hunts around for more pebbles, but can't find any. Finally, he takes
the loose change from his pocket and flings it outwards.*

VINNIE: Go on. Might as well take that as well. Take it
                all! Take the whole shaggin' lot. (*shouts*) That's
                great that's ace –

VOICE: (*OFF*) Will yeh ever shut up down there! It's
                late!

*VINNIE stops chanting and sits down on the road. AMY appears out of
darkness behind him.*

VINNIE: What are you doing out. They'll be worried.

AMY: I got out the window. They doesn't know.

With great ceremony, she takes an envelope from her pocket.

AMY: I told Sr. Joan I needed to have my wisdom tooth
                out. There's forty pounds there Vinnie.

VINNIE: Amy, Amy. I don't want your money.

AMY:	Is my money not good enough.
VINNIE:	It's not that. I just don't want you to lie on my behalf.
AMY:	I don't care if I get into trouble because of you.
VINNIE:	Well you should.
AMY:	Do you not want it so.

He takes the money. She smiles, helps him to his feet and leads him off.

TO BLACK.

At top of ACT TWO, a stepladder stands downstage. Lights up, the living room of MICK and CIARAN's flat. DEIRDRE's skirt hangs haphazardly from a ceiling hook. Her blouse and tights from another. DEIRDRE, wearing a sheet, and MICK, in boxers, lustily paw each other. GINA enters, wearing her costume with CIARAN's coat over it, and holding a single limp helium balloon. DEIRDRE manages to tear herself away from MICK.

DEIRDRE:	Hi! I'm Deirdre. I saw you in the pub last night, but we haven't been introduced.
GINA:	Hi. I'm Gina. It's kind of a long story.
DEIRDRE:	Listen, it's alright. He told us.
GINA:	Told you what.
MICK:	Did they take much?

316

GINA:	Who?

DEIRDRE:	This country...you walk down the street, minding your own business and next thing your handbag is gone.

GINA:	Oh, yeh. He was good to give me his couch for the night. I hope we didn't wake you up, comin' in so late.

DEIRDRE:	No.

MICK:	No.

This prompts another pawing session. GINA takes a piece of paper from her pocket and reads it feverishly. CIARAN enters with trepidation.

CIARAN:	(*mutters*) Mornin'.

MICK and DEIRDRE barely look up, then go back to whispering sweet nothings to each other. CIARAN quickly guides GINA downstage, where they hiss.

CIARAN:	So. I suppose this is it.

GINA:	What?

CIARAN:	Well, goodbye.

GINA:	What?

CIARAN:	I have to get ready. So, like, see yeh. See yeh a round.

GINA:	What!

MICK *and* DEIRDRE *look up.* CIARAN *pulls* GINA *further downstage.*

CIARAN: Gina, what exactly is it yer expectin'? A marriage proposal? I'm sorry, but I'm already supposed to be marryin' someone else. This mornin', in fact.

GINA: Don't flatter yerself. I get hustled out of your bed like I've some kind of contagious disease, I'm shoved down here onto that couch and now you're just going to abandon me? With no clothes? And no way of gettin' home?

CIARAN *fumbles in his pocket and unearths a wad of money.*

GINA: What do you think I am.

CIARAN: I'm sorry, that was awful. I don't normally...look, I'll get you some breakfast and some clothes and then I'll ask Mick to drop you home. Okay? Okay?

GINA: Yeh, okay. It's just that I've to collect me bunny girl outfit from the dry-cleaners for a one o'clock gig. But it's a retirement party so it should be fairly sedate.

CIARAN: I'm really sorry again about last night. Me, in the pub.

GINA: You don't have to keep apologisin'. From some of the stories I've heard from the girls, it can be a lot worse. One of 'em was chased all the way to Phibsboro last week.

CIARAN: You were right to leave when you did.

GINA: No, I wasn't. I was paid to be there, and I shouldn't have run out. Just lost me nerve for a minute. Last night – it was only me third night on the job. Just got to get used to it, that's all.

| | Denise – she works with me – she says that you have to learn how to play it, you have to get into the swing of it and that after a while, you start to enjoy it. |

CIARAN: Ah Jesus, no one could enjoy that.

GINA: And tell me, Mr. High and Mighty, what do you do for a livin'?

CIARAN: I'm...between jobs.

GINA: Well I was too. Startin' work in a restaurant in August – nothin' special, but it's a nice place – and I have to pay the rent in the meantime.

She starts to practise a few steps, looking at the piece of paper.

GINA: Dave, I hear you're hittin' sixty, but you're still pretty nifty –

CIARAN: Who composes that shite?

GINA: This is one of the better ones.

CIARAN: Gina? You didn't say anythin' to Mick or Deirdre, did you?

GINA: Course I didn't. Why would I. Look, I don't normally pick up my customers. And I certainly don't go around braggin' about it.

CIARAN: Well I don't normally do it either.

GINA: Yeh? Could've fooled me, if you don't mind me sayin'.

CIARAN: The night before me weddin'. Oh Jesus.

GINA:	I could be completely wrong here...but maybe you don't feel sure about this woman –
CIARAN:	Well you are completely wrong. I am sure about her.
GINA:	Why did you do it then? Last night, with me.
CIARAN:	Too much drink.
GINA:	You weren't drunk.
CIARAN:	You should have stopped me! You knew all along I was getting married today!
GINA:	I'm not the one gettin' married. I don't even have a boyfriend. And I didn't make the first move in that wine bar last night. Maybe I don't feel brilliant about the whole thing, but I had too much to drink and it just happened, okay?
CIARAN:	But you weren't drunk either, were you?
GINA:	I...look, I've had seven horrible gigs in three days. And last night, we had a laugh and we talked and you treated me like I was somebody. I forgot after a while that I was in this gear. I just needed to be reminded, that's all.
CIARAN:	I've a bit more at stake.
GINA:	Don't even know her, but I pity her. Elaine.
CIARAN:	Why?
GINA:	Here you are, lickin' your wounds and feelin' sorry for yourself when it's her you should be feelin' sorry for.

CIARAN:	(*blurts*) I can't do it with her anymore. Can't sleep with her. I'm marryin' her this mornin' and all I can think of is tonight in Jury's honeymoon suite.
GINA:	And what was I, practice?
CIARAN:	Something like that.
GINA:	Cheers. Listen. I have to go.
CIARAN:	Should I tell her?
GINA:	I'd say she'd probably find out off her own bat tonight.
CIARAN:	No. I mean about you. About last night.
GINA:	Well I don't know. Sorry, but I really have to go. (*to* DEIRDRE) Could I borrow some clothes?
DEIRDRE:	I'll see if I can get you something of Mick's.

She glides out, GINA *following.* MICK *looks dreamily after* DEIRDRE.

CIARAN:	Mick. I'm in a bit of state.
MICK:	Wouldn't expect you to be any other way. And you goin' to be tied lock, stock and barrel to the woman you love in...oh, less than four hours.
CIARAN:	Leave off the sarcasm for once.
MICK:	I'm not bein' sarcastic. You see, Ciaran, I think I've found her. The One.
CIARAN:	Sorry, but I'm not with yeh.

MICK: I was all set for the one night stand, you know,
                         but instead, I found her. The One. Deirdre.

CIARAN: Oh. That's great, but right now –

MICK: Like, it just came out of the blue.

DEIRDRE *arrives in holding a pair of his jeans. She is unnoticed.*

MICK: Cos she's not really my type. You know, where
                         the desperation wafts off 'em like a fog, and
                         they've marriage tattooed across their foreheads.
                         The type who just try too bloody hard, it'd
                         frighten any man off.

DEIRDRE *races out.*

MICK: But it was exactly like you said. You know,
                         when you described how you feel about Elaine.
                         It's like a blindin' light, it's like a part of you was
                         missin' and you didn't realise it until you met
                         her, and then you feel complete. It's like what
                         you said about comin' home –

CIARAN: I know what I said. I know what I fuckin' said!
                         (*pause*) She didn't sleep on the couch. Gina.

MICK: What? You mean...ah Jesus. Ah Jesus Ciaran.
                         You're somethin' else.

CIARAN: It's nothin' you don't do seven nights a week if
                         you get the chance!

MICK: It's different though when you're with someone
                         who matters to you.

CIARAN: Just because you've found true love overnight –

322

MICK:	Yeh, yeh maybe you're right. And I know I wouldn't do that to Deirdre. I wouldn't.
CIARAN:	Look, I feel bad enough as it is. I kinda counted on you for a bitta support. You're supposed to be me friend, me best man. I need some help here Mick!
MICK:	I'm not breakin' it to Elaine, if that's what –
CIARAN:	No. I'll do that myself.
MICK:	Want my advice, keep yer mouth shut. What yer after doin' is bad enough. It'd be ten times worse if you told her on her weddin' mornin'. Don't do it. Don't do it.

But CIARAN *swiftly exits.*

MICK:	Ciaran, it's seven o'clock in the mornin'!

He exits at a run. *GINA* re-enters. She starts to pluck *DEIRDRE*'s clothes from the ceiling hook and put them on. *DEIRDRE* enters cautiously. She sees the clothes and bursts into tears.

GINA:	Sorry. Are these special? I just couldn't find you –
DEIRDRE:	Take them. Burn them. I never want to see them again.
GINA:	Listen, are you alright?
DEIRDRE:	No, I'm not. I'm one of those desperate women, can you not tell? There's nothing worse than being branded that, is there? People can call you plain, or fat, or boring, or stupid, but nothing quite carries the same punch as "desperate". Desperate for somebody. Anybody. Anything.

323

GINA: Whoever told you that, don't mind them –

DEIRDRE: Nobody told me! That's the point! I asked her to
                     tell me if I was doing anything wrong and she
                     swore I wasn't.

GINA: Who?

DEIRDRE: Elaine. I thought she was a friend, I thought
                     she'd tell me the truth if I asked. I asked her
                     yesterday, and she was so smug, now that I
                     think of it, so smug that she'd found someone
                     special and that I had nobody.

GINA: I don't think she's got much to be smug about, to
                     be honest. Listen, Ciaran's friend, I don't know
                     his name...?

DEIRDRE: Yeh? Well I can't remember it either.

GINA: Anyway, Ciaran said he'd ask him to give me a
                     lift home, but I'm just gonna slip out.

DEIRDRE: I'm coming with you.

*They exit. To black. AMY enters in the black and plays the cello, a
mournful version of "Here Comes The Bride". A series of loud hammer
thumps accompanies her. lights snap on. VINNIE stands in the entrance,
in nightclothes, his hand on the light switch. The thumping continues
OFF.*

AMY: This doesn't sound like "Here Comes The
                     Bride". That priest said this would be "Here
                     Comes The Bride" Vinnie.

VINNIE: What's goin' on? What are you doing here at this
                     hour?

324

AMY:	The convent was locked last night so I had to stay here. And he came ten minutes ago.
VINNIE:	What?

PHIL *enters, carrying a metal tray.* AMY *immediately takes it from him.*

AMY:	The steaks go on that. You can't take that.
VINNIE:	What do you think you're doing here?
PHIL:	You knew I'd have to come back this morning. She told me yesterday that you're usually here by seven. Now, if you want to go on back upstairs, I'll finish here.
VINNIE:	But I'm not open today! And me family is asleep upstairs!
PHIL:	You've wasted three days on me already. Wasted them. Now I've another two of these to get through today, so give me a break here, will you?
VINNIE:	No, wait. Please. Just listen to me. What's your name. Your first name.
PHIL:	(*resignedly*) Ah here, don't start that stuff, please.
VINNIE:	Just tell me your name. Come on.
PHIL:	Phil. It's Phil, alright.
VINNIE:	Right. Phil. I'm Vinnie. Vinnie Sands. Pleased to meet you and sorry we got off on the wrong foot. Now Phil, I'm just like you. I've a job, just like you, and a family just like yours – have you a wife? Well my wife's name is Chris. She's

	been sick, very sick, and I don't want her upset, same as you wouldn't want your wife upset.
PHIL:	If I had one, Mr. Sands. Now would you mind –
VINNIE:	Call me Vinnie. And I've a daughter, Phil, her name is Elaine and she's gettin' married this mornin'. Don't do this to me. To them. Can you see where I'm comin' from, Phil? Can you see?
PHIL:	I don't mean to be blunt here, but you can wheel out your dying granny and I'm still going take your stuff.

He takes the tray from AMY's hands. VINNIE snatches it back.

VINNIE:	You're not walking out of here with everything I own in front of my family. No way. No way.
PHIL:	Please move away Mr. Sands. Just doing my job.
VINNIE:	You're not takin' this. Get out.
AMY:	Get out!
PHIL:	Ah Jesus. Do you know what I have to do now? I have to go all the way back to the office, get them hot and bothered enough to ring the guards for me and then I have to traipse back here. All that, Mr. Sands, and I'm still going take your stuff. Now, how about saving me the grief, eh?
VINNIE:	Get out and don't come back here today.
AMY:	(*shouts*) Don't you come back!
PHIL:	Nothing but grief.

326

He exits. VINNIE exits after him, reappearing a moment later with a hammer and a plank of wood. He puts the plank against a solid wall and starts to hammer.

VINNIE: He will not walk off with everythin' I've worked for for fifteen years. He's gonna have to get through this first.

AMY: You could go away.

VINNIE: And where would I go.

AMY: I dunno. Somewhere safe.

VINNIE: Did you think any more about Wexford? You'd get to live in a house, with your family. And Linda would give you a job.

AMY: She gave me a job last Christmas, when I stayed for a week. Takin' out the staples from her mail orders so that they could be photocopied. But she was the one to photocopy them Vinnie, then she gave them back to me and I stapled them all back together again.

VINNIE: Tell her you want a better job –

AMY: No. She doesn't know anything. Not really, Vinnie. Not like you. No.

VINNIE: Sr. Joan thinks it might be best.

AMY: I know they don't want me there any more either. But I'll go off on my own. I'll be alright. I'll go to a safe place. (*pause*) Do you want to come with me Vinnie?

VINNIE: Yeh. Yeh I'd love to. But they always find you.

| AMY: | No. Not some places that I know. |

She skips upstage and starts to play again. VINNIE *hammers.*

| VINNIE: | There was a woman in the ward opposite Chris. She went to the doctor three years ago because she felt a bit tired. They sliced off her left breast. A year later, they sliced off the other one. Eight months after that, they opened her up and scooped out half her insides, then stitched her back up. She was in that ward because they were back for the rest. But she said no, that they weren't goin' to take what was left. They looked at her like she was mad and got the poor husband to sign the form instead. The minute she was conscious after the operation, she was up and out of the bed and staggerin' down the hall, nurses and tubes trailin' after her. She was back ten minutes later cradlin' this plastic bag holdin' whatever they took out. They tried to take it from her but they couldn't. She said that it was hers and that was that. |

He leaves the wood and exits. Lights up in the Sands kitchen. ELAINE stands looking out a downstage window, in nightclothes, drinking a glass of Solpadeine. More thumps bring CHRIS on, also in her nightclothes.

| CHRIS: | What's going on? |

| ELAINE: | I don't know. But I'm not able for it. |

| CHRIS: | You look sick. |

| ELAINE: | I am sick. |

| CHRIS: | Nerves? |

| ELAINE: | Hangover. |

| CHRIS: | Ah, Elaine. Go back to bed and I'll bring you up some tea. |

| ELAINE: | No, I'm fine. |

| CHRIS: | Expecting somebody? |

A bright light suddenly comes up, blinding them.

| ELAINE: | Jesus. Turn that off! |

| KATE: | (*calling from off*) Sorry. |

The light comes back down. KATE scrambles onto the stage from the audience with a blackened bulb in one hand, the camcorder in the other. She's in yesterday's clothes, filthy now. She has dirt smudges on her face and wobbles with weariness.

| KATE: | This is yours. Sorry. I'll replace it. Do you have any children at this wedding? Rascally types? |

| CHRIS: | I don't think we have any children at all coming. |

| KATE: | (*distracted*) Oh. It's just that they add humour, my father says. A humorous touch is very important...I wonder if I could get hold of some... |

She trains the camcorder on CHRIS and ELAINE. ELAINE turns away.

| ELAINE: | Please. I'm really not up to this – |

| KATE: | I've just spent all night getting the lights right! Sorry...sorry...I need a mother and daughter shot. One. |

VINNIE enters carrying the hammer and a padlock. KATE grabs him and positions him at the other side of ELAINE. They stand rigidly.

329

VINNIE: Listen, sorry about the noise –

KATE: Louder please.

VINNIE: (*bellows*) – one of the shutters came loose.

CHRIS: What's going on with you two? One of you was
                        pacing the landing half the night and the other
                        was pacing the kitchen, I couldn't work out who
                        was where.

VINNIE: Did we keep you up? Did you not get enough
                        rest?

CHRIS: Right. I'm going to say this once and once only.
                        I am not an invalid. I am not sick. And I am not
                        going to stand for the two of you running after
                        me all day warning to me to take it easy! I've
                        every intention of getting drunk and dancing
                        until dawn. With or without your permission.
                        Now. Who's going to start?

*FR. JACK wanders on in his night attire. VINNIE and ELAINE use the
distraction to escape. FR. JACK unearths a piece of paper which he
hands to CHRIS.*

FR JACK: I had the most amazing dreams last night.
                        Absolutely amazing. And I got up in the middle
                        of the night and re-wrote the readings for the
                        Mass, Chris. Far too stuffy. Let me know what
                        you think.

CHRIS: Seems like I was the only one actually in bed
                        last night.

FR JACK: Morning Kate! (*loud whisper*) Getting on
                        alright?

KATE: (*whispers*) Yes thank you Father.

The thumping starts up again from OFF. VALERIE enters in a nightgown, followed by ALICE. FR. JACK is momentarily riveted, then bolts out.

CHRIS: Oh don't look at me. Nobody tells me anything around here anymore.

ALICE *manages a dramatic sway, captured by* KATE.

ALICE: My head is splitting, I've a sick stomach and I think I'm coming down with the flu. And who's Kate.

KATE: Me.

ALICE: Here.

She efficiently thrusts a letter at KATE, then sways weakly again. VALERIE puts her hand on her forehead.

ALICE: I already took my temperature. It's a hundred and ten.

CHRIS: If it was a hundred and ten Alice, you'd be dead.

VALERIE: Chris, she does feel a bit hot.

ALICE: And I've been vomiting. All night long. I think I might have food poisoning.

CHRIS: I thought you said it was flu.

ALICE: I'd say it's a combination. You don't know my stomach Chris. Valerie knows it well.

CHRIS: I'd say she does alright. I'll call a doctor –

ALICE: No! I mean, all I need is to go back to bed.

CHRIS:	But you'll miss the wedding.
ALICE:	And it'll kill me. But I don't want to risk ruining it.

She lurches to the table and sits.

CHRIS:	You were looking for humour, Kate?
VALERIE:	Maybe she is sick.
CHRIS:	She doesn't know what sick is. (*to* ALICE) I've the most amazing collection of pills upstairs Alice. I'll get you a selection and I guarantee that you'll be able to come to the wedding.
ALICE:	Oh. Right. Well that'd be great, Chris.

CHRIS *exits.* ALICE *immediately drops all pretence.*

ALICE:	I can't do it, Valerie. I can't go to this wedding.
VALERIE:	It's only for a couple of hours.
ALICE:	A couple of hours of wondering what I did wrong and thinking about him living in my house with that woman.
VALERIE:	Well, you moved out Alice. It was your decision.
ALICE:	Oh what would you know! With your nice safe solicitor who hangs around the house like an old faithful mutt. Sometimes I kick him in passing to see if he's alive. It's easy to give advice when you haven't been cast aside like a mismatched sock, without explanation or apology or warning.

332

VALERIE:	How do you know, Alice? How do you know I haven't? Have you ever asked me?
ALICE:	Well, no, but it's obvious that –
VALERIE:	No! Well you don't have a monopoly, you know!
ALICE:	What? Has the mutt dumped you? You're better off, Val –
VALERIE:	He hasn't. I was just making a point.

ALICE *gets to her feet.*

VALERIE:	Where are you going.
ALICE:	(*evasively*) I think I might go for a walk. Exercise.
VALERIE:	But we'll be getting ready soon.
ALICE:	Cellulite Valerie. We must fight it at every turn.

She exits, VALERIE hurrying after her. KATE turns off the camcorder and slumps onto the table. She opens her letter.

KATE:	Kate. Not feeling too good this morning I'm afraid. But I'll be there, don't you worry, I just need to get up and about. Here are few last minute reminders. This morning, your first priority is the bride's preparations and then her and her father leaving the house. I've sent over a lamp which you can fix high to give you some light. Good luck.

She drops the letter, lays her head onto her arms and nods off. CHRIS re-enters in a flurry. KATE jerks awake.

CHRIS: You haven't seen Nicola, have you?

KATE: Nicola? No. Is something wrong?

CHRIS doesn't answer and exits. KATE climbs the step ladder and during the next scene, readjusts lights. Lighting change to the butchers. AMY enters and plays Jack's version of "Here Comes The Bride." She's wearing a formal dress hat. LINDA enters, carrying a holdall. She stops short.

LINDA: I never knew you still played.

AMY: I play all the time. But only in my room.

She continues to play, oblivious. LINDA moves forward to stand behind her.

LINDA: I packed that for you. The day they drove you to Dublin. I packed that and I packed your pink gingham skirt and your jumpers and a Mars bar. D'you remember, you used to go mad for Mars bars. And Auntie May came in to me as I was packing and she asked was I sure. Was I sure that I wouldn't miss you terribly. I knew she was hoping I'd say no, because she didn't want to have to take in the two of us, she was getting on. But she would have kept you if I'd say yes, she was that kind of a woman. She stood there, waiting for the answer, and all I could think was that all our lives, you were the one to grab all the attention, you were the number one concern, you were the stone around my neck. "Is Amy alright Linda?" "Keep an eye on Amy Linda." "Linda, don't be so selfish, take Amy out to play with you. I saw my chance to grab all the attention for myself. And I said no. Let her go.

AMY: I can't make this sound like "Here Comes The Bride."

LINDA:	Here, Sr. Joan packed your clothes last night. Do you want to get changed out of that dress?
AMY:	No. I like it.
LINDA:	She was up all night, you know. Sr. Joan. She was worried because you didn't go back to the convent. She was worried that you might have been out with somebody. Were you Amy?
AMY:	I was here. With Vinnie.
LINDA:	Did he speak to you? About coming to Wexford?
AMY:	I'd only be in the way, with you and him.
LINDA:	No, you wouldn't. Paul wants you to come as well. He spent all last weekend doing up the spare bedroom.
AMY:	Addled Amy. That's what he said on the phone one day to his friend. I heard him.
LINDA:	What? I'm sorry Amy. You can be sure he won't say it again.
AMY:	I don't care. Because I'm not going.
LINDA:	Please Amy. I can't keep calling back here! Paul's got work this afternoon. We need to go home.
AMY:	Go home then. Nobody asked you to come here Linda.
LINDA:	Oh, that's lovely. I'm only trying to do the best for you Amy. I thought you'd be pleased. I thought you'd be glad! It's not easy, you know,

	arranging everything and pleasing everybody and doing a bloody balancing act!

AMY: You didn't come at Easter and nobody asked you
                  to come now!

She picks up the holdall and childishly throws it at LINDA.

LINDA: (*temper rising*) I didn't come at Easter because
                  Paul and I separated for a while Amy. You see,
                  he thought I was making a mistake. You don't
                  have to do this, that's what he said, you're only
                  young and just married, she's not your
                  responsibility. Well you are my responsibility
                  and I've finally managed to convince him of
                  that! And you're not making any of it easy!

AMY *looks stricken.* LINDA *immediately deflates.*

LINDA: But I want to do it as well. Of course I do! I
                  want you with me Amy.

AMY *runs off upstage.*

LINDA: Amy? Amy!

She gives up and exits downstage. Lighting change to house. The stage is empty, save for KATE on the stepladder.

WILMA: (*OFF*) Mind the hem Elaine!

ELAINE enters, followed by VALERIE, FR. JACK, VINNIE and CHRIS, all in their wedding outfits. WILMA brings up the rear.

WILMA: You all look absolutely fabulous!

She claps loudly and proudly. The group morosely drifts to the four corners of the stage. VINNIE *paces, looking at his watch.* ELAINE

336

stations herself by the window, looking out. WILMA *slowly stops clapping.*

WILMA: I thought it might be best to get you all ready. Thought it might lift the spirits. (*pause*) You've checked everywhere?

CHRIS: Everywhere we could think of.

ELAINE: Twice.

VALERIE: She'll turn up.

Suddenly the stage is plunged into darkness. KATE *screams.*

WILMA: Kate? Kate are you alright up there? (*pause*) Kate!

KATE: (*mumbles*) I'm fine. Sorry everybody. Don't move.

A flashlight beam comes up and plays haphazardly over them all, then KATE *focuses it on wiring. The rest continue talking in the black.*

FR JACK: Did anyone ring the guards?

CHRIS: They won't do anything until she's missing for twenty four hours. They asked me when I saw her last and I had to tell them that I didn't know. I didn't even check on her last night and she with an exam today.

VINNIE: She'd better turn up soon if she knows what's good for her. Sit down, Chris.

CHRIS: Well I would if I could find a chair.

KATE: Two seconds!

337

WILMA:	I hate to ask this, but if she doesn't...do you still want to go ahead with the wedding?
VALERIE:	Is that all you care about?
WILMA:	It's just. that if we're going to cancel, I'll have to make some phone calls, to make it easier on Chris in the next few days, that's all. I am on your side, you know.

The lights come back up.

FR JACK:	Ah. Let there be light. Well done Kate!
KATE:	Thanks Father.

At VALERIE's *knowing look,* FR. JACK *goes over to her, businesslike.*

FR JACK:	Didn't want to ask this in front of everybody, but where's Alice?
VALERIE:	She said she was going for a short walk. She must have covered greater Dublin by now.
FR JACK:	She'll turn up. Like a bad penny.
VALERIE:	At least she told me she was going.
FR JACK:	Valerie. I need to talk to you. To explain.
VALERIE:	Save it, Jack.

FR. JACK is mute. Footsteps approach from OFF. Everyone looks up hopefully, as VINNIE dashes to the exit. DEIRDRE makes a dramatic entrance, the bridesmaid's dress trailing from her hand. She pushes past VINNIE.

CHRIS:	You haven't seen Nicola have you?

DEIRDRE:	No.
WILMA:	Deirdre, you're supposed to be at the church!

DEIRDRE *shoves the bundled up bridesmaid's dress into her hands and marches down to* ELAINE.

DEIRDRE:	You lied to me.
ELAINE:	What?
DEIRDRE:	You know what I mean.
ELAINE:	I'm sorry, but I don't Deirdre. Look, can we talk about this later? Nicola's missing.
DEIRDRE:	What? Missing? Oh, Elaine. I'm so sorry.
ELAINE:	We thought you might have been her. And you know, my first thought was that it might be Ciaran. We had a huge fight. Thought it might have been him coming to say he was sorry. Awful, amn't I? And Nicola missing.
DEIRDRE:	She'll turn up. There's a little while to go yet.
ELAINE:	Anyway, what have I done on you?
DEIRDRE:	No no, that can wait until later.

She sails past them all again, grabbing the bridesmaid's dress from WILMA *as she passes, then exits. Another long tense silence.*

VINNIE: eleven?	Where is she! Doesn't she know that it's at
CHRIS:	Vinnie, calm down please! The main thing is that she's alright, surely?

339

More footsteps from OFF. Everybody looks up hopefully. ALICE *arrives in in her wedding outfit. She carries a miniature ornamental fire shovel.*

ALICE: Not late am I? Good God, you'd swear
                          somebody had died.

VALERIE: Alice –

ALICE: Uno momento, Valerie. Save the lecture for a
                          second.

She hurries down to ELAINE *and thrusts the shovel at her.*

ALICE: I didn't wrap it. They only had wrapping paper
                          with "Happy Birthday" on it in the shop. I hope
                          you like it. It's gold-plated. See, I was looking
                          for something practical, tasteful and that you'd
                          use for years to come. You and Seamus better
                          think of me every time you light a fire.

ELAINE: His name is Ciaran, Aunt Alice! Ciaran!

ALICE: Ciaran. Sorry. (*to herself*) Ciaran-Ciaran-Ciaran.

ELAINE: Anyway, we don't have a fireplace in the new
                          flat.

ALICE: Shit. You can change it. The man in the shop
                          said you could change it. I bought it in...shit,
                          where did I buy it. It'll say it on the receipt. Did I
                          get a receipt? (*hisses*) How did it go last night?

VALERIE: Alice! Nicola is missing. You haven't seen her in
                          your travels, have you?

ALICE: Missing? That's terrible Chris. Do you remember
                          that poor girl who went missing from the house
                          opposite us last year Valerie and...(*she catches*

340

herself on) She'll turn up. Course she will. Here
we are. That receipt.

*She rummages in her bag. An empty can of lager falls out and rolls
across the floor. Into the silence, NICOLA's voice from OFF. Lights up
downstage. NICOLA approaches, a book in her hand.*

NICOLA: (*rapidly*) Not this by no means that I bid you do:
Let the bloat king tempt you again to bed, pinch
wanton on your cheek, call you his mouse, and
let him for a pair of reechy kisses, or paddling in
your neck with his damned fingers, make you to
ravel all this matter out that I essentially am not
in madness, but mad in craft. (*checks the book*)
Yes!

She saunters upstage, lights back to the wedding party.

NICOLA: Am, hi. I suppose I'm cuttin' it a bit fine.

ALICE: There. You see? She's home safe and sound.

CHRIS: I thought you were in a ditch!

NICOLA: What?

*CHRIS flings herself on Nicola, smothering her. VINNIE advances
slowly.*

VINNIE: Where were you? Eh? What were thinkin' of,
doin' this to us all? Doin' this to your mother and
she not well? Doin' it to your sister and she
about to get married? Have you no thoughts for
anybody but yourself!

ELAINE: Ah Da, she's back, it's alright –

VINNIE: It's not alright! Where were you! What gives you
the right to jeopardise this weddin' when the rest

	of us are tryin' so hard to make sure it goes ahead?
CHRIS:	Vinnie!
NICOLA:	Da, I was only in the church. I went in there last night and I fell asleep. Noel fell asleep too and didn't wake me until an hour ago.
VINNIE:	Noel? NOEL?
NICOLA:	Yeh. He's alright, you know, really.
VINNIE:	I'm sure he is. You little –
CHRIS:	Vincent! Stop it now! Do you hear me? Stop it!

VINNIE *gets control of himself and moves away, all eyes on him.*

CHRIS:	Nicola, I know you probably think we're stuffy old parents and all that, but...to spend a night with someone? You' re too young, Nicola!
NICOLA:	What are you talking about?
ELAINE:	(*quickly*) She was studying. Weren't you Nicola.
NICOLA:	Well, yeh, course I was. What else would I be doin'?
ELAINE:	I heard her asking Noel if she could study there.
NICOLA:	What are you talkin' about now?

ELAINE *hustles her upstage.*

ELAINE:	I was trying to cover for you. You and Noel.

342

NICOLA:	What? Elaine, I WAS studin'. Jesus. (*pause, then rapidly*) Ah, listen, I never said it, but I'm happy for you today and – and I hope it all goes well.
ELAINE:	Yeh. Thanks.
NICOLA:	God. You stink of drink.

ELAINE *goes back to the window, where she anxiously looks down.*

VINNIE:	Wilma? Can we get goin' to the church please?
WILMA:	But we're waiting for the cars.
VINNIE:	Well get everybody ready for the cars!
WILMA:	I know how to do my job, Mr. Sands. (*pause*) And have you your wedding speech written?
VINNIE:	(*lying*) Yes.
WILMA:	Oh. Well, right, let's get this show on the road then. Elaine, get that veil on you. Deirdre, get the bouquets, Nicola, get your dress please, you'll have to change in the church, everybody go downstairs and be on standby for the cars! Chris, where's your hat?
CHRIS:	I don't know. I left it on my bed, but it's disappeared.

WILMA swiftly takes off. FR. JACK, DEIRDRE, NICOLA and VINNIE exit.

KATE:	(*calls*) Hold it a second please!

They all automatically trail back on, turns around and exit again, filmed by KATE. CHRIS hands VALERIE the reading.

CHRIS: If you wouldn't mind Valerie, I'll have to ask you to do the reading, because it's obvious that Alice never had any intention of coming to my daughter's wedding.

ALICE *looks like a bold child.* VALERIE *exits as* VINNIE *re-enters.*

VINNIE: The first car is here Chris. Come on.

CHRIS: In just a moment Vinnie. I'm sure it'll wait for me.

Reluctantly he exits. CHRIS *hands* ELAINE *the veil, which she ignores.*

ALICE: Trouble in paradise?

ELAINE: I don't need any more of your advice right now, Aunt Alice.

ALICE: Well you didn't have to take it, you know.

ELAINE: I bet you enjoyed watching that little scene in the pub last night, didn't you?

ALICE: I wasn't even there. But if you want to tell me what happened, I'll listen.

ELAINE: No. No I won't tell you, and do you know why? Because you'd just love it. You'd just love to hear me say that it's all turned out just like you expected so that I can join you in your misery!

ALICE *is frozen for an instant, then blunders out.*

CHRIS: Do you want to tell me what happened in the pub last night.

ELAINE *looks anxiously at* KATE, *who films.*

CHRIS:	Kate. Just give us a moment, will you?
KATE:	Oh. A long shot is more interesting anyway.
CHRIS:	(*to* ELAINE) Well?
ELAINE:	I can't.
CHRIS:	Why not?
ELAINE:	It concerns...sex.
CHRIS:	You're right, I wouldn't know anything about that.
ELAINE:	Oh Mam, it's not bridal nerves about losing my virginity.
CHRIS:	Come on Elaine. I'm not that old.
ELAINE:	It's just that it's not the sort of thing you swap stories about with your mother.
CHRIS:	You don't have to go into the gory details. In fact, I'd prefer if you didn't. Leave me with some illusions.

VINNIE *re-enters.*

CHRIS:	(*briskly*) Out please. We're having a private conversation.
VINNIE:	But the car is waiting –

She stares pointedly at him until he is forced to exit.

ELAINE:	It's Ciaran. He's been avoiding me for weeks and last night, well, he said it was because nobody could keep up with me. That's bad enough, but

it's worse if it's because he just doesn't want me anymore.

CHRIS: He'd hardly be marrying you if he didn't.

ELAINE: Maybe he wanted to call it off only it got too late.

CHRIS: Why don't you ask him.

ELAINE: I couldn't.

CHRIS: You could. That's if you still want to marry him. Do you?

ELAINE: I think so, yes.

CHRIS: Then go.

ELAINE *rushes off, bowling over* VINNIE *on his way back in.*

VINNIE: Where is she gone to now!

CHRIS: Will you try to curb your bad temper this morning. I don't know what's gotten into you but I don't like it.

He checks his watch again and makes for the exit.

CHRIS: Don't you walk away from me. I'm tired of being kept in the dark. It's not fair to me.

VINNIE: Later, alright?

CHRIS: You bet later. I'm sitting down with you tomorrow morning and you'll tell me Vinnie. I can handle the fact that we might be a bit in the red with the bank.

VINNIE:	Maybe. But just a bit, Chris.
CHRIS:	See? That wasn't so hard, was it? Now we can enjoy today. It's a proud day, Vinnie.

She exits. KATE moves down and films VINNIE, her movements assured.

VINNIE:	You're supposed to be in the church.
KATE:	No, I'm not. I have to film you and the bride leaving the house.
VINNIE:	Well I'm paying you and I'm telling you to go to the church.
KATE:	If that's what you want. But you can explain it to Wilma.

She sails out. VINNIE freezes in place as butchers lights come up around him. AMY hurries on with a cluster of knives which she stockpiles, then methodically ties with a piece of string. LINDA enters and watches.

LINDA:	Amy. I'm sorry if you thought I didn't want you, but I do. And Paul does. Just give it a try, that's all.
AMY:	But you don't need me.
LINDA:	What do you mean.
AMY:	You don't really need me Linda. You can get on okay without me. But Vinnie needs me.
LINDA:	Amy. Vinnie told me he wants to see you settled.
AMY:	What?
LINDA:	He told me to take you Amy.

AMY:	You don't know anythin' Linda! You come to see me every three months with your kids' clothes and your Mars bars and you don't know anythin'!
LINDA:	Amy, calm down.
AMY:	Vinnie didn't say that, I know he didn't. He likes me.
LINDA:	Well, of course he does, he's very fond of you –
AMY:	No! Not like that. Properly!
LINDA:	What do you mean, properly?
AMY:	(*excited*) We used to stay late here, him and me Linda, and he'd teach me things and tell me stories and sometimes he'd open a can of Heineken and let me have some. And one night, I let the mincer slip and cut my hands and he washed them for me and bandaged them up and he held them for a long, long time. And he said it was nice to have me there when he felt lonely, cos she was away. Then she came back from the hospital and he stopped, but he promised we'd do it again next week. He loves me Linda. I know he does.
LINDA:	(*carefully*) And did he tell you this Amy?
AMY:	He doesn't have to. I know. We're going away. Me and him.
LINDA:	Going where Amy?
AMY:	Can't say. But it's to a safe place.

She smiles then runs off upstage. LINDA backs out slowly downstage. VINNIE moves forward and takes out a piece of paper and a pen. He paces feverishly and writes.

VINNIE: I'd like to propose a toast to the bride and groom. I've known Ciaran for two years – three years – three years now and I'd like to welcome him into the family –

PHIL enters, followed by Man 1 and Man 2 (MICK and NOEL, in brown delivery coats and caps). They stand with backs to VINNIE, as though outside.

PHIL: Mr. Sands? Now Mr. Sands, listen here to me for a minute. I'm after ringing the guards and they'll be here in two minutes if I have any more trouble. I don't want to, but I'll do it if I have to. Mr. Sands? If you don't answer me, I'll just go and get them and they'll park outside your door with their sirens screaming and their lights flashing and they won't care what your neighbours think. Now come on, what do you say?

VINNIE: (*defeated*) Come in.

The three turn, advance and walk casually out the back. VINNIE goes back to his piece of paper and writes with difficulty.

VINNIE: I'm happy to see me daughter Elaine marryin' such a fine man...am...Elaine is...is me eldest daughter –

The supermarket chant starts from off, interspersed with thumps from the men out back.

VINNIE: I'm proud of her...and I'd like to wish them both every happiness...in their new life together...

The chant and thumps grow louder and faster. He abandons the piece of paper and puts his hands over his ears. AMY enters upstage, carrying her holdall, which is now bulkier and heavier.

VINNIE: Why can't they change it. Why can't they change the fuckin' thing.

AMY: What thing.

VINNIE: The jingle. The jingle from the supermarket.

AMY: But you can't hear it from here. The supermarket is all the way up the town. You can't hear it from here Vinnie.

The chanting abruptly stops. VINNIE looks up, more confused.

AMY: Are you ready?

VINNIE: Yes...is the wedding car outside?

AMY: I don't know. We're goin' away. You and me.

VINNIE: Amy. I'm not sure what you mean.

Man 1 enters upstage and travels downstage with a cardboard box.

VINNIE: (to him) That's mine. I paid five hundred pounds for that. I just want you to know that you're takin' what's mine!

AMY: Vinnie, I've got all the knives and cleavers in here, the new ones, before they found them. So that we don't have to buy them when we start up somewhere else again. And I have the slicer hidden away. It's heavy, but you promised to teach me how to use it. We have to go soon.

VINNIE: Amy... Amy what are you talkin' about?

His attention is fixed on Man 2 who enters upstage and moves down-stage carrying another box.

VINNIE: That's mine too. Thief. You're the one they
                       should have up in court!

AMY: (*insistently*) But Vinnie. We're goin' away.

VINNIE: (*distracted*) What? We' re goin' to the weddin'.

AMY: But you said you wanted to come with me!

VINNIE *ignores her as* PHIL *enters with a third cardboard box.*

VINNIE: That's my mincer. You thief. Going to fuckin'
                       Tenerife on my money. You scavenger.

PHIL: Excuse me please.

VINNIE: You think you can come in here and take all but
                       the ground from under my feet and justify it by
                       tellin' me you're just doin' your job? You
                       spineless lackey. I don't know how you can look
                       yourself in the mirror in the mornin's!

*PHIL goes to move past him. VINNIE hits him. He falls to the ground.
After a moment, he slowly gets up and looks at VINNIE almost in
contemplation. When he speaks, it is with quiet venom.*

PHIL: You said yesterday that I don't care about your
                       situation, and do you know something? You're
                       right. I don't. People like you, you think you've a
                       god-given right to throw your sob-story in my
                       face, expect me to understand, to turn around
                       and go, ah no, it was all a mistake, you' re a
                       decent man after all, you made some bad
                       business decisions but you shouldn't be held
                       accountable. Your sort, blaming the banks and
                       the supermarkets and the system for all your

misfortunes and when all else fails, you turn around and blame me. Because I'm an easy target, amn't I? Don't see you hitting the bank manager who took you to court, or the supermarket boss, or the Judge who made the order. No, because you're not brave enough to do anything except lash out like an animal and then whine behind closed doors about the injustice of it all. You're a coward and a failure, that's what you are Mr. Sands. I've done a lot of these, you know, and you're all the same. Cowards who fuck up and turn into pathetic bitter little men who can't believe for an instant that their mess might have anything to do with themselves. I can look myself in the mirror in the morning, Mr. Sands, precisely because I'm not like you.

VINNIE backs away from PHIL, afraid. PHIL casually proceeds out with his cardboard box. VINNIE hunches over, as if trying to ward off the words.

AMY: Vinnie, are you alright?

VINNIE: Let's go Amy. Let's go.

He takes her hand and dashes blindly out. Lights up on church. The place is again a hive of activity. NOEL sweeps the floor, DEIRDRE puts on make-up and MICK brings on chairs. VALERIE holds the reading, muttering under her breath. FR. JACK does a warm-up, dressed in conventional robes save for a multi-coloured sash around his neck. KATE is up the stepladder. CHRIS paces downstage. ALICE attempts to wrap a present on the ground. WILMA sweeps on with her clipboard. She's in a state of high nervousness.

WILMA: I'm sorry Chris. I simply don't know what's happened.

CHRIS: What did you tell the guests?

WILMA:	That we had technical difficulties. It was the best I could come up with. I sent them across to the pub.
CHRIS:	It's not your fault. I let Elaine go.
WILMA:	I could have explained Elaine away! Said she was just taking the tradition of the bride being late a little too far. But what about the groom? And the father of the bride? And the musician? I'm going to ring Vinnie again...

She hurries off. CHRIS *paces past* ALICE *who is on the floor.*

ALICE:	(*muted*) Chris? I got Ciaran and Elaine this. It's not very glamorous or exciting I'm afraid. I just wanted to get them something they needed.

She takes off what's left of the wrapping to reveal a toaster in its box.

CHRIS:	Believe it or not, nobody else has given them a toaster.
ALICE:	Really?
CHRIS:	Are you sober?
ALICE:	What a question to ask a person. I am actually. But I won't be persuaded into making any rash promises. (*pause*) About what Elaine said. Does it appear to people that I enjoy their misery?
CHRIS:	Yes, Alice, it does.
ALICE:	I must do something about that.

She goes back to her wrapping. MICK *approaches* DEIRDRE.

353

MICK: Deirdre, what's up? Like, I thought we had a
                   really nice night last night, but you left this
                   mornin' without sayin' goodbye and now you
                   won't even meet me eyes.

DEIRDRE: Look. We both got what we wanted last night,
                   let's just leave it at that.

MICK: What? But I'd like to see you again Deirdre.

DEIRDRE: Why? Make you feel good to have a fawning,
                   desperate woman hanging on your every word?
                   Or is it just sex?

MICK: What are you talkin' about? Look Deirdre, I'm
                   not very good at sayin' this stuff...I like you,
                   Deirdre. That's the only way I can put it.

DEIRDRE: You're right. You're not very good at saying that
                   stuff.

He produces a red rose from under his coat.

MICK: I hear it's a custom. In Zambia.

DEIRDRE: Oh. It's beautiful. Thank you.

MICK: Can I see you again. Please.

DEIRDRE: Well...I'll think about it.

MICK: When? I can meet any time, any place, maybe
                   tomorrow –

DEIRDRE: (*airily*) I said I'll think about it, okay?

*The lights dip alarmingly, then go back to normal. WILMA goes to the
foot of the stepladder, looking up suspiciously.*

WILMA:	Kate. Correct me if I'm wrong, but I'm not at all convinced that you know what you're doing.
KATE:	It's a lamp my father sent over. And I think this is really going to work, Wilma.
WILMA:	We'll soon see, won't we? Now go and get changed please.
KATE:	(*blurts*) But I don't need to get changed.

She steals an anxious look towards the entrance.

WILMA:	You do. We can't have the guests seeing you like that.

She takes off her scarf and drapes it around KATE's neck, trying to hide the worse smudges. VALERIE starts to practise her reading aloud.

VALERIE:	(*reading*) She rose from the lake like a Madonna in white...her chestnut hair soft and gleaming and true to memory...she walked on the water towards me, beckoning, I felt that familiar stirring in my heart and in my loins...(*petering out in embarrassment*).

The activity has stopped as everyone looks at her. WILMA dashes over.

WILMA:	Fr. Jack? I don't know whether we might be better off sticking to scripture. I know you've re-written it and all, but don't forget, God wrote it first.

FR. JACK snatches the reading from her. He fumbles in his pocket and unearths another piece of paper.

FR JACK:	No. Wrong one everybody. Sorry. This is the reading.

The activity resumes. JACK *and* VALERIE *converse in hushed tones.*

FR JACK: Sorry about that. This was just...my dreams last night. I often write them down, try and make sense of them later.

VALERIE: That one seems pretty straight forward to me. Feeling the pinch of celibacy, Jack?

FR JACK: Wouldn't be human if I didn't, Valerie. Still, we must all make sacrifices, mustn't we –

VALERIE: Don't spout that pseudo-religious claptrap at me, like I was just another of your adoring congregation. You're talking to Valerie, remember? Remember me Jack? Do you?

FR JACK: Yes. Well, go on.

VALERIE: What?

FR JACK: Go on with the recriminations and the accusations, which you've been dying to get off your chest since yesterday evening. Go on. I deserve them all.

VALERIE: You'd like that, wouldn't you.

FR JACK: I want to explain Valerie. Why I left. It was a terrible thing to do. I need to explain and to apologise to you.

VALERIE: But I don't care.

KATE *moves in with her camcorder, to* FR. JACK*'s discomfort.*

FR JACK: (*hissing*) What? You could at least listen to me Valerie! I deserve that much.

VALERIE: (*loudly*) Jack. You don't deserve the time of day.

She places the bible carefully in his hands and walks away. FR. JACK looks at KATE in embarrassment for a long moment, then slinks out of the glare of the camcorder. WILMA picks up a bunch of discarded flowers.

WILMA: Where's she disappeared to now...Nicola!

Lights up downstage. NICOLA is again hunched at the feet of the front row audience, dressed in her little flower girl outfit. She is buried in a book. NOEL enters, his dustpan poised.

NICOLA: Thanks. For last night. For helping me.

NOEL: You knew it all anyway.

NICOLA: No, not like you. I still wish you could go in there and do it for me.

NOEL: Yes. Well. I never did the Leaving myself. Missed too much school. Illness. Always sick. Terminal O'Toole, that's what they used to call me – casually, unthinking, just another playground jibe. The first time I picked up a dictionary was to find out what terminal meant. Fatal, it said. I had to look that up too. Ending in death. Now, I knew what that meant. Spend years waiting to die. Anyway, as you can see, I didn't. But I never managed to get past Inter, never mind the Leaving.

NICOLA: They have adult classes. You could still do it.

NOEL: Why?

NICOLA: What? Well, to get qualifications.

357

NOEL: There you go again. Making presumptions about other people. Do you really think that a little slip of paper with six honours on it is going to make any difference to me, or to anybody else come to think of it? What am I going to do with it? Put it on my mantelpiece?

NICOLA: I don't know, it might help get you a good job.

NOEL: And what's wrong with the one I've got?

NICOLA: Well, nothin' –

NOEL: Exactly. Now if you'll excuse me.

He carefully tips his dustpan and turns upstage. NICOLA looks doubtfully at her book and closes it, then exits. Lights back to the church.

WILMA: We'll give it another half hour and then I'm going to have to ring the hotel and cancel. They're already on standby.

Downstage, KATE again looks anxiously at her watch, before moving into her first position. She looks down for her mark. It's gone. Across the way, NOEL briskly starts to whip up the masking tape.

KATE: What are you doing? I need that!

NOEL: It's sticking to people's shoes.

KATE: But what am I...you'll mess up everything! This is this all planned out, I've my camera focused for these positions!

NOEL: Sorry. Oh, here. This came for you.

He hands her a letter. She frantically tears it open. NOEL tries to ignore her mumbling.

KATE:	Kate. They told me I had a slight heart attack. Very slight, stress and overwork. I can hardly believe it. And so I'm not going to be there this morning. You'll have to cope on your own. Sorry. Good luck. Dad.

She slumps in despair and worry. NOEL hesitates, then grudgingly stamps back into place a piece of tape he has ripped up.

NOEL:	But you'll have to take this up yourself later on. I'm not doing it. I don't get paid to do it.

He walks quickly off. KATE picks up her camcorder and tries out a few shots. She slowly tracks up the aisle to the entrance upstage, where she comes up against VINNIE and AMY, both still and unsmiling.

WILMA:	Oh wonderful! Everybody? I think we' re ready to start! Noel, run across and alert the occupants of the Horse and Hound, would you?
CHRIS:	Vinnie, isn't Elaine with you?

VINNIE does not answer, but it's obvious she's not with him.

WILMA:	(*wearily*) Cancel that Noel.
NOEL:	Certainly.

VINNIE walks brusquely past the posse to downstage, where he sits in a chair looking at the floor.

CHRIS:	(*to* AMY) And that's my hat! Were you in my bedroom again?
AMY:	Go away.
CHRIS:	I'm sorry, but I won't go away. And I'd like it if you were a little less rude to me.

AMY:	Take your stupid hat. You always take everything. You were meant to die!
CHRIS:	What?
WILMA:	Let me, Chris. (*gently*) Amy, I gave you a dress. A lovely dress. Why aren't you wearing it?
AMY:	(*on the verge of tears*) Because we were supposed to be goin' away. Instead he brought me here!

WILMA takes control, by putting a comforting arm around AMY and leading her to her cello.

WILMA:	Come on Amy, let's get you settled.

She continues murmuring to her, calming her down. CHRIS goes to VINNIE.

CHRIS:	What's going on?
VINNIE:	Nothin'.
CHRIS:	(*angry*) What is the matter with you?
VINNIE:	Nothing. Nothing, alright? I said I'd tell you tomorrow so I'll tell you tomorrow. Let's just get this wedding over with. Please Chris. Just leave me alone. Please.

He goes back to looking at the floor. NOEL passes by WILMA.

NOEL:	There's another wedding due here in about an hour. I don't know if you knew that.
WILMA:	How could I know that when you didn't tell me?
NOEL:	Slipped my mind. Sorry.

WILMA *hurries down to* VINNIE, *oblivious to his mood.*

WILMA: Your wedding speech Vinnie. Can I have a look over it.

VINNIE: Haven't got it written.

WILMA: (*lightly scolding*) I ask you to do one thing and you can't even manage that. I asked you this morning if you had it written, and like a coward, you said you had.

VINNIE *jerks at the mention of the word "coward".*

VINNIE: (*low*) Get away from me. Just get away and leave me alone. Can you understand that? Get away.

WILMA *backs away, shocked, bumping into* KATE, *who is looking up the stepladder.* WILMA *vents her frustration and anger on* KATE.

WILMA: And you! You've never done a video before in your life, have you?

KATE: No.

WILMA: No! I probably know more about lights than you do! Out of my way. Quick!

She brushes past KATE *and huffs up the ladder. In her haste, she slips and falls. She sits sprawled on the ground, the wind taken from her sails.* KATE *jumps into action, takes off* WILMA'*s right shoe and examines the ankle.* WILMA *calmly tosses away her clipboard and unearths a cigarette. She puffs in contemplation.*

WILMA: You know, I'd like to be able to say that I did a wedding like this before, but I can't. This is the first where I've had no bride, no groom, and up to recently, no father of the bride and no musician. Not to mention a hundred and fifty two irate wedding guests sitting in the pub across the road eating free ham sandwiches and getting drunk, twenty two temperamental chefs waiting with dried-up crepes suzette, a limousine driver who's thrown in the towel and gone to pick up his mother, and two photographers who are outside photographing each other.

KATE *deftly wraps the scarf* WILMA *has given her around the ankle.*

KATE: (*with practised ease*) It's just a sprain. That'll support the ligaments for now, but try not to put any weight on it. You may have a little swelling later on, but that'll disappear in a day or two.

WILMA *looks at her suspiciously.*

KATE: (*apologetically*) I'm a nurse.

Gradually, all become aware of a mumble. They look at one another, then slowly all eyes turn to VINNIE. *He has his head in his hands, mumbling the supermarket slogan. The wedding party stay like this as lighting changes to downstage.* ELAINE *hurries on from one side,* CIARAN, *the other.*

CIARAN: I've been lookin' everywhere for you!

ELAINE: And I've been looking everywhere for you! There're a few things we need to straighten out right now.

CIARAN: We do. The first is that I slept with another woman last night. (*pause*) I know, and I'm completely disgusted with myself, I hate myself, I can't bear what I've done to you and you'd be absolutely right not to marry me. (*pause*) Elaine, you're takin' it very well.

362

ELAINE whirls around and slugs him on the chin. He falls to the ground.

ELAINE: You bloody bastard. Who.

CIARAN: A kissogram.

ELAINE: A kissogram? You slept with a kissogram?

He struggles to his feet just in time for her to floor him again.

ELAINE: Why.

CIARAN: I don't know.

ELAINE: It's because you can't bear me anymore, isn't that right? Because I'm too demanding. I'm always "after it", wasn't that how you put it?

CIARAN: What? No! I'm sorry I said that in the pub last night, I didn't mean it, honestly! It's nothin' to do with you. It's me, Elaine. Since losin' the job, and dependin' on you for money, I'm just not able.

ELAINE: Oh haul out the violins.

She turns and paces back and forth a couple of times.

ELAINE: How do you think I feel right now?

CIARAN: I've a pretty good idea of how you feel.

ELAINE: I don't think you do. Or how I've felt for the last month, with you putting me off, avoiding me, giving me brotherly kisses on the cheek. I used to go home some nights Ciaran and have a look in the mirror just to check that I wasn't completely repulsive.

CIARAN:	Never meant to make you feel like that. But it's me, Elaine. I don't come from people who live off their wives.
ELAINE:	And I don't come from people who are too proud to work somewhere they think is beneath them.
CIARAN:	I'm gettin' a job. Any job.
ELAINE:	That doesn't make it alright!
CIARAN:	No, but at least I'll be able to look you in the eye over the cornflakes in the mornin'.
ELAINE:	I'm not talking about that. I'm talking about last night. How am I to know you won't do it again?
CIARAN:	I wouldn't have told you if I was going to do it again. I'd have come into this church and married you with a big smile on me face as if nothing had happened. But I wouldn't do that to you.
ELAINE:	And how am I to know that you're not going to freeze up on me every time we set foot in a bedroom?
CIARAN:	I don't know. I suppose we could try it tonight and see.
ELAINE:	Oh, so you actually think I still want to marry you?
CIARAN:	No. Sorry. Course you don't.
ELAINE:	You' re not wriggling out of it now! I bloody well will marry you! That is, if you'll marry me.
CIARAN:	Fine! I will bloody marry you then!

364

They turn and face upstage. Lights back to the church. ELAINE *and* CIARAN *move forward, into the church.*

CHRIS: Elaine! And Ciaran! What's going on?

ELAINE: It's alright Mam. Wilma?

WILMA: What is it now. Be quick, because I'm going to the pub.

ELAINE: Well, we want to get married. Now. If that's okay.

CHRIS: Of course it's okay. Vinnie! They're here. Vinnie?

VINNIE *ignores them.* ELAINE *makes to go to him.*

CHRIS: No. Just leave him. He'll be alright in a minute.

WILMA *has gotten slowly to her feet and hobbles doubtfully to* ELAINE *and* CIARAN, *unsure whether it's all a macabre joke at her expense.*

WILMA: You...want to get married.

CIARAN: Yeh.

ELAINE: Yes.

WILMA: Oh. Oh I see. So you want to get married. That's wonderful! Right. Everybody! We're about to get started. Noel, ring the pub and tell those guests to get over here, Nicola and Deirdre look lively please, everybody into position! Fr. Jack? Would you like to take over the proceedings now?

FR JACK: Right! Listen up everybody! While we're waiting for the guests to join us in the celebration of this

365

wonderful occasion, I'd like to get the ball
rolling so to speak with a warm-up lap of the
grounds. Okay? Ready? Music Amy!

*He cues her and she plays the mournful version of "Here Comes The
Bride". The wedding guests start to dance out, led by* FR. JACK. CHRIS
links VINNIE *firmly and attempts to drag him out, but he refuses.*

VINNIE: Chris. Just need to get meself together, alright?

CHRIS: I'll be outside if you want to...well, if you want
anything.

She follows the wedding party as all exit save for VINNIE *and* AMY.

VINNIE: Amy? I'm sorry if you took me up wrong. Amy?

AMY *deliberately plays louder, ignoring him.* LINDA *enters. She goes
straight to* AMY, *and crouches down by her. She doesn't look at*
VINNIE.

LINDA: Amy. Paul's waiting for us outside. We're going
                         to stop for lunch on the way. Wherever you
                         want, alright? But we have to go now.

AMY: No.

LINDA: Amy. I'm doing what's best for you here. You
                         mightn't realise it, but I am. And I mightn't have
                         been around much in the last few years and I can
                         see that I should have been. Anyway, I'm here
                         now. So come on.

VINNIE *finally looks up.*

VINNIE: Can she at least stay and play at the weddin'?
                         She was lookin' forward to that.

LINDA:	Oh, there'll be other weddings, won't there Amy? Other weddings and other people. Good people. Come now.
VINNIE:	What's goin' on? Why are you lookin' at me like that.
LINDA:	Like what.
VINNIE:	Like I was dirt beneath your feet, that's what.
LINDA:	I'm just taking her away, alright? Sr. Joan said to just take her away.
VINNIE:	What's she done?
LINDA:	She hasn't done anything. She's not capable of doing anything, as you well know. (*pause*) I trusted you. With her. We all did. Sr. Joan, Paul, me.
VINNIE:	What?
LINDA:	She told me. About the nights you spent with her while Chris was in hospital. About the scratches on her hands and the drink. Sr. Joan thought it was just the local boys, but she was wrong. You won't see her again Vinnie.
VINNIE:	What? Linda, you've got somethin' badly wrong here.

LINDA gets to her feet, pulling AMY with her. VINNIE makes to go to them.

LINDA:	You stay away. You know what you are? Nothing more than scum. Worthless scum.

VINNIE: Amy? What have you been tellin' her? What lies have you been tell in'!

LINDA: Come on Amy –

AMY *resists her and whirls around to* VINNIE.

AMY: You were the one who lied. You said you wanted to go to a safe place. I thought you meant it. I thought you were different Vinnie. But you're just like all the rest. I hate you now. I hate you.

When LINDA *pulls her hand again, she does not resist. They exit.*

Alone in the church, VINNIE *slowly moves to centre stage. He jams his hands over his ears, even though there is absolute silence. In his own head now, the wedding party roar back in around him, along with* LINDA, AMY, PHIL *and* GINA, *their dance grotesquely distorted. They whirl around him, chanting the supermarket slogan and taunting him with "coward" and "failure",* LINDA *and* AMY *taunting him with worse.* VINNIE *turns and runs.*

Lighting change to butchers, the wedding party in a freeze upstage. VINNIE *re-enters, breathing laboured as though after running hard. Slowly, he wanders around the empty space, calming down in the familiar surroundings. He grows more and more detached.*

VINNIE: You know when you have a nightmare where you're fallin'. From the top of buildin', or off a cliff, or the ground suddenly collapses beneath you. And you're gone, down, plungin', tryin' to scream but nothin' comes out. Turnin' over and over in the air and you can feel your heart goin' wild and your stomach risin' as the ground rushes up to meet you. But you know the way you feel yourself fallin', but you're watchin' yourself at the same time? Completely detached, yet the terror is yours? Funny, that. And now the

368

ground is close, you're about to crash into it, you're starin' death in the face. But you always manage to jerk yourself awake just before that moment arrives. You sit up, sweatin' and pantin' with your heart comin' out of your chest. And in the darkness, you slowly realise that you're under your own duvet, in your own bedroom, and you're alright, you're safe. You're in a safe place.

The wedding party close in and accompany VINNIE *with sound as he climbs onto* KATE's *stepladder and hangs himself.*

LIGHTS DOWN. END.

WHAT THE DEAD WANT

BY

ALEX JOHNSTON

CHARACTERS

NEIL, mid 20s

KAREN, early 20s

MAGGIE, mid 20s

RENEE, early 20s

BOBBY, early 20s

JOE, early 20s

DOCTOR, 30

DYER, 17, a dead soldier, Cockney accent

CARL, early 20s, American accent

WALTER, late 20s, a dead German literary critic

MC, 20s

CUSTOMS OFFICERS, m/f, 30s

THE DEAD, all ages

SETTING.

DUBLIN

TIME.

NOW

For Amy, Barry, Dave, Jay, John Paul, Katie, Matthew, Nonie and
Peter

Is there life before death?
- Graffiti, Belfast, 1970s

Is love worse living?
- James Joyce

PROLOGUE.

An immigration office. Two bored CUSTOMS OFFICERS. *One by one, with increasing urgency, the* DEAD *arrive, crowding together.*

THE DEAD: Stalingrad January forty-three / what day is it today / I get these headaches / shema yisroel, adonai elohaynu / my husband very sick / is this a good place to stand / I swear to God I almost had him / have you seen my daughter / we are in a vertical dive / oh God oh God / everyone / we all / burning / my English very bad / who is in charge here / no surrender, no fuckin / 2000 at 6.4, do you have a fax I can use / can you pass me a drink of that water / I'm just a patsy / God be merciful to me a sinner / hit me in the wing, started burning / my brother and my father and my sister / I was only going for some chips / hate the Americans, want to eat their skin / just need one more hit / jumped the median, must've been doing a hundred / is there someone / can you help us / who's in charge

C. OFFICER: All right, all right. Silence there please. One at a time.

A YOUNG WOMAN *steps forward. She is dressed in shabby clothes and has bare feet.*

YOUNG WOMAN: Do you know who we are?

C. OFFICER: No.

YOUNG WOMAN: Can you find somebody who can tell us?

SCENE ONE:

A hospital waiting room. Row of seats.

KAREN *is sitting.*

NEIL *comes in. He carries an overnight bag. He stops. They see each other. She stands up. He goes over to her and they hug for a long moment.*

They disengage and sit.

Pause.

MAGGIE *comes in.* NEIL *and* KAREN *stand up. She goes over to* KAREN *and gives her a big hug. They disengage.* MAGGIE *turns to* NEIL *and hugs him too. They disengage. She blows her nose. They sit,* KAREN *in the middle.*

Pause.

RENEE *comes in. She goes straight over to* KAREN *and hugs her before* KAREN *has had time to stand up.* KAREN *pats her on the back.* MAGGIE *stands up and* RENEE *hugs her. She gives* NEIL *a quick hug as well. She sits down.*

Longer pause.

BOBBY *comes in. He is eating Hula Hoops. He stops and looks at them. They all see him, but* RENEE *ignores him,* NEIL *only nods at him and* MAGGIE *actively snubs him.* KAREN *stands up, goes over to him, gives him a quick hug and sits down again.*

He sits down some distance away and eats Hula Hoops. When there are only a couple left:

BOBBY: Would anyone like a Hula Hoop?

Total lack of reaction from the others.

BOBBY: There's two left.

Still no reaction. He eats the Hula Hoops. Pause. He crumples up the bag and goes off.

MAGGIE: (*to* KAREN) Sorry.

KAREN: Why? Not your fault.

MAGGIE: He's such an asshole.

BOBBY *comes in again, empty-handed. He sits down.*

Pause.

The DOCTOR *comes in from the opposite side.*

DOCTOR: You can come in now.

The women get up. NEIL *and* BOBBY *remain seated. A look passes between* NEIL *and* KAREN. *The women follow the* DOCTOR *out.*

Pause.

BOBBY: How you been, man?

NEIL: Oh, you know.

BOBBY: I thought you'd gone.

NEIL: My flight's not till evening.

Pause.

BOBBY: What you been up to?

NEIL: Just waiting.

BOBBY:	Yeah? (*Pause*) I went to see *The Waste Land* at the Savoy.
NEIL:	...Was it good?
BOBBY:	Surprisingly. Yeah. You wouldn't think they could make a blockbuster action movie out of a modernist poem but it works really well.
NEIL:	What's...whatshername like.
BOBBY:	Oh, she's a bit shit, just nags all the time. (*nag voice*) "What are you thinking? What are you thinking?" Pain in the hole. It's kind of a relief when she gets pushed out of the Zeppelin. - Oh. Sorry.
NEIL:	Hm?
BOBBY:	I just gave away loads of the plot.
NEIL:	Doesn't matter.
BOBBY:	How is everyone?
NEIL:	You saw yourself, Bobby, they're not the best, you know?
BOBBY:	Right. (*Pause*) Do you think it's something to do with me?
NEIL:	I wouldn't say so, no. I'd say it's more to do with the fact that Joe is about to die.
BOBBY:	Yeah.
NEIL:	Although it doesn't help that you tried to chat up Karen while he was on a ventilator.

377

BOBBY: No, that wasn't clever, was it. How *is* Karen?

NEIL: You ask her.

BOBBY: She doesn't like me.

NEIL: I don't blame her. I don't like you very much either.

BOBBY: Oh. (*Pause*) For what it's worth, I like you.

NEIL: I'll bake a fucking cake.

Pause.

BOBBY: Why don't people like me?

NEIL: They think you're a selfish, egotistical prick. And frankly, I agree with them.

BOBBY: Fair enough. (*Pause*) Stupid thing to do. I really like Karen.

NEIL: It's the weirdest thing, I really don't have much sympathy right now?

Pause.

BOBBY: You didn't tell Joe about it?

NEIL: Thought about it. Then I decided not.

BOBBY: Right. Cheers, man.

NEIL: I didn't do it for you. I did it for him. He doesn't need any more bad news.

BOBBY: Course, yeah. (*Pause*) People can be really weird sometimes.

NEIL:	If people are acting weird, I think there's quite a good reason, don't you think?
BOBBY:	What.
NEIL:	Bobby. Dunno if you watch the news, at all, but the world is going through a bizarre transformation. The basic laws of the universe appear to have changed. The dead have risen, Bobby, and they are walking amongst us. The most brilliant scientific minds –
BOBBY:	Oh, *that*.
NEIL:	- are at a loss to explain it.
BOBBY:	Sure.
NEIL:	You know who's playing the Point Depot next month?
BOBBY:	No.
NEIL:	Legends of Irish music. Phil Lynott, Turlough O'Carolan and Ruby fucking Murray. So don't tell me that things aren't a tad off-kilter at present.
BOBBY:	Could be a good gig.

Pause.

NEIL:	I just don't think that a...cosmic, sub-quantum-mechanical superstring anomaly is any excuse for behaving like a prick, that's all.
BOBBY:	Well, it's obvious to me what's going on.
NEIL:	Yeah?

BOBBY:	I mean fuck this stupid name they've given it, the Koop –
NEIL:	The "Koop-Shriver Harmonic Reversal".
BOBBY:	It's not exactly catchy.
NEIL:	No.
BOBBY:	When we already have a perfectly good name.
NEIL:	Ah, not you too.
BOBBY:	Judgement Day.
NEIL:	I never took you for religious.
BOBBY:	I'm not religious. It makes more fuckin' sense, Neil.
NEIL:	Superstitious bullshit.
BOBBY:	Common fucking sense.
NEIL:	Somebody has to keep their brain working.
BOBBY:	Oh, and you, because you're –
NEIL:	Cause I can see you've given up.
BOBBY:	- Mister fucking Moral Centre, I've just started man, watch me.

Pause.

NEIL:	Well I'm not fighting today. I'm going in to see Joe.
BOBBY:	So am I.

NEIL:	Fine.

They go in.

SCENE TWO.

A hospital bed. KAREN, MAGGIE, RENEE, NEIL *and* BOBBY *are gathered around JOE, who is dying.* KAREN *sits closest to him, stroking his hand.* JOE *is asleep. A machine registering his heartbeat goes "beep" regularly. A sign hangs over him: DO NOT RESUSCITATE.*

RENEE:	I thought his folks would've come.
KAREN:	He doesn't have any. He's an orphan.
RENEE:	Oh Jesus.
KAREN:	It's okay.
RENEE:	I totally forgot. (*Pause*) Still...they could've showed up.
KAREN:	They died when he was really young. He doesn't remember them.
RENEE:	Oh. Poor Joe.
BOBBY:	That's the thing about the dead. Never around when you want them.
MAGGIE:	Shut up.
BOBBY:	Sorry. Hi Karen.
KAREN:	Bobby. Thanks for coming.
BOBBY:	Not a problem.

Pause.

KAREN:	Look, guys, this isn't about Bobby, this is about Joe, so will you all please... stop standing there like you've got, fucking...pencils up your arseholes.

They others try to stop registering silent disapproval of BOBBY.

BOBBY: Cheers Karen.

KAREN: Bobby.

BOBBY: Yeah.

KAREN: Shut up.

BOBBY: Okay.

KAREN: Joe? You there? Your friends are here. Joe? You wanna wake up and say hello to your friends?

JOE *wakes up slowly. He is very weak.*

JOE: ...Hi guys...

RENEE: Hello Joe.

NEIL: Hi Joe.

KAREN: Hello love.

She kisses JOE *on the forehead.*

JOE: ...Jeez...sorry I'm not more fun...

NEIL: How you doing, man?

JOE: Ah...bit under the weather tell the truth...

BOBBY:	All right, Joe?
JOE:	Bobby man...what's the crack...
BOBBY:	Not too shit, you know.
JOE:	Good to see you. Jeez, everybody here...
KAREN:	We're all here.
JOE:	Ah, lads...shouldn't have...

He drifts off to sleep.

KAREN:	It's okay. He's just tired.
BOBBY:	Why's it say "Do not resuscitate"?
KAREN:	Joe and I agreed a long time ago, if anything happened to either of us, and we were on a life-support machine, whatever, that we didn't wanna do things that way. We wanted to say goodbye to each other properly, and that would be that.
NEIL:	Good thinking.
KAREN:	Yeah. Well...it's a bit different, now.
NEIL:	What do you mean?

Pause.

NEIL:	Karen?
KAREN:	Ssh.

JOE wakes up again.

383

KAREN:	Joe?
JOE:	Oh...still here.
KAREN:	It's okay. You're not going anywhere.
JOE:	I was having a dream.
KAREN:	Yeah?
JOE:	I dreamed I was going home with you.
KAREN:	Did you?
JOE:	What time is it?
NEIL:	(*looks at watch*) Half five.
JOE:	Cheers...sorry to keep yous all waiting...
KAREN:	Don't talk if it hurts.
JOE:	Nah, doesn't really...so, lads...what do yous reckon...famous last words?
MAGGIE:	(*upset*) Oh, Joe.
JOE:	Serious...could use a suggestion...
NEIL:	I've always, uh, liked that general in the American Civil War who stuck his head over the lip of the trench to look at the enemy and his last words were "They couldn't hit an elephant at this dist."
JOE:	(*grins*) Good one.
KAREN:	Wasn't it some English king who said "I think I could eat one of

	Bellamy's veal pies."
JOE:	Class.
MAGGIE:	Tony Hancock had the best.
KAREN:	What was that?
MAGGIE:	"Things just seemed to go wrong too much of the time."

Silence.

| **JOE:** | Well...I just want yous to know...I had a fuckin' brilliant time. And you're all great. |

They mumble variations on "Thanks".

| **JOE:** | And I don't want yous to be sad cause...as long as you remember me...I'm gonna be around. |

| **KAREN:** | We'll never forget you. |

| **JOE:** | I know babe. |

She squeezes his hand.

| **JOE:** | Yeah...think this it, lads... |

| **KAREN:** | Don't fight it. |

| **JOE:** | Nah...boldly go...where none of yous bastards...have gone before... |

A pause.

The beeping machine emits a continuous tone. JOE is very still. He has died. Pause.

KAREN:	Yep. That's it.

MAGGIE *starts to cry.* NEIL *comforts her.* RENEE *puts a hand on* KAREN*'s shoulder.* BOBBY *puts a hand on* RENEE*'s shoulder but she shrugs him off.*

A quiet moment.

The DOCTOR *comes in discreetly.*

DOCTOR:	Hello?
KAREN:	(rousing herself) Hi. Yes. He's gone.
DOCTOR:	I'm very sorry.
KAREN:	It's fine. Thank you.
DOCTOR:	If I could just...(*They step aside. He leans over the body.)* Yes. Time of death: five thirty-three p.m. Thank you. Who is the next of kin?
KAREN:	That would be me.
DOCTOR:	Right. I have some forms for you to sign. I'll get them.

He goes. Pause.

MAGGIE:	I'm so sorry, Karen.
KAREN:	It's okay.
JOE:	Listen guys, I'm really sorry as well.
KAREN:	I know, love...
JOE:	I mean, this is hardest on yous. I feel really bad about it.

386

MAGGIE:	We'll miss you so much.
JOE:	Ah stop that.
BOBBY:	Joe?
JOE:	Yeah?
BOBBY:	What's it like?
JOE:	Being dead?
BOBBY:	Yeah.
JOE:	It...it doesn't hurt or anything. It's just...(*He trails off, as if not really interested. To* KAREN) How you doin?
KAREN:	(*smiling at him*) I'm okay.

The DOCTOR *enters.*

DOCTOR:	Hi. Yes. The documentation. This is a form certifying the, ah, the demise, I just need you to sign that, and this is to register the handover of the deceased to our remembrance centre, where you will of course have full visiting privileges –
KAREN:	I'm not signing that one.
DOCTOR:	I, you, well. What? Okay. Sorry?
KAREN:	Joe's not going with you. He's coming home with me.
DOCTOR:	Yes. Now. We strongly advise against that.
KAREN:	I don't care.

DOCTOR:	It, you see, yes, ah, studies, have shown, that continued cohabitation with the, uh, differently deceased, interferes with the natural process of mourning.
KAREN:	I don't fucking care.
DOCTOR:	I would really, ahm, urge you, don't do this.
KAREN:	Look, if Joe were dead in the normal way he wouldn't be here anymore and I wouldn't have him and I'd be saying goodbye to him. But it's not like that now, he's still here and I'm keeping him with me. Cause I love him. And you can't make me let him go.
DOCTOR:	Technically that's correct.
KAREN:	Thank you.
DOCTOR:	But. The Koop-Shriver Harmonic Reversal is a very complicated phenomenon which we don't really understand, and this is why guidelines have been put in place –
KAREN:	Look, piss off, all right? I want his clothes.
DOCTOR:	There's no need to be intense about it.
NEIL:	Have to say, Karen, I think he's right, this is nuts.
KAREN:	Mind your own fucking business!
RENEE:	I agree with Karen, I don't see why –
NEIL:	But Renee –

KAREN: Listen! If the Christians are right then we're all
                    gonna get judged in a few weeks anyway. So
                    what difference does it make. He's mine and I'm
                    taking him.

Pause.

DOCTOR: Well I can't force you.

KAREN: No you can't.

BOBBY: I think we're forgetting something here.

KAREN: What.

BOBBY: What does Joe want.

MAGGIE: What *do* you want, Joe?

JOE *shrugs and smiles. He seems a good deal livelier than he did
earlier.*

KAREN: Joe and I agreed. He's coming with me.

Pause.

DOCTOR: I, uh. I have to let you go then. He *will* have to
                    wear the armband.

KAREN: That's fine.

DOCTOR: I'll take you to his clothes.

KAREN, JOE *and the* DOCTOR *exit.*

BOBBY: Does anybody else think there's something a bit
                    necrophiliac about all this?

MAGGIE: Oh, shut up, we all know what you want.

BOBBY: I'm just saying.

NEIL: It's true though. I really think this is a bad idea.

MAGGIE: It *is* a bad idea.

NEIL: What are we going to do about it?

Pause.

BOBBY: What do you mean "we", paleface?

NEIL: We're her friends, we should be doing
                     something.

BOBBY: Well, personally speaking, I'm going down the
                     pub. Anyone?

RENEE: What the fuck. I'll join you for one. Today's just
                     been too weird.

BOBBY *and* RENEE *go.* MAGGIE *prepares to go.*

NEIL: Where are you going?

MAGGIE: Home. I want to think.

NEIL: But don't you think we should –

MAGGIE: Oh Neil will you just leave it. So bloody
                     responsible the whole time.
                     (Pause) The main thing is, Joe is dead. That's
                     not the real Joe, that's just...memories of Joe. I
                     think Karen is insane but I'm not telling her
                     what to do with her life. I'm going home. You
                     do what you like.

She goes.

NEIL: Hang on. Somebody has to...hello? We have to
               do something. (*Pause*) Doesn't somebody have
               to do something?

SCENE THREE:

The train. MAGGIE *is seated next to* CARL. *It is crowded.*

CARL: Are you all right?

MAGGIE: Sorry?

CARL: Do you want a handkerchief?

MAGGIE: No thank you.

Pause.

CARL: Are you washed in the blood of the lamb?

MAGGIE: Excuse me?

CARL: Are you washed in the blood of the lamb?

MAGGIE: I, uh, you mean, am I a Christian?

CARL: If you like.

MAGGIE: No, I'm not very, uh...no.

CARL: Nah, me neither really. (*Pause*) I really like your
               country.

MAGGIE: Oh. Thank you.

CARL:	Celtic spirituality is really important to me. I know it's under threat right now but it'll fight back.
MAGGIE:	Is it under threat – I suppose, yeah.
CARL:	Oh yeah. We live in great days.
MAGGIE:	You think.
CARL:	"Behold, I show you a mystery, we shall not sleep, but we shall all be changed, in a moment, in the twinkling of an eye, at the last trump, for the trumpet shall sound, and the dead shall be raised incorruptible, and we shall be changed."
MAGGIE:	Will we?
CARL:	Paul's first letter to the Corinthians.
MAGGIE:	Right.
CARL:	That's the King James version. It's based on the William Tyndale version. Tyndale was burned at the stake on 22nd November. You know?
MAGGIE:	I don't – it doesn't – sorry.
CARL:	Four centuries later, 22nd November 1963. Dallas. Kennedy. Bang. *(Slaps his own forehead)* Pow.
MAGGIE:	Ah.
CARL:	"Back, and to the left."
MAGGIE:	Oliver Stone.
CARL:	*Yes.*

MAGGIE:	You think there's a connection.
CARL:	"The eyes of the blind shall see out of darkness." Isaiah.
MAGGIE:	You really know your Bible.
CARL:	My parents. Same chapter, twenty-nine, verse one: woe to Ariel, the city where David dwelt. The North Tower of the World Trade Centre had a what?
MAGGIE:	I'm sorry?
CARL:	It had aerial on it.
MAGGIE:	Ah.
CARL:	A lotta multinationals had offices in there. You ever hear of the Bilderberg Group?
MAGGIE:	No.
CARL:	...Okay, not actually them but those guys have a lot of connections. Notice it was mostly banks that got hit? The international finance system.
MAGGIE:	Mm.
CARL:	A lot of these guys, they go to the same country clubs, they go to the same schools, you can't tell me they're not carving up the world in these places.
MAGGIE:	I think it's best to look at specific corporate structures, and actual documentary evidence of relations between business and government, I don't really believe

in conspiracy theories, sorry, I've had a hard
day.

CARL: Are you a leftist?

MAGGIE: Well, yes.

CARL: Shame. You seemed pretty sensible.

MAGGIE: Oh.

CARL: You agree that the federal government's for shit,
                    right.

MAGGIE: The American, well, yeah.

CARL: Ever look at the streets and think, what is
                    happening to my country?

MAGGIE: Look, um...I'd kind of prefer just to sit here. A
                    friend of mine's just
                    died, and I'm a bit –

CARL: There is no more death.

MAGGIE: There is but it's different.

CARL: And you know what swung it for me, where are
                    the, where are the six million?

MAGGIE: The what?

CARL: The six million dead Jews? *I* don't see them. Do
                    you?

MAGGIE: Are you one of those people who think the
                    Holocaust didn't happen?

CARL:	I'm just telling you the facts. In 1989, an Italian biochemist did tests on the so-called gas chambers at Auschwitz, and proved conclusively –
MAGGIE:	Look, I, um, I'd really sooner not have this conversation, if that's okay –
CARL:	*(explodes)* Oh and what makes you so fuckin high and mighty? You and your fuckin liberal bullshit, how does it feel to be on your high fuckin horse the whole time –
MAGGIE:	Excuse me.
CARL:	Fuckin Irish retards, we bailed your ass out in two world wars that Hitler *never* wanted to start, *by* the way –
MAGGIE:	Oh that is such bullshit –
CARL:	But no, the Nazis have to be *totally* wrong, spooky monsters under the bed, what about the bombing of Dresden, what about Hiroshima, what about the Jewish conspiracy in the media, the occupation of Palestine –
MAGGIE:	I'm against the occupation of Palestine.
CARL:	- but you don't even have the courage to face a few simple facts, did you *know* five thousand Jews were evacuated from the World Trade Centre on the morning of –
MAGGIE:	That is total crap, that has been *so* disproved –
CARL:	Don't tell *me* they didn't know what was gonna happen, and *all* you fucking liberals, somebody

comes along with well-researched *facts* and you shut them up, free speech my ass.

MAGGIE: Look, if you're gonna be like that about it.

CARL: I know your kind. Jew-lover.

MAGGIE: Okay. You're a lunatic, right? And I'm getting off the train.

CARL: Always the same, will *not* listen to a few facts.

MAGGIE: Listen to me. The man I love died, right? He *died*. And he didn't love me, and the woman he did love is never gonna let him go, and I'm not gonna be allowed to forget about him, so excuse me if I say I don't give TWO SHITS for your FUCKING INSANE BULLSHIT! Now GOODBYE!

She stands up and gets off the train. The carriage empties. CARL runs to the window.

CARL: You're all gonna BURN! In HELL! GOD WILL SPIT YOU OUT OF HIS MOUTH!

The train pulls out. He is alone. He sits down again and drums his fingers on his knees.

SCENE FOUR.

BOBBY *and* RENEE *in the pub.* BOBBY *has a pint,* RENEE *a glass of wine.*

BOBBY: You know when they say "Nothing will ever be the same again" and it's usually bullshit cause things are.

RENEE: Yeah.

BOBBY: I mean the World Trade Centre.

RENEE: Yeah.

BOBBY: Fact, right. The first attack on the mainland USA since 1812 or something.

RENEE: What about Pearl Harbour?

BOBBY: Doesn't count. Wasn't a state at the time.

RENEE: Oh.

BOBBY: And look what happened, Jesus. You'd think nobody had ever been killed before. And what do they do, they bomb the fuck out of a country populated largely by goats...all because a couple of thousand Americans got hit by a falling building.

RENEE: It wasn't just Americans.

BOBBY: Mostly.

RENEE: Cousin of mine got killed in the South Tower.

BOBBY: Oh. *(Pause)* Sorry about that.

RENEE:	It's all right. I didn't know her that well.
BOBBY:	You seen her since? What with the whole –
RENEE:	Yeah. She turns up at the house, now and again. Everyone cries and says how they miss her. I try and stay away.
BOBBY:	Yeah. But this is exactly it, dead people walking around, this is one of those things where things are never the same after. Fairly fucking unprecedented in human history.
RENEE:	But they say that it's not really literally the dead, it's some sort of sub-atomic thing to do with perception and memory.
BOBBY:	*(dismissively)* Oh, scientists. Nah. Call it what you want. Definitely the weirdest thing that has ever happened.
RENEE:	I think you're right. *(Pause)* That's still no excuse for you trying to hit on Karen.
BOBBY:	Oh, *that*. Jesus. Let it *go*. I'll never live that down. Strictly a one-off.
RENEE:	Was it.
BOBBY:	Even more stupid than normal for me.
RENEE:	I don't think you were being stupid, I think you knew exactly what you were doing.
BOBBY:	Karen seems to be cool about it.
RENEE:	Karen loves Joe. Plus, Karen is probably a nicer person than me.

BOBBY:	Well. (*Pause*) I mean, you're dead right. I'm just a shithead.
RENEE:	You're young.
BOBBY:	Oh. "Miaow".

Pause.

RENEE:	I don't know. Karen's in love. What do you do.
BOBBY:	I think what you *don't* do is shack up with your dead boyfriend.
RENEE:	Well, no.

Pause.

BOBBY:	Being a bit of a tit runs in my family. I'm not making excuses.
RENEE:	Well, my mother's a bitch and so am I.
BOBBY:	Take my great-grand-uncle Billy. He lied about his age to get into the Army and he was killed on the first day of the Battle of the Somme.
RENEE:	You're not serious.
BOBBY:	Yeah, really. I mean, king and country, yeah. But at the same time...what a dick.

Pause. A figure in WW1 British battledress comes slowly forward. It is a young man, muddy and very confused, BOBBY*'s great-grand-uncle Billy, a.k.a. Rifleman* W. T. DYER.

DYER:	Hello?
BOBBY:	All right man? (*looks closer*) Oh fuckin' hell.

RENEE:	What?
BOBBY:	It's my great-grand-uncle Billy. (*to DYER*) Are you Billy Dyer?
DYER:	That's right – what – where am I?
BOBBY:	It's all right. You're in Dublin.
DYER:	Dublin? Nah, we were...we were supposed to take the salient...I'm not fightin the Micks, am I?
BOBBY:	It's all right, Uncle Billy. Don't worry about it.
DYER:	What's goin on?
BOBBY:	Something really weird happened a few months ago. You were dead, but you've come back. Sort of. Or we're remembering you in a new way, or something.
RENEE:	Nobody's totally sure.
BOBBY:	This is my friend Renee.
RENEE:	Hello. I'm not really his friend, I just tolerate him.
DYER:	It was bloody horrible, I was in this big shop an it was all brightly lit, and I could hear some girl screamin, nobody minded her. Horrible it was.
BOBBY:	Yeah?
DYER:	What was it she was, yeah, "Hit my babies one more time."
BOBBY:	Oh yeah. That's muzak.

DYER:	What?
BOBBY:	It's sort of like the wireless only even more shit.
DYER:	Ere, mind your language. There's a lady present.
BOBBY:	Sorry.
DYER:	Who are you anyway?
BOBBY:	I'm your nephew Bobby.
DYER:	I don't ave a nephew.
BOBBY:	No, see, your brother Harold had two sons, Jim and Martin, and Martin had a daughter called Linda, and Linda came to Ireland and married an Irish guy, and I'm her son Bobby. So I'm your great-grand-nephew.
DYER:	No, you got it wrong. Harold's only a little feller, he ain't even got a girl yet.
BOBBY:	No. Ahm - (*to* RENEE) what's the best way to put it?
RENEE:	See, Mister Dyer, you were...you were killed. In the first world war. In, (*to* BOBBY) when was it?
BOBBY:	1916.
RENEE:	1916. And this is 2002.

Pause.

DYER:	You're jokin.
RENEE:	No. Really.

DYER:	Flippin ell. (*to* RENEE) Scuse my French. We livin on the moon yet then?
BOBBY:	No.
DYER:	Oh. Pity about that. I always liked that, Jules Verne an that, yeah, my dad used to read that. What time is it?
BOBBY:	It's about half-seven.
DYER:	I've got to go up the line in ten minutes.
BOBBY:	We're not in France, Billy, we're in Dublin.
DYER:	Dublin? Bloody ell. I'm sposed to be in France. (*Pause*) It was a fuckin shambles. (*to* RENEE) Scuse me.
RENEE:	It's all right, what was?

Pause.

DYER:	The attack.
RENEE:	What happened?
DYER:	It was bloody orrible. We was supposed to go round the back of the hill and join up with the Midlands. So five nights before we go over, we start shellin the German wire. They reckoned the shells would cut the wire, see, knock out the Jerries, be a cakewalk. They said, you'll be able to walk it in ten minutes. So five nights, the noise...head like a bloody drum, you know. Scuse me. So, seven thirty in the morning, first lot of lads goes over the top, what happens, bloody German machine guns open up, not just from the trenches, whole fuckin hill on our left

402

side. I couldn't see cause I was in the second wave. But I heard the shootin. I heard the blokes dyin. Then we get the whistle an we go over an, it was mad. Just bloody mad. Everywhere, blokes fallin down like they were slippin, but they wasn't, they was gettin shot. Stan Morton, bloke in our company, he got about ten feet an then he got caught in the wire, our bloody wire, stupid, then a machine gun got him an he was just hangin there, he was just shakin...I was comin up behind an I could...I could see through him. An then we got to the German wire. An it wasn't bloody cut, and I thought hold hard, someone's buggered up, we're in the wrong bit. An then I saw all these things stuck in the ground, yellow things covered in mud. It was our shells. Five days of em. Most of em hadn't even gone off. (*Pause*) What a fuckin waste. So I started looking for a hole in the wire and I don't remember what after that.

BOBBY: (*not really interested*) Oh yeah? Yeah, that'd be about right. Yeah.

RENEE: (*to* BOBBY) How do you know that?

BOBBY: Cause I've read about him. In fact I've read all that before. It's all in standard history books. Family history as well.

RENEE: (*Pause*) Mister Dyer?

DYER: Rifleman Dyer to you, miss.

RENEE: Yeah – what do you think of 2002?

DYER: Oh, that's a long way off. (*Looks around*) Where's me rifle, I ave to get up the...

RENEE:	What would you say if I told you that the war ended in 1918?
DYER:	(*gets up, starts looking for his rifle*) Did it? There's a thing.
RENEE:	And there was another war twenty years later and it was even worse, and there've been wars ever since but not as big, in fact there's one going on now.
DYER:	(*indifferently*) That doesn't sound too cheerful...you seen my rifle? I ave to get back to the lads. Don't say I've lost it. They'll bloody kill me.

He wanders off. Pause.

BOBBY:	You can't tell him anything. That all happened after he died, he's not interested.
RENEE:	But this is history. This is his future.
BOBBY:	He doesn't have a future. He's dead. All he has is his memories. All he can talk about is what we remember about him.
RENEE:	Yeah but Jesus Christ can they not see what's going on around them?
BOBBY:	I think they can a bit, but they're not interested. They just want us to remember them.
RENEE:	And otherwise they just fade away. So am I supposed to go on remembering my...granny, who died when I was six, I can't even think what she looked like?

BOBBY:	Nah, you can't. But somebody else might. And she'll come back and visit them.
RENEE:	Lucky them. (*big gulp of wine*) You know what else. This Karen and Joe thing is totally, what's the word? Unhealthy?
BOBBY:	You used to think it was a great idea.
RENEE:	Oh look, don't...pick on me. You were right and I was wrong. (*Pause*) I never thought you were interested in history.
BOBBY:	You never asked. Yeah, the first world war. I've always had this thing about it.
RENEE:	Boys and war. Like flies on shite.
BOBBY:	Nah, it's more than that. I mean...world war two makes a sort of *sense*, you can sort of see why that happened, to stop Hitler, though why the Japanese got involved I frankly have no fucking idea, but world war one – I mean, do you *know* why it happened?
RENEE:	That guy shot that guy.
BOBBY:	Yeah, but how did that lead to global war?
RENEE:	(*thinks*)...I don't know.
BOBBY:	Exactly. I have read, I dunno how many history books, and none of them can explain exactly why it all had to happen in the first place. And after four years, millions dead. Millions. And you've got the conditions for the second world war, which led to the Cold War, which led to what we have now.

RENEE:	I suppose so.
BOBBY:	And I always come back to these guys in the trenches, fighting a war that makes no absolutely no fucking sense, and going over the top and dying, or if they don't go over the top they get shot for cowardice. I just don't understand why that had to happen. I dunno. I wannabe able to...save them. Or something.

Pause. He drinks.

RENEE:	This is so unlike you.
BOBBY:	What?
RENEE:	Actually seeming like you give a shit about something.
BOBBY:	Yeah. Well, don't tell anyone, will you.
RENEE:	Okay. (*Pause*) I like it. I mean, slightly. Hidden depths.
BOBBY:	Hidden shallows.
RENEE:	So why do you have to be such a prick the rest of the time?
BOBBY:	I'm just protecting my own interests.
RENEE:	It wouldn't kill you to be nicer to people.
BOBBY:	It's too late. They'd just think I was tryna get something off them.
RENEE:	They'd probably be right.
BOBBY:	Yeah.

406

Pause.

RENEE: This is fun. Deconstructing Bobby.

BOBBY: I'm enjoying it. You want another drink?

RENEE: I could use one, yeah.

BOBBY: I'll get em. Don't think about dead people.

He goes.

RENEE: (*to herself*) Right. Don't mention the war.

SCENE FIVE.

JOE *and* KAREN *in* KAREN*'s place.* KAREN *is bouncing all over the room.* JOE *is wearing a black armband with a cross on it – a government initiative to identify the officially recognised dead.*

KAREN: Here we are.

JOE: Home again, yeah.

KAREN: I'm having wine, do you -? No.

She goes off.

JOE: I always liked this room.

KAREN: (*off*) Sit down. Won't be a sec.

JOE: Remember that time we shagged on this sofa?

KAREN *laughs, off.*

JOE:	And then we couldn't be arsed to get a blanket and we fell asleep and nearly froze.

KAREN *dances in with a glass of wine.*

KAREN:	And I got a cold the next day.
JOE:	Yeah.

KAREN *dances over to him.*

KAREN:	That was fun, though.
JOE:	It was.

KAREN *kisses him on the lips. They curl up on the sofa together.*

KAREN:	I am not letting you go.
JOE:	I like this sofa.
KAREN:	Never never never never never.
JOE:	What about some music.
KAREN:	Oh, good call.

She drinks some wine and goes to the stereo.

KAREN:	What would you like?
JOE:	Ah, anything. What was it that was playing that day in Howth? On the radio, that I liked.
KAREN:	Nick Cave.
JOE:	Yeah. That was great.
KAREN:	Yeah. That's too sad though.

JOE:	I always said that all his songs sound the same, but it doesn't matter cause it's a good song.
KAREN:	Yeah...ooo yeah, what about Sly and the Family Stone?
JOE:	Sure, yeah. That always makes me think of breakfast.
KAREN:	Me too.
JOE:	You always used to play that at breakfast. Yeah.

Pause.

KAREN:	How about the Avalanches?
JOE:	Sure, yeah. Whatever you like.

She puts on "Since I Left You" by The Avalanches, dances over to him and sits on the sofa with him, curling her arms and legs around him.

KAREN:	Now you're mine.
JOE:	Now I'm yours.
KAREN:	Trapped. Like a...dog in a...bus. Jesus, I'm talking complete bollocks, I'm sorry, I'm so happy.

JOE smiles. Pause.

KAREN:	Are you happy?
JOE:	I love you.
KAREN:	I know.

They kiss and cuddle.

409

KAREN: What was it like?

JOE: What was what like?

KAREN: You know. When it...happened.

JOE: Ah...(*not really interested*) You 're just going
              along, you know. And then it ends. It's over.

KAREN: Yeah but is there like a light, or do you hear
              music, or –

JOE: Couldn't, eh, couldn't, couldn't say really. Just...

Pause.

KAREN: And of course it's not over. Cause you're here.

JOE: Yeah. (*smiles*)

KAREN: Oh guess what's on tonight.

JOE: What.

KAREN: *All the President's Men.* Shall we watch it?

JOE: Sure, yeah.

KAREN: Or, we could go out.

JOE: I'm grand. Either way.

Pause.

KAREN: This is gonna be great, isn't it?

JOE: Yeah.

KAREN: You're not going away.

JOE:	No.
KAREN:	If it was like before. If you'd gone, and you were in a morgue or a funeral home now or – I don't think I would have been able to stand that. But you're here.
JOE:	Yeah.
KAREN:	(*hugs him*) I love you so much.
JOE:	I'll always love you.

Pause.

KAREN:	This song's doing my head in.

She gets off the sofa and turns off the music. Sits back down with him again.

KAREN:	What'll we do?
JOE:	I don't mind.
KAREN:	Okay. I think we should stay in.
JOE:	Okay.
KAREN:	I'll have some dinner, and you can, um –
JOE:	You could make that chicken thing I always liked.
KAREN:	Yeah. Mm...No, I think I'll make something I've never had before.

SCENE SIX.

BOBBY *and* RENEE *are still in the pub, several drinks later.*

RENEE: No way.

BOBBY: Liar.

RENEE: Absolutely no way.

BOBBY: For a million quid. Sterling, not euros.

RENEE: No.

BOBBY: A billion quid.

RENEE: ...Okay, I *would* play strip poker for a billion quid –

BOBBY: Ha!

RENEE: On *condition*, and I have to be very strict about this, I am playing it with John Cusack, in a locked room, with nobody else around.

BOBBY: Good condition.

RENEE: No hidden cameras, nothing.

BOBBY: Ah, you're no fun.

RENEE: In fact for him I wouldn't even need the cards, more like Take me now you unbelievable ride you.

BOBBY: Oh yeah? Got a thing for Johnny, have you?

RENEE: Yes, and not just his looks, also, because: very intelligent, and sense of humour.

BOBBY:	Well yeah. By the same criteria, I would shag Susan Sarandon.
RENEE:	Really? Yeah, good choice...what about Cameron Diaz?
BOBBY:	No.
RENEE:	No? You liar. You so would.
BOBBY:	Cameron Diaz is not beautiful.
RENEE:	She is gorgeous, what are you –
BOBBY:	She's skinny, her mouth is too big and her eyes are too pale.
RENEE:	Every guy in the universe would shag Cameron Diaz.
BOBBY:	No they would not, and I am living proof, and if they did they'd be wrong, cause she is not that beautiful. For example, you are much better-looking than Cameron Diaz.
RENEE:	That is a total fucking lie and you know it.
BOBBY:	No. It's true. What, you don't think you're good-looking?
RENEE:	*(Pause)* I don't think I'm *bad-looking*.
BOBBY:	Well, I think you're exceptionally good-looking.
RENEE:	*(smiling)* You are a complete bullshitter.
BOBBY:	No, I bullshit a lot, but I am in fact an incomplete bullshitter, because this is the truth.

Pause.

RENEE:	You think I'm good-looking?
BOBBY:	Yes.
RENEE:	Do you fancy me?
BOBBY:	Yes.

Pause.

RENEE:	And, so, we've know each other for three years and there's a reason why you've never said this before?
BOBBY:	There is. You thought I was a total arsehole.
RENEE:	I still think you're an arsehole.
BOBBY:	Just not a total one.

Pause.

BOBBY:	There is of course another question at stake here.
RENEE:	What's that.
BOBBY:	Do *you* fancy *me*.

Pause.

RENEE:	Yes. There have been times when I – yes.
BOBBY:	When you what.
RENEE:	...When I've caught myself looking at your arse. Big deal.

414

BOBBY:	It's funny how women fancy men's arses. It's supposed to be the other way around.
RENEE:	Don't you fancy women's arses?
BOBBY:	Yes. Yours in particular.
RENEE:	Shut up.
BOBBY:	You're not even supposed to like me, remember.
RENEE:	I know. I don't.
BOBBY:	That's okay. I don't really like you, either.
RENEE:	Fine then.

They look at each other for a long moment.

RENEE:	I'm really hungry.
BOBBY:	Me too.
RENEE:	You wanna get some fish and chips.
BOBBY:	I could do that.
RENEE:	Actually, I'm not really all that hungry.
BOBBY:	Neither am I.
RENEE:	I really do think you're an arsehole, you know.
BOBBY:	I know.
RENEE:	But I think you should kiss me anyway.
BOBBY:	No. I think *you* should kiss *me*.

415

RENEE:	Why?

BOBBY:	Cause I made the first move.

RENEE:	You definitely are a total arsehole.

She grabs him and they kiss.

SCENE SEVEN.

MAGGIE *is in her and* RENEE's *living room. She is reading.*

The DEAD *approach diffidently. They are all wearing armbands. They bicker quietly amongst themselves about who is going to be the spokesperson. Finally a man in a shabby 1930s suit, with dark hair, round glasses and a small moustache, is pushed forward. This is* WALTER. *He tries to protest but the rest of the dead offer him silent encouragement. He comes up behind* MAGGIE *nervously.*

MAGGIE:	(*without looking up*) Don't even think about it.

WALTER:	It's not me.

MAGGIE:	I don't care.

He goes back and tries to argue out of it. The others shove him back again. He stumbles slightly.

WALTER:	They're very insistent.

MAGGIE:	I. Don't. Fucking. Care.

WALTER:	I don't want to disturb. I was always very bad in social situations. I had a wife and son, you know – how that happened has always been a bit of a mystery to me. I must have been thinking about

something else at the time. Do you mind if I sit down?

MAGGIE: Yes.

WALTER: Right. (*Pause)* My name is, ah, Walter. (*He pronounces it with a hard "W" - "Valter" - and a short "a".)*

MAGGIE: I know who you are. I did you in college.

WALTER: I find that highly unlikely.

MAGGIE: It's true. You're famous now, in academic circles. Your complete works have been published in seven volumes. You know that book you never finished? On Paris in the Nineteenth Century? They published it. All your notes and drafts, just like you left them.

WALTER: How embarrassing.

MAGGIE: I wouldn't worry. Hardly anyone's read it.

WALTER: Good. I would hate to think I'd become a success, in spite of all my efforts.

MAGGIE: Listen, okay, who, what, who, what are you doing here anyway? I mean if dead people are going to be making a claim on my attention, why couldn't I have a woman? Lorraine Hansberry? Sylvia bloody Plath? Or someone Irish? Constance Markiewicz? Maud Gonne? Well, maybe not Maud Gonne.

THE DEAD: Tell her / important / sorry to be / urgent matter of / tell her.

WALTER:	(*to the* DEAD) In a moment. (*to* MAGGIE) Maud...Gonne? I'm sorry, I don't know these people. I know your novelist, Joyce. Not personally though. The whole social thing. I gather he was even more shy than me.
MAGGIE:	It doesn't matter.
WALTER:	No. Well, the reason we came, is, we understand you are thinking of joining us.

Pause.

MAGGIE:	Possibly.
WALTER:	I see.
MAGGIE:	What do you care?
WALTER:	Me personally? I, well, you could say, I represent, as it were, your, your wish to go on living. In spite of, you know. Everything.
MAGGIE:	Oh. Yeah, that figures. My desire to live is embodied as a dead male German literary critic.
WALTER:	Is that an insult? I'm not good with them.
MAGGIE:	Sorry. (*Pause*) You're not like the others. You're actually having this conversation.
WALTER:	Yes. You could say that I always had a vested interest in the future. Professionally speaking, anyway.
MAGGIE:	Not personally, though.
WALTER:	Well, no.

418

MAGGIE:	You killed yourself.
WALTER:	...Yes. I did.

Pause.

MAGGIE:	Some role model you are.
WALTER:	There's a very beautiful line in Gustav Janouch's book "Conversations with Kafka". Of course the book itself has dubious provenance –
MAGGIE:	Just quote the fucking line.
WALTER:	Sorry. Kafka is supposed to have said "There is an infinite amount of hope, but not for us."
MAGGIE:	Yeah, I've always liked that too. Seems to me fairly applicable in my case.
WALTER:	(*sitting down*) What exactly is your case?
MAGGIE:	My life is going to shit, the world is going to shit, I may as well deal with my life. It doesn't look like the world is getting fixable. Also I didn't say you could sit down.

WALTER *stands.*

WALTER:	Excuse me. (*Pause*) So. How are you going to go about it?
MAGGIE:	I don't know. I was thinking of taking about fifty paracetamol, because it causes fatal liver damage. But apparently it takes a long time and it's very painful.
WALTER:	I see. I used morphine, at least I think I did.

MAGGIE:	You can't get morphine these days. Only hospitals.
WALTER:	Failing these, there are other methods, the tall building, the knife, the gun, the speeding vehicle.
MAGGIE:	I don't fancy them. There are only two buildings in Dublin that are tall enough for you to be sure you'd die if you jumped off them.
WALTER:	What are they?
MAGGIE:	The Central Bank and the trade union headquarters. Ironic isn't it?
WALTER:	That is a misuse of the concept of irony. I find it "significant" rather than "ironic".
MAGGIE:	We do that a lot. It's got to the point where anything happens at all anywhere and some stupid shit will say it's ironic.
WALTER:	You have my sympathy. Kierkegaard is interesting on the topic –
MAGGIE:	I don't want to know about bloody Kierkegaard. I want a reason to live.
WALTER:	Well, he's interesting on that topic too –
MAGGIE:	Jesus! I want help, not a fucking...philosophy tutorial!
WALTER:	... But you admit you want help.

Pause.

MAGGIE:	Yeah.

WALTER: I'm sorry I'm not more useful. *(Pause)* "The help goes away without helping." Kafka.

MAGGIE: Full of quotes, aren't we. Are you going away?

WALTER: I think that's up to you, isn't it?

Pause.

MAGGIE: A friend of mine said, oh you'll get over him. Like he's a fence. It doesn't work like that. I know why the symbol for love is a heart, it's stupid but I think about Joe my heart hurts, like someone's stuck a, not a knife but something. I'm never gonna be able to forget this, it's never gonna go away. You wrote a good line about it.

WALTER: Did I?

MAGGIE: You said "The only way to know a person is to love them without hope". Jesus. I know that man, how he laughs, I've seen him sleep, the way he walks, terrible handwriting, fucking dreadful taste in books, I had an argument with him about Catcher in the Rye, it's his favourite book, I tried to persuade him it was defeatist bullshit but he just kept saying "To each his own" and even when he annoys the piss out of me I still love him. I fucking love him. And I know Karen loves him but I love him more. You know?

WALTER: Yes. *(Pause)* Although I think you misquoted me, I would never have used a plural pronoun to refer to a singular object.

MAGGIE: Shut up. *(Pause)* You know what's the worst? It's that he's still here. If he were dead like before, I think I could handle it. Maybe. But the idea that I'm still going to see him...I can't stand that.

WALTER: And so you think you can solve it by killing yourself.

MAGGIE: Yeah. - I don't know. Maybe. I just want to stop feeling like this, all the time.

Pause.

WALTER: You know, there's something about you people that strikes me as odd.

MAGGIE: What people?

WALTER: The living. I began to notice this when I was alive. You seem to feel that the fact that you can now see us around you all the time, and talk to us, is in some way strange or unprecedented. That, shall we say, it represents a radical change in the order of the world. But from our perspective, it has always been like this. The only difference is that nowadays, you pay us a little more attention.

MAGGIE: What do you mean?

WALTER: You'll find out.

RENEE *and* BOBBY *both fall into the room, drunk.*

RENEE: Hello.

BOBBY: Hello.

RENEE: We're a bit pissed.

BOBBY:	Whoa. Dead guy. Outstanding. How you been.
WALTER:	Excuse me?
BOBBY:	Never mind. Listen. Maggie. Listen.
MAGGIE:	I'm kind of busy, guys.
BOBBY:	You're busy, the fuck could you be doing, it's the weekend. Listen.
RENEE:	We have had the most –

RENEE *falls next to* MAGGIE.

BOBBY:	...Fucking brilliant idea. [*to* RENEE] You tell them.
RENEE:	No, you tell them.
BOBBY:	No, you tell them.
RENEE:	No, you tell them.
MAGGIE:	Guys, whatever it is, I really don't –
BOBBY:	Oh shut up, wait. Okay. We have sorted out this Karen thing. I am such a fucking genius. This is what we should do:

SCENE EIGHT.

KAREN *and* JOE *are making love on the sofa.*

KAREN:	(*panting*) Oh yeah – right there –
JOE:	Remember West Cork? On the beach?

KAREN:	Yeah – go on –
JOE:	Remember you coming out of the sea? And me taking you into that little foresty bit, it was a really hot day, remember?
KAREN:	Yeah – oh –
JOE:	And I peeled that swimsuit off you and you were all wet and naked and we lay down on the ground and had sex? And the sun coming through the trees, and the feel of the dry leaves on your naked body?
KAREN:	Oh God yeah –
JOE:	And then you got a bit of leaf or something inside you, and you got an infection and had to go on antibiotics and you couldn't drink anything for the rest of the holiday?
KAREN:	Hang on – go back –
JOE:	What bit? Where?
KAREN:	Me on the ground and you fucking me –
JOE:	Okay. (*Pause*) Yeah, you were on the ground and you were afraid someone was gonna come along, especially since you were naked and I wasn't and that made it more sexy.
KAREN:	Yeah, go on –
JOE:	Yeah. Uh...and I don't think I actually came, but you did. Did I? I can't remember.
KAREN:	Please...just a bit more –

424

JOE:	Mmmmyeahhh...aaand, when we were finished you put your swimsuit on again and you were ages trying to get all the bits of dead leaf off your arse.

KAREN *stops. This isn't working.*

JOE:	You remember?
KAREN:	I remember, yeah.

Pause.

JOE:	Remember the time you tied me to the bed?
KAREN:	Oh yeah. That really didn't work, did it.
JOE:	Remember the first time we kissed?

KAREN *thinks.*

KAREN:	...Yeahhh...where was it, was it in Thomas Read's or was it in the Olympia?
JOE:	It, eh...wasn't it in the Olympia?
KAREN:	Yeah, I think it was, who had we gone to see? Sonic Youth.
JOE:	Sonic Youth.
KAREN:	And you bought me a t-shirt.
JOE:	Yeah.
KAREN:	But where did we...cause, no, I remember kissing you in the Olympia, but we'd already kissed before then.

425

JOE:	That was a great gig.
KAREN:	Yeah, but, Joe, concentrate. Where did we kiss, was it in Read's or was it on the way to the gig, or...
JOE:	I, uh...
KAREN:	Was it outside? In the queue?
JOE:	I don't, uh...
KAREN:	Where was it. I forget.

Silence.

KAREN:	You still with me?
JOE:	Yeah.
KAREN:	Don't drift away. Please don't.

JOE *smiles and shrugs.* KAREN *hugs him.*

KAREN:	You're all I have. Just stay. And everything'll be fine.

Long pause. Knock at the door.

KAREN:	Stay there.

She gets up, adjusts her clothing and answers the door. RENEE *and* BOBBY *burst in, followed by* WALTER, MAGGIE *and the* DEAD.

RENEE & BOBBY:	SURPRISE!
KAREN:	Hi guys. What's –
BOBBY:	We have had this fucking brilliant idea.

426

RENEE *hugs* KAREN.

KAREN: ...Yeah? Who are all these –

RENEE: This is Walter, he's a friend of Maggie's.

KAREN: (*to* WALTER, *who bows*) Hello – hi, Maggie –

MAGGIE: Hi Karen, look, I can't stay, I think I might go –

BOBBY: (*putting an arm round* MAGGIE) Bullshit,
                    bullshit, bullshit, listen, (*to* KAREN) what we
                    have to do is, we have to have a proper wake.
                    For Joe.

KAREN: A wake?

RENEE: Isn't it brilliant?

THE DEAD: A wake / party party / drinks on him / woman in
                    the bed more porter

KAREN: Who are this lot?

MAGGIE: They keep following me around, I'm sorry.

WALTER: They're with me.

KAREN: Who are you? (*sees his armband*) Oh, excuse
                    me.

WALTER: Not at all.

KAREN: Well, um...we were actually thinking of turning
                    in.

MAGGIE: So was I –

JOE: Did someone say party?

MAGGIE:	Joe, hiya.
THE DEAD:	Jooooe / compadre / buddy / one of us, one of us
BOBBY:	Joe, we wanna have a wake for you.
RENEE:	You'd be the guest of honour.
JOE:	Cool.
BOBBY:	Joe wants to.
KAREN:	Well, okay – I'm so not dressed though –
RENEE:	Oh, come on. We'll sort you out.

She drags KAREN *off.*

BOBBY:	Gotta take a wizz. Back in a sec.

BOBBY goes off MAGGIE stands. JOE is lying on the sofa smiling at the ceiling.

WALTER:	I think, if you had anything you wanted to say, this might be a good time.
MAGGIE:	You reckon. (*to* JOE) Joe?
JOE:	Yeah?
MAGGIE:	I know there's no point saying this now cause I never told you before you – before you went away, but...the thing is, ever since we first met I've sort of had really strong feelings for you and...(JOE *has stopped listening. He stares at the ceiling and hums cheerfully)* This is ridiculous.
WALTER:	Yes. Go on.

428

MAGGIE:	(*to* JOE) I mean, can you think, was there ever a time when you knew that I...do you remember noticing the way I looked at you, or did anybody ever tell you that...like Neil or anyone. It would've been Neil, I only told Neil. Did you know I loved you. (JOE *does not respond. Long pause)* You never knew. (Pause) Okay. Never mind.
Pause.	
WALTER:	So.
MAGGIE:	I don't want to stay here. I don't want to go to any fucking wake or anything.
WALTER:	Where are you thinking of going?
MAGGIE:	I might just, I might just take a hike down the late-night chemist, you know? For some...Pain Killers. I think I might just do that. Yeah.
Pause.	
WALTER:	Why don't you.
MAGGIE:	I'm scared it'll hurt.
WALTER:	You know it will hurt. But only for a while. And then – nothing.
Pause.	
MAGGIE:	No, not nothing. I end up as a memory. Clever Maggie who was a bit dull. Unlucky with men. Good cook. Good daughter. Good sister.
WALTER:	Kind.
MAGGIE:	Oh, yeah. That one, yeah.

WALTER: Intelligent.

MAGGIE: Oh, fierce intelligent, yeah. A book is a party, a book and a cup of coffee is an orgy.

WALTER: These are all good things, no?

MAGGIE: Fucking brilliant, yeah. All the great sexy virtues. (*Pause. Crying*) It's so pathetic. I'm so fucking boring. How did I get to be like this, I only wanted to be happy. (*to* JOE, *who doesn't respond*) This is your fault. I had to fall in love. Shithead. Everything's grand, and then one day love comes along and knocks you down and rolls over you.

Pause. The DEAD have quietly come up behind her. After a long moment, a thin, mousy dead woman tugs at the back of MAGGIE's coat.

DEAD #1: Scuse me? Young one? (*Pause*) I just wanted to say, it could be worse.

MAGGIE: That's no help.

DEAD #1: Well, but you could have been me.

MAGGIE: What happened to you.

DEAD #1: I had desperate migraines me whole life.

DEAD #2: I drowned in a ferry accident on my honeymoon.

DEAD #3: My husband beat me to death.

DEAD #4: I had a burst appendix.

DEAD #2: Oh, they're a killer.

DEAD #5:   I was poor and hungry and cold, all the time, and I ended up being killed by a bomb dropped from an aircraft flown by people from a country I thought was supposed to be our friend.

Pause.

MAGGIE: Yeah, well life is not fucking fair.

DEAD #3:   She's right.

DEAD #4:   Got a point.

DEAD #5:   Yes, but all I'm saying is I don't need *her* telling me that.

DEAD #4:   It's true though.

DEAD #1:   Life *isn't* fair.

DEAD #5:   I'm not arguing. I'm just saying.

DEAD #4:   Well, good.

DEAD #5:   Everyone has problems, no need to bite my head off.

DEAD #4:   I wasn't.

DEAD #1:   Ssshh!

Long pause.

MAGGIE: No. Life is not fucking fair. We deserve better. (*to* WALTER) What do you think?

WALTER: About what?

MAGGIE: I want more life. Do you approve? Probably not, right? You probably think I'm...shallow or something. You probably think I'm betraying something. Right?

Pause while WALTER *thinks.*

WALTER: ...I find this metaphor of "shallowness" very interesting.

MAGGIE: Oh will you stop doing that! Just tell me what you think!

Pause.

WALTER: You look to me for advice. Or approval. But what am I. Just one of your memories. Not even a very accurate one. If you want hope, the past is probably the wrong place to look for it.

MAGGIE: So where do I look for it.

WALTER: I can't tell you. But on the subject of hope, suppose, for a moment, that the world really isn't like paradise. I'm not being glib, listen. Suppose there really is no chance of building utopia – in fact, that the world is a lot more like hell than like heaven, which I admit does seem more likely – what difference would it make? Would we really give up trying to make it better? I don't think so. I think the only difference is that our hopes wouldn't be quite so – um – wild, and our disappointments wouldn't be quite so crushing.

MAGGIE: (*Pause*) Did you write that?

WALTER: Unfortunately not, no.

MAGGIE: I like it.

432

WALTER:	Good. Now, I think you need to find something to wear to this party.
MAGGIE:	Are you coming?
WALTER:	Oh yes. (*He offers her his arm*) Did you know I once succeeded in drinking a Spanish bar hostess under the table?
MAGGIE:	(*taking his arm*) Yeah, I read that. Where was that again?
WALTER:	A little island in the Balearics, interesting place. It was called Ibiza.
MAGGIE:	Yeah. You really don't want to go there now.

SCENE NINE.

A Departure lounge in Dublin airport. NEIL *is sitting reading a paper.* CARL *comes by and takes the seat next to him.*

PA: Ladies and gentlemen, Flight LD 245 to Frankfurt is now boarding at Gate 23. Would Business class passengers please proceed to the gate with their boarding cards. Thank you.

Pause.

CARL: Crazy, isn't it?

NEIL: Sorry?

CARL: The news.

NEIL: Usual weirdness.

CARL: Ever think that the whole world has gone totally insane?

NEIL: Well, you've seen the front page.

CARL: No.

NEIL: It seems that somebody identifying himself as Jesus son of Mary has turned up on the West Bank. The Israelis won't let him have a travel permit cause they say he has a criminal record. The Vatican says that he doesn't have any doctrinal authority because he's Jewish. He's issued a press statement, but because it's written in first-century Aramaic, nobody can agree on the right translation. It's a bit pathetic all round.

CARL: I agree.

NEIL: I dunno. Somebody ought to do something.

CARL *smiles.*

CARL: Somebody will.

SCENE TEN.

This scene revolves between three locations: A Karaoke bar, with a table near the performance space; a cubicle of a unisex toilet in the same bar; and the economy section of a passenger aircraft.

The bar. The MC *is working the customers. He speaks into a hand mic.*

MC: Come on now. This isn't rocket science. The book is going round, just choose the song you like, write the number on the slip, and give it to me or the beautiful Angela, who is not available for private dances, guys, in case you were wondering- is it me or is it a graveyard in here? Come on now, folks, let's see some action. Otherwise I'm gonna have to sing myself and we don't want that. Death by a sweeter name.

KAREN, JOE, MAGGIE, WALTER, BOBBY, RENEE and *THE DEAD* enter.

MC: There's a bunch of likely-looking layabouts. Any of you lot singers? No? Folks, we have some, ah, deceased in the building, so if you're in their vicinity, a bit of respect please. Thank you. Just a reminder that shots are available at the bar for the knock-down price of seven-fifty for five.

MAGGIE: I'll have a Slippery Nipple.

BOBBY:	Whoa, Maggie. I bet you will. Karen?
KAREN:	Just a red wine.
BOBBY:	(*to* RENEE, *nuzzling her*) What would you like?
RENEE:	(*nuzzling back*) Red wine. I'll give you a hand.

They go.

WALTER:	What is the function of the man with the microphone?
MAGGIE:	This is karaoke. They invented it in Japan. They play songs, pop songs, and people sing along with them.
WALTER:	In public?
MAGGIE:	Yeah. Sorry, bit of a nightmare.
WALTER:	No no no. I approve. Truly democratic.
MAGGIE:	Wait till you hear them sing.
WALTER:	That's not the point. Although, it would be better if you could make up the words yourself.
MC:	Come on. Are we men or mice. Three thousand songs, something for everyone, give it a spin, this is pathetic. Let's get somebody up here. Not a single request so far, folks. We're gonna come down amongst you and see if we can't raise some spirits.

He puts down the mic and goes.

KAREN:	Joe? You still with us?

JOE:	Hm?

KAREN:	You still there? Hah?

JOE:	Yeah, yeah. Just...sitting.

KAREN:	...Okay.

The plane. NEIL *and* CARL *are sitting together.*

NEIL:	So this friend of ours...he died. And his girlfriend brought him back to her place, and is trying to keep it going, and I think it's just...insane. You know? I mean you just can't hang on to things like that. It may seem like he's there, but he's not really. You know what I mean?

CARL:	So you would go for the secular version? The dead aren't really risen?

NEIL:	Yeah. I don't believe this Judgement Day stuff. I just don't. I mean I have respect for religion. – Well, no, I don't really. I just think that stuff is fucking nuts.

CARL:	Oh yeah?

NEIL:	Yeah.

CARL:	So what about this thing of Jesus coming back?

NEIL:	Well, I dunno about that, but look what's happened. Nothing's changed. It's still the same bloody bickering. I don't think it makes any difference.

CARL:	You don't, huh?

437

NEIL: No.

CARL: Well, Neil, you know, every apocalypse needs a little bit of human intervention.

NEIL: How do you mean?

CARL: I'll show ya.

CARL stands up and rips his shirt open. There is a bomb strapped to his chest.

CARL: TAKE THIS PLANE TO ISRAEL OR I BLOW US OUT OF THE FUCKING SKY!

The toilet in the bar.

BOBBY *and* RENEE *are sharing a joint.*

RENEE: Do you think this is gonna work?

BOBBY: Dunno. But it's worth a go.

RENEE: If it'll get Karen's mind off Joe, I suppose.

BOBBY: Yeah. (*has a drag*) I shouldn't be doing this. I'm fairly pissed as it is.

RENEE: So am I. Not so much that I don't wanna take you home at the end of the night and shag your brains out.

BOBBY: Me too. (*Pause*) Of course, we could just do it right here.

RENEE: Oh that's so tacky.

BOBBY: I know.

Pause.

RENEE: Okay then.

They start to snog furiously.

The bar. JOE *is writing down a song slip. He hands it to the* MC.

MAGGIE: I'm curious about something.

RENEE: Yeah – yeah –

BOBBY: Oh God –

RENEE: Oh Jesus –

BOBBY: Oh Karen –

RENEE: What?

BOBBY: I – what?

RENEE: What did you call me?

BOBBY: (*still going*) I didn't – hold on –

RENEE: (*disengaging*) You called me Karen!

BOBBY: No I didn't! What are you –

RENEE: YOU FUCKING ARSEHOLE!

BOBBY: I never did!

RENEE: You were thinking about her!

BOBBY: I was not! I dunno where that came from –

RENEE: I am, I don't, you fuckin, I can't believe, get out
                    of here! Just go! Now! Go! No. Wait. Don't.
Pause.

BOBBY: What's wrong.

RENEE: Right. Um, I think I'm gonna vomit. Hold my
                    hair.

BOBBY: Okay.

She turns, kneels and sticks her head in the toilet. He holds her hair.

*The music gets louder. Bright light. A roaring sound, as of a low-flying
plane. They look up in fear.*

The plane. It lurches. The music is still quite loud.

CARL: Take me to the cockpit!

NEIL: Don't do it, man.

CARL: I'll fucking kill you all, man, I don't care.

NEIL: For what, for –

CARL: Faith, man! Haven't you been *listening*? Can't
                    you see what's around you? The *signs*?

NEIL: I don't see any signs.

CARL: "For the trumpet shall sound, and the dead shall
                    be raised incorruptible, and we shall be
                    changed." We shall be *changed*.

NEIL: No we won't, we'll just all get killed.

CARL: I'm gonna do it. I'm gonna do it. God protect me.

NEIL:	Protect *you*? What about *us*?
CARL:	God be merciful.
NEIL:	Don't do it.
CARL:	God be praised.
NEIL:	I'm warning you.
CARL:	God forgive me.

He reaches for the detonator. NEIL *dives at him. Blackout on the plane. Sound of an explosion.*

The bar.

JOE *is leading the* DEAD *in the chorus. They sway a little, hold up lit cigarette lighters etc. As the song winds down, they leave the stage one by one. Finally* JOE *and* WALTER *are left.*
KAREN *walks up to* JOE. *He "sings" the last line to her, then kisses her.*

JOE:	See you, babe.

END.

Author Biographies

MARINA CARR

Marina Carr's plays to date are ULLALOO, 1989; LOW IN THE DARK, 1991; THE MAI, 1994; PORTIA COUGHLAN, 1996; BY THE BOG OF CATS, 1998; ON RAFTERY'S HILL, 1999; ARIEL, 2000; WOMAN AND SCARECROW, 2004; THE CORDELIA DREAM, 2006; MARBLE, 2007; 16 POSSIBLE GLIMPSES, 2009. Her two plays for children are MEAT AND SALT, 2003 and THE GIANT BLUE HAND, 2004. The RSC produced the world premiere of her reimagining of HECUBA at the Swan Theatre in September 2015, and in August 2015 the Abbey Theatre produced a major revival of BY THE BOG OF CATS.

Her work has been produced by The Abbey Theatre, The Gate, Druid, The Royal Court, Wyndhams Theatre, The RSC, The Tricycle, The MacCarter Theatre, San Diego Rep, Milwaukee rep.

She is translated into many languages and produced around the world.

Prizes include THE SUSAN SMITH BLACKBURN PRIZE, THE AMERICAN/IRELAND FUND AWARD, THE E.M FORSTER AWARD from the AMERICAN ACADEMY OF ARTS AND LETTERS, THE MACAULAY FELLOWSHIP, THE PUTERBAUGH FELLOWSHIP. She is a member of AOSDANA.

She has taught at TRINITY, at VILLANOVA, at PRINCETON. Currently she lectures in the English department at DUBLIN CITY UNIVERSITY.

She is published by THE GALLERY PRESS, NICK HERN BOOKS and FABER & FABER.

GAVIN KOSTICK

Gavin is an award-winning playwright. He has written over a twenty plays which have been produced in Dublin, on tour around Ireland, the UK and New York. Recent works include *The End of the Road* for

Fishamble, *This is What we Sang* for Kabosh, *An Image for the Rose, Trilogy* outdoors for Whiplash Theatre Company and *Fight Night, The Games People Play* and *At the Ford* for RISE Productions. *The Games People Play* received the Irish Times Award for best new play. He has written a number of plays for The Gaiety School of Acting, including *Fox and Crow, Aoife* and *Isabel*, and *The Drowning Room.*

Gavin also wrote the libretto for *The Alma Fetish*, composed by Raymond Deane, which was staged by WideOpenOpera at the National Concert Hall. As a performer he performed *Joseph Conrad's Heart of Darkness: Complete*, a six-hour show for Dublin Fringe, Dublin Theatre Festival and The London Festival of Literature at the Southbank.

As Literary Officer at Fishamble: The New Play Company, Gavin works with new writers for theatre through script development for production, readings and a variety of mentorship programmes such as *Show in a Bag* and *The New Play Clinic*.

MARY ELIZABETH BURKE-KENNEDY
Mary Elizabeth Burke-Kennedy began her professional theatre career in Dublin's Focus Theatre, where she acted and worked as resident director for many years. She established Storytellers Theatre Company, which toured throughout Ireland and for which she wrote and directed a large body of work, including an adaptation of The Mayor of Casterbridge, Esther Waters, and her own version of Oedipus Rex. She also wrote for Focus Theatre, Team Theatre Company, Cork Opera House, Theatre of Open Secrets and RTE television. She taught acting in GSA from 1988 until 2010. She now teaches playwriting in NUIG. She is a board member of The Gaiety School of Acting.

PAUL O'BRIEN
Paul O'Brien is a writer from Wexford, Ireland. His *Blood Red Turns Dollar Green* trilogy of novels have been #1 bestsellers in Canada, Australia, Germany, Mexico, Spain, Italy, U.K., Ireland and the U.S. He has been commissioned or produced as a playwright by The National Theatre of Ireland, Druid Theatre, Red Kettle Theatre Company, The National Acting School of Ireland and Spare Key Productions in New

York. Currently, Paul has two US TV pilots in development — one based on his *Blood Red Turns Dollar Green* novels in LA and the other is a black-comedy based out of NY. In 2016 Paul signed to write a screenplay for the Sundance award winning Barnes Brothers. *Staid*, Paul's first feature film that he wrote, produced and directed will be released in 2016. Paul is currently writing WWE Legend, and Hall of Famer, Jim Ross' autobiography. In 2016 Paul's Blood Red Turns Dollar Green novels will be re-written and published by Skyhorse Publishing in New York.

CLARE DOWLING

Clare Dowling writes contemporary fiction, stage plays and televisions scripts. Her previous career as an actor provided inspiration for bestselling novels 'Fast Forward' and 'Too Close For Comfort.' Her television writing credits include 'Roy' and 'Fair City'. She lives in Dublin with her family.

ALEX JOHNSTON

Alex Johnston is a playwright and actor. Some of his previous plays include *Melonfarmer*, which won the Stewart Parker Award in 1998, *Royal Supreme*, *What the Dead Want* for the Gaiety School of Acting, and *Entertainment* which was nominated for an Irish Times Theatre Award.

Complete List of All Plays Staged
1986-2016

Year	Title	Writer	Director
2016	*Proclamation*	Ronan Dempsey	Ronan Dempsey
2015	*The Full Moon Hotel*	Philip Doherty	Paul Brennan
2014	*Dirty Laundry*	Chris Edmund	Chris Edmund
2013	*Town*	Gary Duggan	Liam Halligan
2013	*Country*	Gary Duggan	Liam Halligan
2012	*Another Twin*	Lally Katz	Liam Halligan
2011	*Toxic*	Michelle Read	Liam Halligan
2010	*Casa Lisa*	Ken Bourke	Liam Halligan
2009	*When the Hunter Returns*	Lally Katz	Liam Halligan
2009	*The Fire Room*	Lisa Tierney-Keogh	Patrick Sutton
2008	*God's Lap*	Paul O'Brien	Susanna Dowling
2008	*The Muse Unbidden*	Roger Gregg	John Delaney
2007	*Playground*	Lisa Harding	Patrick Sutton
2007	*End-Time*	Sean McLoughlin	John Delaney
2006	*Olive Skin, Blood Mouth*	Gavin Kostick	Patrick Sutton
2005	*Whose House?*	Mary Elizabeth Burke Kennedy	Liam Halligan
2005	*A/S/L*	Paul O'Brien	Tara Derrington

2004	*Universal Export – Day Shift*	Alex Johnston	Patrick Sutton
2004	*Universal Export – Night Shift*	Ionna Anderson	Liam Halligan
2003	*to be confirmed*	Alex Johnston	Patrick Sutton
2003	*Elysian Juniors*	Ken Harmon	Jimmy Fay
2002	*What the Dead Want*	Alex Johnston	Jimmy Fay
2002	*Requiem for Lena*	Veronica Coburn	Veronica Coburn
2001	*Aoife*	Gavin Kostick	Jimmy Fay
2001	*Isabel*	Gavin Kostick	Eric Weitz
2000	*Under the Stars*	Martin Maguire	Eric Weitz
2000	*Lower Than the Heart*	Michelle Read	Tara Derrington
1999	*The Man Who Couldn't Cross Roads*	Gavin Kostick	Patrick Sutton
1999	*The House in Gourtnashee*	Ken Bourke	Maureen White
1998	*Cult Movie*	Roger Gregg	Tara Derrington& Patrick Sutton
1997	*Fox and Crow*	Gavin Kostick	Caroline McSweeney& Patrick Sutton
1996	*Blood*	Clare Dowling	Patrick Sutton
1995	*The Beloved*	Ken Bourke	Patrick Sutton
1994	*The Drowning Room*	Gavin Kostick	Patrick Sutton

1993	*Tear Up the Black Sail*	Colin Teevan	Patrick Sutton
1992	*The Grogan Budgies*	Conor Norton	Mary Elizabeth Burke Kennedy
1991	*The Quirk Estate*	Michael West	David Byrne
1990	*The Deer's Surrender*	Marina Carr	Maureen White